Caring for America's Children

Caring for America's Children

Proceedings of
The Academy of
Political Science

Volume 37
Number 2

ISSN 0065-0684

Edited by Frank J. Macchiarola
and Alan Gartner

New York, 1989

Library of Congress Catalog Card Number 88-83632

Cover design by Cynthia Brady

Printed by Capital City Press, Montpelier, Vermont

Dedication

We dedicate this volume to the memory of Ronald Edmonds. Friend, teacher, and colleague to both of us in the New York City public schools, Ron was devoted to the well-being of all children. A powerful critic of the schools' failure, he forcefully asserted the capacity of schools to serve children. Indeed, his work—which became the basis of the school effectiveness movement—is the bedrock on which current education-reform efforts build. He thought that school professionals, workers in other child-serving institutions, and people in general could succeed in helping children. He asserted that it was not that society lacked the knowledge to do it; rather, the issue was how society felt about the fact that it had not done so. Serving children with better schools was a matter of caring and will, he said. And so it continues to be. In A. Bartlett Giamatti's recent book about the university, written before he followed the higher calling of commissioner of baseball, a saying of Rabbi Tarphon in *Pirke Avot* is cited: "You are not required to complete the work, but neither are you free to desist from it." That was Ron's message, and in that spirit we continue his work.

FRANK J. MACCHIAROLA
ALAN GARTNER

Contents

Preface

This volume portrays the condition of America's children with examples of how some individuals and institutions have succeeded in serving them. Despite these successes, however, the status of children today is far from satisfactory. Many children are in desperate need of care, and there is little by way of government policy and programs that addresses itself comprehensively to these needs.

There can be no question that the United States wants to do a better job of serving its children, but a commitment has been lacking largely because of doubts about the effectiveness of programs and policies that claim to advance the cause of children. The Academy therefore invited experts to share their insights and offer suggestions for improving the delivery of children's services. We are grateful for their response.

The Academy commissioned Professor Alan Gartner of the City University of New York Graduate School and University Center to coedit *Caring for America's Children*. Professor Gartner, who distinguished himself as executive director of the Division of Special Education in the New York City Public Schools from 1981 to 1983, has spent his life in the service of persons in need. He is the author of numerous books and articles reflecting this interest.

The editors strongly believe that if more Americans become aware of the needs of children they will be willing to meet them. We encourage both voluntarism and public support that can be more significant, more meaningful than dollars alone. We also encourage reaching out to children to let them know that we care about them and their successes.

The views expressed in this volume are those of the individual authors and are not necessarily those of any organizations with which they are associated. The Academy of Political Science, founded in 1880, serves as a forum for the development and dissemination of opinion on public-policy questions. It is a nonpartisan, not-for-profit organization, and it does not make recommendations on political and social issues.

The Academy thanks the Primerica Foundation, the Smith Richardson Foundation, the J.J.G. Foundation, and the Forest House Fund for their financial support of this project.

Finally, the Academy is grateful to William V. Farr for his editorial direction of this project and to Eric C. Banks and Adam Karpati for their editorial assistance.

FRANK J. MACCHIAROLA
President

Contributors

GERALD BENJAMIN, professor of political science, State University of New York at New Paltz, is majority leader, Ulster County (New York) Legislature. He is coeditor, with Charles Brecher, of *The Two New Yorks: State and City in a Changing Federal System* and coauthor, with Robert H. Connery, of *Rockefeller of New York*.

A. R. COLÓN is professor of pediatrics, Georgetown University School of Medicine. He is coeditor, with Mohsen Ziai, of *Pediatric Hepatology* and the author of *Pediatric Pathophysiology*.

P. A. COLÓN is research associate, Georgetown University School of Medicine.

JAMES J. DIGIACOMO, S.J., teaches theology at Regis High School in New York City. He is also adjunct assistant professor of religion and religious education at Fordham University. He is senior author of the *Conscience and Concern* series and coauthor, with Father John Walsh, M.M., of the *Encounter* series.

MARIAN WRIGHT EDELMAN is president, Children's Defense Fund. She is the author of *Families in Peril: An Agenda for Social Change*.

AZRA FARRELL is administrator, Coordinated Children's Services, Ulster County, New York.

ALAN GARTNER is professor and director of research, the Graduate School and University Center, the City University of New York. Formerly executive director, Division of Special Education, New York City Public Schools, he is coauthor, with Mary Conway Kohler and Frank Riessman, of *Children Teaching Children* and coeditor, with Tom Joe, of *Images of the Disabled/Disabling Images*.

ROBERT M. HAYES is counsel for the National Coalition for the Homeless.

DIANE P. HEDIN is director of community relations, the Pillsbury Company, and former professor, Center for Youth Development & Research, University of Minnesota. She is the author of *Experimental Education and Youth Participation*.

NAT HENTOFF, the author of *Our Children Are Dying*, is a columnist for the *Washington Post* and the *Village Voice* and a staff writer for the *New Yorker*.

TOM JOE is director of the Center for the Study of Social Policy and former special assistant to the under secretary, U.S. Department of Health, Education, and Welfare. A recipient of a MacArthur Fellowship Award, he is coeditor, with Alan Gartner, of *Images of the Disabled/Disabling Images*.

MICHAEL JUPP is executive director of the Defense for Children International – USA and former consultant on children's rights, United Nations Children's Fund (UNICEF). His most recent book is *Children Under Apartheid*.

SHARON L. KAGAN is associate professor, Bush Center in Child Development and Social Policy, Yale University, and former director of the Mayor's Office of Early Childhood Education, New York City. She is coeditor, with Edgar Klugman and Edward Zigler, of *Children, Families and Government: Perspectives on American Social Policy*.

ALFRED J. KAHN, professor of social planning and social policy at the Columbia University School of Social Work, is codirector, with Sheila Kamerman, of the Cross-National Studies Research Program. He is coauthor, with Sheila Kamerman, of *Mothers Alone: Strategies for a Time of Change*.

SHEILA B. KAMERMAN is professor of social policy and social planning and chair of the doctoral program, Columbia University School of Social Work. She is codirector, with Alfred J. Kahn, of the Cross-National Research Studies Program and coauthor, with Alfred J. Kahn, of *Mothers Alone: Strategies for a Time of Change*.

DOROTHY KERZNER LIPSKY is senior research scientist, the Graduate School and University Center, the City University of New York, and assistant to the superintendent, Bellmore (New York) Public Schools. She is the author of *Family Support Services* and *Family Supports for Families with a Disabled Member* and coeditor, with Alan Gartner, of the forthcoming *Beyond Separate Education: Quality Education for All*.

FRANK J. MACCHIAROLA, formerly chancellor of the New York City school system, is president and executive director of the Academy of Political Science and professor of business at Columbia University.

STEPHEN MORRIS is probation director of the Ulster County (New York) Probation Department and former director of training and development, Office of Probation for the Courts of New York City.

DOUGLAS W. NELSON is deputy director of the Center for the Study of Social Policy and former assistant secretary, Wisconsin Department of Health and Social Services. He is the author of *Heart Mountain*.

ANN ROSEWATER is staff director, House Select Committee on Children, Youth, and Families.

ROSEMARY C. SALOMONE is professor of law at the St. John's University School of Law. She is the author of *Equal Education Under Law*.

JULE M. SUGARMAN, formerly director of the National Head Start Program, is secretary, Department of Social and Health Services, State of Washington.

JOSEPH P. VITERITTI is senior research scientist, Urban Research Center, and associate research professor at the Graduate School of Public Administration, New York University. The author of *Across the River: Politics and Education in the City*, he has served as special assistant to the chancellor of the New York City school system and as director of a transition team for the superintendent of the Boston public schools.

Failing America's Children: Responsibilities and Remedies

FRANK J. MACCHIAROLA
ALAN GARTNER

One of the ironies of the present period of educational reform is that it was launched by a report entitled *A Nation at Risk*, but we now discuss children "at risk" and see school failure as children's failure. True, the failure of the schools (and other child-serving institutions) disproportionately affects certain children—those of color, those living in poverty, and those who do not fit in an ever-narrowing mainstream. Yet, so long as the focus is on those who suffer the effects of school failure and not on the failure of the institutions, we will continue to fail children.

Evidence of America's failure of its children is pervasive—in daily newspaper stories, in an overflowing river of reports and mountains of data, and even in the recent presidential campaign, when both candidates asserted concern and put forth programs, though neither seemed willing to propose any that was commensurate with the needs. More promising is the response of some in the business community and of many governors. Private companies and states are now at risk, as schools and other child-serving institutions fail. These leaders and others are raising questions about the fundamentals of our child-serving institutions.

Not only our public institutions fail children. The family is also increasingly strained and little supported. The demographic data are clear—greater numbers of children are growing up in families where both parents work, where there is only one parent, or where there is no family at all. Service systems continue to behave as if the 1950s stereotype of *the* American family remains true; the stereotype was not entirely true even then, and fewer than one in ten families fit the model today. By 1995, more than three-quarters of all school-age children will have mothers in the labor force. Seventy-one percent of employed mothers with children under eighteen now work full time, and more than a quarter of the children under thirteen must care for themselves during a part of the day. Between

1973 and 1986 young families experienced a 27 percent decline in income, and today nearly one in four children is poor.

Social institutions seem unable to support, much less substitute for, the family. Child welfare agencies are underfunded, poorly staffed, and more often than not swamped beyond their capacity. In New York City between 1984 and 1988, for example, the number of children eligible for adoption grew by 20 percent, while those adopted fell by nearly 50 percent.

Increasingly, there are questions about the responsibility of public agencies charged with protecting children. A case currently before the U.S. Supreme Court involves a deceased boy named Joshua DeShaney, whose father is suing the Wisconsin Department of Health and Rehabilitation Services. He claims that the state knew that the young boy was being abused by his stepfather, but it failed to intervene. And in New York City, the failure of school personnel to see or act on the obvious bruises of Lisa Steinberg confirms the view of an NBC investigative reporter, Michelle Gillen, that "the majority of children being abused today are getting no help in the system despite billions of dollars pumped into it."[1]

In the first section of this volume, the authors describe in different ways the condition of children. Ann Rosewater draws on her work as staff director of the House Committee on Children, Youth, and Families, a unique group led by George Miller (D-Calif.) that has focused on children's issues when few others cared to notice. Among those organizations that did care was the Children's Defense Fund, shaped by Marian Wright Edelman into a powerful instrument of analysis and prescription. Her essay draws on her work with that organization. Michael Jupp offers an international focus, while P.A. Colón and A.R. Colón examine the health of children and Robert M. Hayes the condition of homeless children, with comments from the children themselves. Sharon L. Kagan, after assaying the data on children, suggests we may be on the brink of a "paradigm shift": from a fragmented and limited system of children's services to entitlements, a shift not unlike the one in public education in the early nineteenth century.

In the section on public policy, Sheilia B. Kamerman and Alfred J. Kahn contrast developments in the United States with those in other industrialized countries concerning income supports, child or family allowances, housing allowances, child health care, child support, and maternity and parenting policies. Jule M. Sugarman, who served at the national level and is now a state commissioner in Washington, maps a new set of relationships in the federal system. Joseph V. Viteritti proposes a new model for urban services, one that would place the school at the center. Gerald Benjamin, Stephen Morris, and Azra Farrell give insiders' views of efforts at the county level to deliver children's services.

In the section on the schools, Nat Hentoff uses some students' testimonies to portray the limiting nature of a lot of school practice and suggests several promising programs. Dorothy Kerzner Lipsky and Alan Gartner present a new conceptualization of the organization of schooling, one that places the student in the center of the process. James J. DiGiacomo, S.J., addresses the need for moral development in the schools and proposes ways to do this while honoring the diversity among students. Frank J. Macchiarola describes the new meaning of schooling in contemporary society, how the school can work, and what adults and children must do to build a school community.

The concluding section returns to a wider focus. Rosemary C. Salomone traces the recent decline in students' constitutional rights and proposes ways to balance judicial intervention and unfettered school administration. Diane P. Hedin examines the array of community-service programs, assesses the evidence of their academic and social outcomes, describes the components of effective programs, and argues that such programs deserve a prominent place in schools. Tom Joe and Douglas W. Nelson, in the context of the Annie E. Casey Foundation's "New Futures" program that they designed, argue for basic institutional reform in the concept, organization, and operation of comprehensive services for children.

The contributors present the best data on the current condition of America's children, examine those conditions as well as the institutions that most affect children, and offer not only a critique but also positive approaches for the future. While the authors' views differ, they share a common perspective on two matters: first, that America is failing its children and, second, that both the responsibility for that failure and the locus of its remedy are in the public and private institutions of the society. In short, the problem is not with the children.

NOTE

1. "NBC Nightly News," 10 Oct. 1988.

Child and Family Trends: Beyond the Numbers

ANN ROSEWATER

The generation of children growing up in the United States today faces a different world from the one in which its parents were reared. Sweeping economic and demographic changes since the 1960s have fundamentally altered traditional assumptions about the family and have changed significantly the way American families work, the way they live, and the world in which their children grow and learn. At every income level, in every ethnic group, and in every geographic region of the United States, families are becoming increasingly diverse because of divorce, remarriage, and delayed childbearing. Economically, they have been affected by multiple changes, including declining family income, growing numbers of women in the work force, the greater impoverishment of children, and the increasing vulnerability of young children.

Many of the statistics on America's families and children — more children in poverty, more children bearing children, new family structures, and the like — have become part of the conventional lexicon. Beyond the statistics is a story that is both complex and drastic; it encompasses both alarming data and hidden courage and tenacity. Behind the data are the lives of real parents and their children. To find solutions to their problems, one must address not the statistics but the people and their lives.

While there appears to be a surplus of data, the statistical base on children has significant gaps. Unfortunately, these gaps have grown wider in recent years as resources to collect and analyze data have been cut. The only way to understand what is happening to children in the latter half of the twentieth century is to synthesize various data sources and look at children's issues comprehensively. This has been one of the chief missions of the Select Committee on Children, Youth, and Families, established by the U.S. House of Representatives in 1982, on whose work this essay draws heavily.[1] While considerable data are available to the public and policymakers, that does not mean that they have acted on this knowledge.

This essay provides a statistical portrait of America's children and families and analyzes how major social, economic, and demographic trends of the past two decades have affected their circumstances. In addition, it acknowledges the relationship between economic circumstances and demographic conditions. Finally, it considers the implications of these interdependent trends and posits an analytical framework that will help make sense of these numbers.

Demographic Shifts: Changing American Family Arrangements

American families are adjusting to new economic realities and profoundly different family structures. All families have, to some extent, been affected by economic and social trends, but economic security for increasing numbers of families with children has become more precarious. For the first time in more than forty years, families with children — especially young families — face an uncertain future with lowered expectations.

Family composition has changed dramatically in the United States. One out of every two marriages now ends in divorce; the failure rate for second marriages is even higher, at 60 percent.[2] More than a third of American children now live in step relationships,[3] and nearly a fourth of all children live with only one parent. As recently as 1960, only one child in ten lived in a single-parent household, but estimates now indicate that more than half of American children will live in a single-parent household at some time during their childhood.[4] The proportion of black children living only with their mothers remains substantially higher than it is for white children, though it has risen for both.

Children are a decreasing proportion of the United States population. Over the last two decades, the total number of children in the United States has fallen to about 64 million, representing only 26 percent of the total population, compared with 36 percent in 1960. Women of childbearing age are entering the labor force in record numbers, and many have deferred pregnancy until later years. In 1986, about one-third of all twenty-five-year-old women had never been married, more than twice the rate of 1970.[5] But there has been a substantial increase in the number of children born to unmarried teenage mothers, 35 percent since 1970.[6] In the 1990s, the number of children is expected to rise as a result of the "baby boom echo," with preschool children constituting the largest age group among the young. Nevertheless, the number of children will not approach the baby-boom high recorded in 1957.

While the majority of American children are white, growing numbers are black and Hispanic. Nearly one child in five is a member of a minority group. The proportion of children of Spanish origin, now 10 percent of all American children, will climb to 13 percent by the year 2000. The number of black children is expected to increase by 19 percent by 2000.[7]

Data on the number of children with disabilities are particularly scarce. While different estimates are based on different definitions, the federal government's health-statistics unit defines *disability* as referring to "limitations of activity." According to this definition, about 3.2 million children have limitations of activity as a result of chronic health conditions, and about 2.3 million of them are limited in a "major activity." Thus, between 3.5 and 5.0 percent of all children have a disability that falls within this definition.[8] The government's data based on this definition do not generally include emotional disabilities. The most recent survey of children with serious emotional difficulties estimated that 7.5 million to 9.5 million children (12 to 15 percent of those under eighteen) suffer mental health problems severe enough to require treatment.[9]

These demographic trends seem to have become permanent features of American family life. Yet social institutions—schools, hospitals, religious groups, employers, and government—have yet to catch up with them. And it is rapid economic changes combined with these demographic changes that has made it difficult for millions of today's families to provide adequately for their children.

Economic Shifts: Altering the Way Families Work

During the post-World War II period, the United States experienced unparalleled economic expansion and a rising standard of living. Between 1947 and 1973, the "traditional" American family was supported by a booming economy that, in many cases, enabled one parent—usually the father—to earn enough to support the family while the other parent—usually the mother—worked at home, caring for their children. In the economy of the 1950s and 1960s, a working father saw his real earnings rise by 25 to 30 percent. Family income rose, setting new records every year.[10]

Beginning in 1973 with the international oil price increases, the United States experienced three recessions, and in 1982 unemployment reached a post-Depression high of 11 percent. Global competition and economic recession spurred businesses to move manufacturing production out of the country to cheaper labor markets. Families and communities across the United States have suffered measurably as a result. With the decline of steel, automobile, and other heavy industries, for instance, millions of workers lost their jobs and are still unemployed; many others are working in service-sector jobs at a fraction of their prior wages, with minimum benefits and little job security. In agricultural communities, many families lost their farms, and the banking and service sectors that supported these farmers were similarly dislocated.

Today, nearly three in four workers are employed in the service sectors—both public and private. The manufacturing and farming proportion of total employment is at a record low of 22 percent. While many new jobs in such fields as computer science or financial consulting carry high earnings, most new jobs are in the lower-paying retail-trade and personal-service industries. In fact, half of the full-time jobs created since 1979 pay less than $12,000 a year.[11] Accompanying structural employment shifts has been the resurgence of a "contingent" work force— a fourth of today's jobs fall into this category. Companies, motivated by a desire to increase productivity and reduce labor costs, are hiring greater numbers of part-time, temporary, and contract workers who receive lower wages and fewer benefits than do permanent full-time employees.

The gap between the richest and the poorest in the United States has reached its widest point in forty years and is greater than in most industrialized countries. In 1987, the wealthiest 40 percent of American families received 67.8 percent of the national family income, while the poorest 40 percent of families received 15.4 percent. The growth of income inequality is particularly stark, given the varying rates of income growth among different family types. The income of the average family in the lowest two quintiles of the income distribution fell $741 between 1978 and 1987, while the income of the average family in the upper two quintiles rose $3,031. The income of the typical family in the top 10 percent rose $8,119 during this period.[12]

The effects of economic recession and underemployment (typified by the growth of less than full-time work) have reduced the ability of two-parent families with children — especially young families — to survive on only one income. The median annual earnings of the head of a family under age thirty with children declined by 39 percent between 1973 and 1986, compared with 14 percent for those without children. For all family heads ages thirty through sixty-four, median annual earnings dropped by nearly 15 percent.[13] When these trends are taken together, the impact on the majority of the families is a life lived closer to the margin — increasing their economic and psychological vulnerability.

Married women with children have dramatically increased their labor-force participation rate, from 41.7 percent in 1973 to 65 percent in 1987. Motivated by economic need and encouraged by the success of the civil rights and women's movements, mothers with young children in the labor force nearly doubled, growing from 32.7 percent to 57 percent over this period.[14] While there is nothing objectionable per se about women working, it creates new needs for families that the social system does not fill. Women whose husbands earn low wages are far more likely to work, as they always have been, than are wives of more affluent men. Forty-three percent of working wives with children are married to men who earn less than $20,000 a year. And more than half of all working wives with children are married to husbands with annual incomes of less than $25,000.

Yet, despite the significant efforts of working mothers to compensate for the declining earnings of their husbands, real family income has remained below 1973 levels for over a decade. This is a dramatic change from the 1947-73 period, when real median family income doubled. According to a congressional study, the loss in family income between 1973 and 1985 would have been more than three times as great during this period if mothers had not gone to work.[15]

In the aggregate, the increased work effort of women has slowed the decline of family living standards. Real median family income for all types of families has registered a slight growth in recent years. However, young families with children and the growing number of mother-only families have fallen behind significantly. Work, even full-time employment, is no longer enough to keep many of

these families out of poverty, and while six years of economic growth have reduced unemployment, high child-poverty rates persist.

Since 1973, young families — especially young minority families — have suffered
the most from changing economic structures. According to research by Andrew
Sum of Northeastern University, the median income of families with children
headed by a person less than thirty years old was 29.2 percent lower in 1986 than
the income of that age group in 1973. For young black families with children,
real median annual earnings have declined by one-half and for Hispanic families
by one-third.[16] While median income for all families with children declined by
6 percent between 1973 and 1986, median family income for young families with
children (where the family head is under age thirty) declined by 26 percent.[17]

Lower wages and the unparalleled growth of mother-only families in recent decades have significantly decreased the economic security of young American families with children. The federal minimum wage has lost a fourth of its relative
value since 1979. Consequently, the minimum wage no longer lifts any family above
the poverty level. The number of persons who are working yet poor has increased
by nearly 40 percent since 1979. In almost half of all poor families and in over
two-thirds of rural poor families, at least one parent is working. One in five American families with children is headed by a mother only, and 23 percent of young
families are headed by single females. The disproportionately low earnings of this
group — $11,560 in 1986 — has also had a significant effect on declining family
income.[18]

This whole range of economic shifts means that parents are more vulnerable
and particularly that children — including young children — are growing up in families with fewer means. The combined effect of young parentage, single parentage,
teenage parentage and unemployment, underemployment, casual employment,
and even more emphatically the succession of economic factors makes the day-to-
day lives of young children a challenge. If one looks integrally at the impact of
each of these changes, the net effect is grave indeed.

Along with declining family income, the rising cost of basic family obligations
has made it far more difficult for American families to feed, house, protect, and
educate their children than just a decade ago. The contemporary reality of dual-
earner families has profoundly changed the way American families work and how
they raise their children. Their annual child-care expenditures now exceed $11
billion — averaging nearly $3,000 a child. The National Institute of Child Health
and Human Development has estimated that American families spend an average
of 11 percent of total family income on child care for their preschool children
while poor families spend an average of 20 to 26 percent.[19]

The cost of housing has risen dramatically over the past fifteen years, exceeding
the rate of inflation nearly every year. The median price of a first home approached
$67,000 in 1986, an increase of more than 92 percent since 1975.[20] In 1973, pay-
ments on the average home mortgage took 21 percent of a typical thirty-year-old
man's income; today it takes 44 percent.[21] The housing affordability crisis has severely affected rates of home ownership and the availability of shelter for lower-
income families.

As a result of economic shifts in employment, the growth of contingent work, and health-care cost containment, health benefits for American workers and their families have significantly eroded since 1979. In 1986, 36.9 million Americans had no private or public health-care insurance, a 31 percent increase over 1980.[22] According to the Employee Benefits Research Institute, the fastest growing group of persons without health insurance are children of a working parent with employer-based coverage.[23] Personal health-care costs as a fraction of personal expenditures are projected to triple between 1986 and 2000, from an average of $1,837 a person to $5,557.[24]

For the eighth consecutive year, college costs have outstripped inflation, increasing by 77 percent since 1980.[25] At the same time, the availability of federal grants to students has declined, as has the average amount of the award. To pay for higher college costs, parents and college-age youth have tripled their personal debt. And many lower-income families have been forced to forgo a college education for their children.

Children in A Changing Economy

A striking fact of the 1980s is the dramatic increase in the number of children in poverty. While the unemployment rate has declined to 1978 levels, there are nearly 3 million more poor children today than there were in 1978. Despite the economic recovery, economic shifts and changing demographics have institutionalized high rates of child poverty in America. Children are now the poorest group of Americans; in 1986, 20 percent of American children lived in poverty, compared with 12.4 percent of persons sixty-five years and older and 10.1 percent of persons between the ages of eighteen and sixty-four. Between 1978 and 1986, the number of children living in families with incomes below the federal poverty level ($11,200 for a family of four in 1987) increased by 16 percent, bringing the total to nearly 13 million children.[26]

The youngest children are the most vulnerable. About one-fourth of all babies are born into families living in poverty.[27] And 25 percent of today's preschool children will be poor in the year 2000.[28] Children in single-parent families are especially vulnerable to poverty. A child born to a single mother is five times more likely to be poor than one born to a married couple. Teenage single mothers face particular risks of poverty and diminshed life chances. In 1986, two in every three young children under the age of three living with a teenage head-of-household were poor. And in the early 1980s, one in five young poor women with below average basic skills was a teenage mother.[29]

Indeed, despite increasing efforts to work and smaller family size, poor families are getting poorer. In 1986, nearly 40 percent of all poor persons had incomes below half of the federal poverty level.[30]

Two in every three poor children are white. Contrary to the stereotype, a disproportionate number of poor families, most of whom are white, live in rural areas. In 1986, nearly 25 percent of rural children were poor. Since 1978, poverty in rural areas has grown at twice the rate in urban areas.[31] Nevertheless, the stereotypes are not all wrong. Black and Hispanic children suffer disproportionately higher rates of poverty. One in every two black children and one in every three Hispanic children are poor, compared with one in every six white children.[32] And poverty rates in the central cities are significantly higher than in other parts of metropolitan areas. Nearly 43 percent of poor persons live in central cities, where poverty rates approximate 19 percent. William Julius Wilson, for example, finds an underclass in these older cities. He defines that underclass as those left behind in urban areas and isolated from other income groups. In 1970, only 15 percent of low-income blacks in New York City lived in high-poverty areas. By 1980, that figure had jumped to 45 percent. In Chicago, the proportion doubled from 25 to 50 percent.[33]

According to Wilson, economic and social dislocations in the central cities are primarily responsible for the emergence of underclass families. The exodus of manufacturing jobs from the central cities has resulted in higher unemployment and lower earnings for young black males. This in turn has discouraged marriage among young blacks and increased the number of mother-only families.[34]

Immigrant children are an increasingly significant minority of the population. And many newcomers to the United States — most recently from Mexico, Central America, Southeast Asia, and the Carribean — also tend to cluster in isolated, poor, urban settings.

The convergence of the major trends — worsening economic circumstances, the growth of single-parent families, and increasing conflicts between home and the workplace — has placed a growing number of children in increasingly precarious circumstances. All families and children are struggling with significant changes in their daily lives, including fewer or changed relationships between children and adults and more limited economic options. While all families face such stress, for those whose resources are extremely limited, these stresses and challenges can often become insurmountable.

Almost every indicator of health and well-being shows that disadvantaged children fare poorly: Low-income children are three to four times more likely to drop out of school than their affluent peers.[35] They are 50 percent more likely to have a disability.[36] Low-income teenagers are 250 percent more likely to become teenage parents.[37] In sum, poor children suffer more frequently from infant mortality, recurrent and untreated health problems, learning disabilities, psychological and physical stress, malnutrition, and child abuse.

Economic and demographic realities have created new challenges that families and society have to address. They raise questions about how society will ensure an adequate standard of living for its children and how to enable them to fulfill their aspirations. But they also raise more immediate questions concerning the ability of families — especially low-income families — to maintain a productive and nurturing family unit. Adequate living arrangements, basic health care, and education have long been essential elements to familial well-being. Yet in the economy of the 1980s, each has become more difficult to obtain for millions of families with children. In addition, child care has become as essential a service for families as any of the traditional basics of shelter, schooling, and medical care. Child care is one of the most pressing issues facing families on a daily basis. Whether parents care for their children at home or arrange for care outside the home depends on a variety of factors, including family work schedules, the availability of other family members, and access to affordable quality care in their community or workplace. National statistics on child-care availability are limited and do not provide a clear picture of actual child-care supply. In addition, information about parental preferences for child care is very limited. Even what limited information is available, however, reveals that the supply is inadequate and the "care" may be harmful to children's safety.

In 1987, more than 10 million children under age six and nearly twenty-five million ages six through eighteen were in need of some type of child care while their parents were working.[38] Between 2 million and 7 million latchkey children, including an estimated 1.5 million under the age of five, cared for themselves during all or part of each school day.[39] Existing spaces in licensed child-care centers and regulated family day-care homes, however, can accommodate only an estimated 2.9 million children.[40] Millions of children are cared for in settings that may not meet even the most basic health and safety standards; 37 percent of preschool children spend their days in family day-care homes, 75 to 94 percent of which are not state-regulated at all.[41]

The data raise some major questions. Is the United States going to develop a comprehensive, publicly supported child-care system comparable to the public education system? What mix of public and private resources will be engaged in providing care for children? How will the quality of children's care outside their own homes be ensured, and what level of government will be responsible for protecting children in these circumstances? Is there an adequate supply of child-care providers who are trained in the area of children and who have an understanding of child development? Are there certain circumstances, such as the age or needs of a child, which dictate that provisions should be made for the child to be at home with a parent, rather than supervised outside the home? What kind of qualitative barometers are needed? By addressing these questions, society will begin the process of providing for the increasing number of families who, regardless of income, require assistance in meeting their child-care responsibilities.

The United States is the only major industrialized nation other than South Africa that does not aid new parents upon the birth or illness of a child. Instead, new parents are often penalized by losing their jobs or wages or forfeiting critical benefits like health insurance when a new baby is born, adopted, or becomes critically ill. In addition to parental-leave policies, workplace policies that would help accommodate parental needs include flexible schedules, part-time work, and the possibility of working at home.

As a consequence of the increasing burden that housing costs have imposed on families, children are living in different and less secure settings than in previous generations. Nearly 65 percent of all children living with a parent live in housing that is owned by their parents or another member of the household.[42] But the number of renter households with children grew more than four times faster than the rate for all households between 1973 and 1987.[43]

The affordability crisis in housing has hit low-income families particularly hard. Half of the estimated 15 million low-income families with children paid more than the generally recommended 30 percent of their incomes for housing.[44] Of the 35 percent of children living in rented housing, 4 percent are in publicly subsidized housing. There is a wide discrepancy between the housing conditions of white and black children. About 60 percent of black and Hispanic children live in rented housing; 17.7 percent of black children and 5.6 percent of Hispanic children live in publicly subsidized housing.[45]

The supply of low-income housing units has decreased dramatically in recent years, causing a shortfall that is 120 percent larger than at the beginning of the decade.[46] More people are living in housing that does not meet basic standards and more families are doubling up.[47] Out of 174,000 public-housing units in New York City, as many as 50,000 are illegally occupied by more than one family.[48] Families with children have become the fastest growing group of the homeless, now accounting for one-third of the total.[49]

Unlike most other industrialized countries, where health care is guaranteed by the government, the United States links the provision of health care to employment. With the rapidly changing economy and employment patterns in the United States, the number of families without health-care benefits is growing. Thirty-seven million Americans, including 12 million children, lack health insurance.[50] Even when an employer provides health benefits, coverage for family members is not guaranteed. More than 50 percent of uninsured children live in families with a full-time, full-year worker.[51] In 1986, one-third of all children in poor families had no health-insurance protection of any kind,[52] including Medicaid, the federal-state health insurance program for low-income Americans.

Consequently, millions of children now begin life at great risk of poor health. Low birth weight is the leading cause of infant mortality and childhood disabilities. The percentage of low birth-weight babies increased in 1985 for the first time in twenty years. The United States now has the highest infant mortality rate among twenty industrialized countries. This is not surprising, since nearly a fourth of all pregnant women receive no prenatal care in the critical first trimester of pregnancy. In fact, black babies are more than twice as likely to suffer from low birth weight as white babies.

After a dramatic and successful national effort to end the ravages of hunger in the late 1960s and early 1970s, hunger and malnutrition have reemerged as phenomena of the 1980s. It is estimated that malnutrition affects almost 500,000 American children.[53] A recent study of one poor neighborhood in New Haven, Connecticut, found that a fourth of families with children were either chronically hungry or faced this risk. The study also documented that hungry children suffered from almost twice as many health problems such as ear infections, dizziness, colds, and weight loss, which were strongly associated with school absences.[54]

While low-income children also suffer more health problems, they make at least 50 percent fewer physician visits than higher-income children with similar health problems.[55] Overall, low-income children suffer higher mortality rates from all causes, including low birth weight, respiratory problems, congenital anomalies, accidents, poisonings, and violence.[56] Furthermore, infants and preschool children at risk of brain damage due to elevated levels of lead in the blood are nine times as likely to come from low-income families than from higher-income families.[57] (For a detailed discussion of children's health care, see the essay by P.A. Colón and A.R. Colón in this volume, pages 45–57.)

Like child care, housing, and health care, participation in education, from the early grades through college, is affected by demographic, economic, and social trends. Between 1970 and 1986, the number of children enrolled in preprimary schools increased significantly. While there are about 6.3 million children in such programs,[58] almost half of the three-to-five age group are not enrolled in full- or part-time day preschool programs.[59] Because families are having fewer children, enrollment in elementary and secondary schools has declined in recent years.[60] But it has begun to increase, particularly in the elementary grades. During the period 1986 to 1990, the elementary school-age population (ages six through thirteen) is expected to increase by over 2 million after having decreased by 5 million since 1970.[61]

In 1987, nearly 1 million young people left public school without graduating. For the past twenty-five years, high-school dropout rates have been relatively stable, with about a fourth of all students not graduating on time. The approximately 20 million youths who do not go to college are often forgotten in reviews of student educational status. While most of these students graduate from high school, they generally have lower academic skills.[62] Less than half of high-school seniors read at levels considered adequate to carry out even moderately complex tasks, and 80 percent have inadequate writing skills.[63] Given the current and future job market, these graduates are unlikely to secure jobs that pay decent wages.

The experience of poverty, particularly for a long time, places children at a significantly greater educational disadvantage than children who are not poor or who are poor for a shorter time. The likelihood of falling behind in school is increased by two percentage points a year spent living in poverty.[64] Children disadvantaged by poverty, low educational achievement, and other hardships are also at increased risk of dropping out of school. Findings indicate that at-risk students are three times more likely to drop out than other students, and, according to a recent review, the more poor children in a school, the higher the dropout rate.[65]

Continued high immigration rates and larger families among immigrants suggest that growing numbers of children may enter school disadvantaged by low income, cultural as well as social isolation, and limited English proficiency. Between 2.1 million and 2.7 million school-age immigrant children (five through eighteen years) now reside in the United States.[66] It is estimated that by the year 2000, more than half of the children in California's public schools will be members of minority groups.

College enrollment is directly affected by economic and social trends. Between

1978 and 1983, while college enrollment students with family incomes over $30,000 increased, the number of lower-income students decreased.[67] College attendance among minority students has also been deeply affected. After rising substantially during the 1970s, black enrollment in college declined by 11 percent between 1980 and 1984.[68]

Increased Stress on Families

The economic and demographic transformations of the past two decades have affected day-to-day family functioning, especially since workplace and government policies have not yet adequately responded to these changes. The stress of meeting both work and family responsibilities has had some effect on most families and has visibly overwhelmed others. There is increasing evidence that the inadequacy of workplace policies to accommodate these dual responsibilities is significantly associated with higher levels of job dissatisfaction, personal stress, and ill health.[69] Extreme examples of the consequences of such stress are child and spousal abuse, alcoholism, and drug abuse — all of which are exacerbated by economic dislocation and new family arrangements.

More than 2.2 million children were reported as abused or neglected in 1987, about 2 percent more than in 1986.[70] Most child abuse and neglect continues to be perpetrated within families and by persons known to the child. The traditional stereotype of abuse by a stranger or the currently sensationalized image of child abuse in institutional settings remains a small fraction of the physical, sexual, and emotional abuse and neglect that children experience. (P.A. Colón and A.R. Colón discuss child abuse in their essay in this volume.)

Statistics on spousal abuse are inconclusive, since there are no uniform reporting requirements across states. Nevertheless, the phenomenon appears to be disturbingly widespread: the U.S. Department of Justice has reported that a woman is beaten every eighteen seconds.[71] More than 2 million women are beaten every year, one in twelve while pregnant.[72] Both spouses and their children are victims: nearly two-thirds of the residents in community-based shelters for battered women are children.[73]

Seven million children under age eighteen live with an alcoholic parent. These children are four times more likely to develop alcoholism than children of nonalcoholics.[74] Alcohol and drug use are also still prevalent among teenagers. About one-third of all twelve- to seventeen-year-olds reported drinking alcohol at least once in the preceding month.[75] Despite a recent decline among high-school seniors, 57 percent of the 1987 senior class had tried an illicit drug, and over one-third had used an illicit drug other than marijuana.[76] The use of cocaine has dropped little from peak levels: annual prevalence is 6 percent among high-school students, 17 percent among college students, and 20 percent among all young adults.[77] Since most of the statistics on drug and alcohol use are based on students in school, the data inadequately reflect the behavior of young people who have dropped out of school, many of whom are the teenagers who are more likely to engage in substance abuse.

A small but significant number of children are growing up without a family at all or in exceedingly troubled households. In many instances, the state has effectively become their parent. Data on these children are extremely limited, but even rough estimates and anecdotes suggest that their numbers are increasing. After some years of decline, the number of children in foster care increased 2.6 percent in two years. An estimated one-day count in June 1988 found 375,000 children in foster care. This also represents a significant increase, partially fueled by the rapid increase of serious drug abuse and AIDS.[78] Nearly 50,000 children were held in public juvenile correctional facilities in 1985, a slight increase from 1979. Most of these youths are teenage males.[79] During recent years, the number of juveniles arrested for violent crimes (homicide, rape, robbery, and aggravated assault) increased after a large decline during the prior decade.[80] Almost 1.2 million children run away from home each year. According to the U.S. Department of Health and Human Services estimates, at least 500,000 youths are homeless at some time during the year. Seventy percent of runaway youths who come to shelters have been sexually or physically abused, and 85 percent are depressed.[81]

Thus, for a variety of reasons, and in most instances through no fault of their own, a small number of children are in the public's charge. As the United States begins to reconsider social policies, it is vital to include these children in the scope of the reforms. It will be essential to address how to prevent their becoming public wards, and if they must enter state custody, how to give them the proper health care, education, and nurturing that they, like all other children, need.

Policy Considerations

The daily struggles of American families reveal certain basic facts that must be considered when planning future policy directions. It is common for mothers to work, for families to spend almost half of their income on housing, and for families to have no health insurance or to be underinsured. Child care is now widely required for families of all income and racial groups. Affording a college education for their children is a common hurdle for families. These facts demonstrate the increasing possibility that many families with children need certain types of supports, including child care, housing assistance, health insurance, and access to postsecondary education, if they are to meet the basic needs of their children.

Furthermore, workplace policies must accommodate the current economic and demographic circumstances of families. The General Accounting Office has documented that offering parental leave, for example, yields benefits to employers by reducing job turnover and enhancing productivity.[82] Corporate prenatal-education seminars and support services for pregnant employees are beginning to affect the incidence of premature births. Average medical costs for maternity and nursery care were reduced by 86 percent at one such company.[83] Repeated studies of employer-supported child care have confirmed that improved recruitment, reduced job turnover and absenteeism, and improved employee morale and productivity are among the benefits.[84] But, despite this evidence, even the largest firms have made only token efforts to meet parental needs.

Special consideration is required for the increasing proportion of American children who face impoverishment and disadvantage. Persistently high rates of school failures are costly to society in two respects. Most directly, since earnings are highly correlated to levels of educational attainment, each year's class of dropouts costs the United States more than $240 billion in lost earnings and foregone taxes over their lifetimes.[85] Over the years, this lack of basic skills could impair the ability of these students to learn high-order tasks, and they will be ill-equipped to rebuild America's competitive edge in world markets. This has significant implications for the nation because the entry-level labor pool is projected to shrink by 25 percent over the next ten years. Consequently, the country cannot afford to squander the talents of any child.[86]

Recognizing the urgency to address the needs of disadvantaged children, American business leaders recently called for reforms in many sectors, giving "highest priority to early and sustained intervention" in the lives of these disadvantaged children. This noted group of executives, drawing on strong evidence that these investments are cost-effective,[87] recommended major strategies, such as prenatal and child care, school restructuring, enhanced compensatory education, outreach and support for at-risk children to keep them in school and to assist those who drop out to reenter, and skills training and retraining.[88] These recommendations underscore the fact that very young children, because of their vulnerability, demand special protections and comprehensive services.

Clearly, the extraordinary swiftness and scope of the economic and demographic changes affecting children require equally far-reaching changes in public policy. These policies must be carefully crafted, so that they work within the framework of children's families and communities, not in a vacuum. The nation has a strong economic interest in ensuring that the next generation will be well educated, able to work productively and to raise a healthy family in an increasingly complex, technological society. At the same time, policies to further that goal must respect children for their own sakes, both as individuals and as the bearers of our dreams for the future.

NOTES

1. House Select Committee on Children, Youth, and Families [hereafter referred to as House Select Committee], *U.S. Children and Their Families: Current Conditions and Recent Trends*, 98th Cong., 1st sess., May 1983, and 100th Cong., 1st sess., March 1987.

2. Arthur J. Norton and Jeanne E. Moorman, "Current Trends in Marriage and Divorce among American Women," *Journal of Marriage and the Family* 49 (February 1987): 3–14.

3. Stepfamily Foundation, "Stepfamily Foundation Statistics: The Numbers Tell the Story" (New York, 1988).

4. U.S. Bureau of the Census, *Marital Status and Living Arrangements*, 1987.

5. Ibid.

6. House Select Committee, *U.S. Children and Their Families*, March 1987.

7. Ibid.

8. Ibid.

9. U.S. Congress, Office of Technology Assessment, *Children's Mental Health: Problems and Services — A Background Paper*, OTA-BP-H-33 (Washington, D.C.: GPO, December 1986).

10. Frank Levy, testimony before House Select Committee, *American Families in Tomorrow's Economy*, 100th Cong., 1st sess., July 1987.

11. Cathy Schoen, ibid.

12. U.S. Bureau of the Census, *Money, Income and Poverty Status of Families and Persons in the United States: 1987*, August 1988; and Center on Budget and Policy Priorities, "After-Tax Income Gap Widens between Rich and Poor," 1988.

13. Children's Defense Fund and the Center for Labor Market Studies, *Vanishing Dreams: The Growing Economic Plight of America's Young Families* (Boston: Northeastern University, 1988).

14. U.S. Bureau of Labor Statistics, *Over Half of Mothers with Children One Year Old or Under in Labor Force in March 1987*, Report 87-345, U.S. Department of Labor, 12 August 1987.

15. Joint Economic Committee, *Working Mothers Are Preserving Family Living Standards*, 99th Cong., 2d sess., May 1986.

16. Andrew Sum (Unpublished paper, Northeastern University, Center for Labor Market Studies, 1988); and Children's Defense Fund and the Center for Labor Market Studies, *Vanishing Dreams*.

17. Ibid.

18. Ibid.

19. Sandra Hofferth, testimony before House Select Committee, July 1987.

20. William C. Apgar, Jr., et al., *The State of the Nation's Housing 1988* (Cambridge: Joint Center for Housing Studies, Harvard University, 1988).

21. House Select Committee, *American Families in Tomorrow's Economy*.

22. Ibid.

23. Ibid.

24. Ibid.

25. *New York Times*, 7 Aug. 1988.

26. Sum.

27. National Center on Clinical Infant Program, *Infants Can't Wait: The Numbers* (Washington, D.C., 1986).

28. Children's Defense Fund, *A Children's Defense Budget* (Washington, D.C., 1987).

29. Ibid. (1988).

30. Center on Budget and Policy Priorities, "Gap Between Rich and Poor Widest Ever Recorded" (July 1987).

31. U.S. Bureau of the Census, *Poverty in the United States: 1986* (June 1988).

32. Ibid.

33. William Julius Wilson, *The Truly Disadvantaged: The Inner City, the Underclass and Public Policy* (Chicago: University of Chicago Press, 1987).

34. Ibid.

35. Children's Defense Fund, *A Children's Defense Budget*.

36. Harriet B. Fox, "A Preliminary Analysis of Options to Improve Health Insurance Coverage for Chronically Ill and Disabled Children" (Washington, D.C.: Fox Health Policy Consultants, September 1984).

37. Children's Defense Fund, *A Children's Defense Budget*.

38. U.S. Bureau of Labor Statistics, *Over Half of Mothers with Children*.

39. House Select Committee, *Families and Child Care: Improving the Options*, 98th Cong., 2d sess., 1984; Census, 1987; and Douglas Baird, testimony on behalf of Child Welfare League of America

before Subcommittee on Children, Drugs and Alcoholism of the Senate Committee on Labor and Human Resources, 100th Cong., 1st sess., 11 June 1987.

40. Hofferth.

41. House Select Committee, *Families and Child Care*, 99th Cong., 2d sess.; and House Select Committee, *Hearing on Child Care: Key to Employment in a Changing Economy*, 100th Cong., 1st sess., March 1987.

42. House Select Committee, *U.S. Children and Their Families*.

43. Apgar.

44. Congressional Research Service, "Housing Programs: Issues in Low and Moderate Income Housing Assistance" (Washington, D.C., 1988).

45. House Select Committee, *U.S. Children and Their Families*.

46. National Low-Income Housing Coalition, "Rental Housing Crisis Deepens For Low Income Renters," newsletter, 3 Mar. 1986.

47. Sandra Newman et al., "Subsidizing Shelter: The Relationship Between Welfare and Housing Assistance," *Urban Institute Report* 1 (Washington, D.C.: Urban Institute Press, May 1988).

48. Chester Hartman, "Affordability of Housing," *Handbook on Housing and the Built Environment* (Westport, Conn.: Greenwood Press, 1988).

49. U.S. Conference of Mayors, *The Continuing Growth of Hunger, Homelessness and Poverty in America's Cities: 1987* (Washington, D.C., Dec. 1987).

50. Congressional Research Service, "Health Insurance and the Uninsured: Background Data and Analysis," May 1988.

51. Employee Benefits Research Institute, *Public and Private Issues on Financing Health Care for Children*, Issue Brief No. 179 (June 1988).

52. Ibid.

53. Physician Task Force on Hunger in America, Harvard School of Public Health, 1986.

54. Matthew E. Melmed, testimony before House Select Committee, *Children and Families in Poverty: The Struggle to Survive*, 100th Cong., 2d sess., February 1988.

55. Paul W. Newacheck and Barbara Starfield, "Morbidity and Use of Ambulatory Care Services among Poor and Nonpoor Children," *American Journal of Public Health* 78 (August 1988): 927–33.

56. Barbara Starfield et al., "Child Health Status and Risk Factors" (Washington, D.C.: The Foundation for Health Services Research, October 1983).

57. National Center for Clinical Infant Programs, *Infants Can't Wait: The Numbers* (Washington, D.C., 1986).

58. House Select Committee, *U.S. Children and Their Families*.

59. Census, CPR Series P-20, no. 426, 1988.

60. Ibid. 409 and earlier reports.

61. U.S. Department of Education, Center for Education Statistics, *Projections of Educational Statistics* (biennial) and *Digest of Education Statistics*.

62. W.T. Grant Commission on Work, Family, and Citizenship, *The Forgotten Half: Non-College Youth in America* (Washington, D.C., 1988).

63. Committee on Economic Development, "Children in Need: Investment Strategies for the Educationally Disadvantaged" (Washington, D.C., 1987).

64. Steven Chaikind, *Poverty, Achievement and the Distribution of Compensatory Education Services* (Washington, D.C.: U.S. Department of Education, 1986).

65. U.S. Department of Education, Center for Educational Statistics, *High School and Beyond*, survey, 1980.

66. National Coalition of Advocates for Students, *New Voices: Immigrant Students in U.S. Public Schools* (Boston, 1988).

67. John B. Lee, "Student Aid & Minority Enrollment in Higher Education," a report prepared by the Applied Systems Institute, Inc. (Report no. ASI 2251) for the American Association of State Colleges and Universities (Washington, D.C., January 1985).

68. Katharine Mohrman, "Unintended Consequences of Federal Student Aid Policies," *Brookings Review* (Fall 1987): 24–30.

69. Dana E. Friedman, "Work vs. Family: War of the Worlds," *Personnel Administrator* (August 1987):36–38; Ellen Galinsky and Diane Hughes, "The Fortune Magazine Child Care Study" (New York: Bank Street College, 1987); and U.S. Department of Commerce, Bureau of the Census, *Who's Minding the Kids? Child Care Arrangements: Winter 1984–85*, Household Economic Studies, Series P-70, 9, May 1987.

70. National Committee for the Prevention of Child Abuse, newsletter, April 1988. See also House Select Committee, *Abused Children in America: Victims of Abused Neglect*, 100th Cong., 1st sess., March 1987; American Humane Association, *Protecting Children*, newsletter, Denver, Colo., 1987; and Andrea J. Sedlak, *Study of National Incidence and Prevalence of Child Abuse and Neglect*, final report, December 1987.

71. U.S. Bureau of Justice Statistics, "Preventing Domestic Violence Against Women," Special Report, August 1986.

72. Anne Stewart Helton, *Protocol of Care for the Battered Woman* (White Plains, N.Y.: March of Dimes, 1987).

73. *New York Times*, 31 May 1987.

74. Children of Alcoholics Foundation, Inc., *Children of Alcoholics: A Review of the Literature* (New York, February 1985).

75. National Institute on Drug Abuse, U.S. Department of Health and Human Services, *National Trends in Drug Use and Related Factors Among American High School Students and Young Adults*, 1987.

76. Ibid.

77. Ibid.

78. CRS Inc., "Indian Child Welfare: A Status Report" (Washington, D.C., April 1988); Maximus Technical Consultants to Management, "State Child Welfare Abstracts 1980–1985," December 1987; telephone interview with Charles Gershenson, Center for the Study of Social Policy, 11 July 1988; and House Select Committee, *A Generation in Jeopardy: Children and AIDS*, 100th Cong., 1st sess., Dec. 1987.

79. House Select Committee, *U.S. Children and Their Families*, 100th Cong., 2d sess., March 1988.

80. House Select Committee, *Youth and Violence: The Current Crisis*, 100th Cong., 1st sess., March 1988.

81. June Bucy, executive director, National Network of Runaway and Youth Services, Washington, D.C., testimony prepared for House Select Committee, *The Crisis in Homelessness: Effects on Children and Families*, February 1987.

82. William J. Gainer, U.S. General Accounting Office, testimony before Subcommittee on Children, Families, Drugs, and Alcoholism of the Senate Committee on Labor and Human Resources, April 1987.

83. *Wall Street Journal*, 12 July 1988.

84. House Select Committee, *Families and Child Care*.

85. James S. Catterall, "On the Social Costs of Dropping Out of School" (Stanford, Calif.: Institute for Research on Educational Finance and Governance, School of Education, Stanford University, December 1985).

86. Education Commision of the State, Business Advisory Commission, *Reconnecting Youth* (Denver, October 1985).

87. House Select Committee, *Opportunities for Success: Cost Effective Programs for Children, Update 1988*, 100th Cong., 2d sess.

88. Committee for Economic Development, *Children in Need: Investment Strategies for the Educationally Disadvantaged* (Washington, D.C., 1987).

Children at Risk

MARIAN WRIGHT EDELMAN

Parents generally accept and even cherish the fact that each child has his or her unique personality, likes and dislikes, strengths and weaknesses, and needs. Within the family these individual differences are accepted. Most parents attempt to respond to each child's needs and welcome the child's special contributions to the life of the family. At the broader level of public policy, however, the uniqueness of each child is not recognized. Public policies, to a large degree, have yet to acknowledge that every child is special and important, not just to his or her family but also to the country. Both individual children and groups of children — by virtue of their race, family income, or other circumstances — have special needs that society must recognize and address.

Despite the inadequacy of existing public policies to meet the varied needs of children at risk, there has been some progress in defining the characteristics of children with special needs and in devising strategies for helping them. More than two decades of research, data collection, judicial activity, and restructuring state and national legislation and budgets have at least helped identify the types of children who are special and who, without a national commitment to help them, are likely to fall through the cracks to a life of poverty. The list of children at risk includes minority children, poor children, teenage parents and their children, the physically or emotionally handicapped, abused and neglected children and others in the child welfare system, and the homeless.

As society changes and analyses become more sophisticated and more perceptive, the list both changes and grows. Twenty-five years ago it would probably not have included abused and neglected children. And although the child welfare system has long targeted orphans and young vagrants among those with special needs, as recently as 1985 the list would probably not have included homeless children in the sense that they are defined now — those who are still with their parents but in family units that are consigned to a nomadic, often squalid existence on the streets and in shelters that can never be a substitute for a stable family home.

But one must not oversimplify. The problem with making lists is that many children belong to several categories, increasing their jeopardy of falling into the group that has become a synonym for hopelessness—the underclass.

The Importance of Every Child

The first high-school graduating class of the twenty-first century entered the first grade in September 1988. They are the country's future workers, parents, college students, taxpayers, soldiers, and leaders. Yet millions of them are already beginning to lose hope:

- One in five of them (a total of 12.4 million) is poor.
- One in five is at risk of becoming a teenage parent.
- One in five is nonwhite; among nonwhites, two in five are poor.
- One in six has no health insurance.
- One in seven is at risk of dropping out of school.
- One in two has a mother in the labor force, but only a minority have safe, affordable, quality child care.

No society that considers itself civilized or moral can condone the victimization of millions of children by discrimination, poverty, and neglect. Help should be extended to children not only because of moral obligations but also because of faith in the future of society, its progress, its values, and its traditions and because children should have every possible opportunity, as they mature, to participate in the society and contribute to it. But as the last decade of the twentieth century approaches, there are also compelling demographic reasons to reject and reverse these trends. In addition to the moral motivation of alleviating human suffering, one must add the motivation of national economic self-interest.

Because of dramatic social changes in the past century, parents no longer expect their own children to support them directly when they are elderly. Rather, they rely on Social Security, Medicaid and Medicare, tax-supported pensions, and retirement benefits financed by employers. Many will require contributions to these programs from the next generation as a whole and from that generation's children. It is therefore in everyone's self-interest that today's children—and their children—are healthy, educated, productive, and compassionate. Yet the society is aging, and the number of children and youths in relation to other age groups in the population is declining.

The William T. Grant Foundation Commission on Work, Family and Citizenship, which is examining the status and future of American youth, documented these trends in its June 1987 publication, "American Youth: A Statistical Snapshot." Among the points made by the commission:

The number of American youth is shrinking dramatically. Between 1980 and 1996, our youth population, ages 15-25, is expected to fall 21 percent, from 43 to 34 million. Young people as a percentage of the nation's population will also decline from 18.8 to 13 percent. . . .

These falling numbers will drastically alter the characteristics of the nation's labor pool, higher education enrollments. . . .

The problems facing minority youth will take on even greater importance as they account for larger and larger proportions of America's youth population. . . .

Children are not only a precious resource, then, but an increasingly scarce one. Until recently, America's youth population has been relatively plentiful, allowing the society to survive and the economy to grow, despite the waste of many young lives through society's neglect. That margin for error no longer exists. The ratio of workers to retirees has shrunk and will continue to shrink in the coming decades. And one in three of the new potential workers is a member of a minority group.

Minority Children

For many blacks, recent years have been good. Black per-capita income is at an all-time high, black purchasing power — now at $200 billion a year — exceeds the gross national product of Australia and New Zealand combined, and there are more black elected officials than ever. Blacks head the House Budget Committee of the U.S. Congress, the Ford Foundation, and the marketing activities of the Xerox Corporation, and they represent the United States on the Olympic Committee. These are important, tangible gains of the civil rights movement. But there is another black community for which these have not been good years — a community, in fact, where life is getting worse.

Today, black children are more likely than in 1980 to be born into poverty, to have been deprived of early prenatal care, to have a single mother or no employed parent, to be unemployed as teenagers, and not to go to college. They are twice as likely as white children to be born prematurely, to suffer low birth weights, to live in substandard housing, or to die in the first year of life. Black children are three times as likely as white children to be poor, to live in a female-headed family, to have no parent employed, or to be murdered between five and nine years of age. They are five times as likely as white children to rely on welfare and nine times as likely to live with a parent who has never married.

While black children's plight is the worst, the fast-growing population of Hispanic children in this country also suffers much higher rates of poverty than their white counterparts. The U.S. Bureau of the Census reported the following poverty rates for 1987: for all American children, 20.6 percent; for white children, 15.6 percent; for Hispanic children, 39.8 percent; and for black children, 48.8 percent.

Some other key indicators further tell the story of problems faced by minority children. For example, National Center for Health Statistics data on infant mortality in 1985 reveal that for all races, per 1,000 live births, there are 10.6 deaths; for whites, 9.3; for blacks, 18.2; and for nonwhite infants, 15.8. Other data show that Hispanic youths as well as blacks are less likely to be employed than whites and are more likely to become teenage parents than their white counterparts.

The Spread of Poverty

The tide of misery that poverty breeds and that blacks have borne disproportionately throughout history has now enveloped a critical mass of white American families and children. Thirty-three million individuals—one-seventh of all Americans—are now poor as a result of economic recession, followed by slow growth, structural changes in the economy, declining real wage rates, federal tax and budget policies that favor the rich at the expense of the poor, and changing family demographics. One in every five American children lives in a female-headed household, and one in four will be dependent on welfare at some point in his or her lifetime.

Most Americans now realize that poverty is not just the result of personal inadequacy, laziness, and unworthiness, despite some national leaders' attempts to portray the poor as culpable. Iowa farmers, Detroit autoworkers, Youngstown steel workers, South Carolina textile workers, and small-business people have lost their livelihoods as a result of the economic dislocations afflicting the United States. They have been surprised to find themselves in unemployment lines or bread lines or new jobs paying a fraction of their former earnings. Of those 32.5 million poor, more than 13 million are children. Children make up the poorest age group in America. Nearly half of black children, almost two-fifths of Hispanic children, and nearly one-seventh of white children in the United States are poor. These figures are appalling.

For a growing number of Americans, moreover, working does not mean escaping poverty. The ranks of the working poor have also grown. In 1979 a parent working full-time at the minimum wage earned enough to lift a family of three above the poverty line. By 1986, a full-time, minimum-wage job yielded a paycheck equivalent to only 75 percent of the poverty-level income for a family of three and 61 percent of the poverty-level income for a family of four. (The poverty-level income for a family of four in 1986 was $11,203.) In 1986 more than a million Americans supported families on full-time, year-round jobs that did not raise them out of poverty. And fully half of the country's 7 million heads of poor households worked at least part-time in 1986.

Young parents and their children have been squeezed by changes in the economy and the job market in the past decade and a half. Young families have borne almost all of the income losses caused by the resulting turmoil. The median income for all American families declined by only 1 percent between 1973 and 1986. Among young families (those headed by persons under age thirty), however, median income dropped by 14 percent during this period. Young families with children suffered the greatest income loss—nearly 26 percent.

Not surprisingly, poverty among young families and their children has also increased far more rapidly than for older American families. The poverty rate for all young families nearly doubled between 1973 and 1986, rising from 12 percent to 22 percent. The chances of being poor are even greater for young families with children—their poverty rate jumped from 16 percent in 1973 to 30 percent in 1986. In contrast, the poverty rate for older families with children increased more gradually, from 9 percent to 13 percent. As a result of the growing economic plight of young families, one-third of all poor children in the United States now live in young families. And among the youngest families—those headed by persons under age twenty-five—a staggering 54 percent of all children are poor.

For a child of poverty, the most ordinary needs—from health care to housing—

become extraordinary. Testifying in April 1988 before the U.S. House of Representatives' Select Committee on Children, Youth, and Families, twelve-year-old Yvette Diaz of New York City painted a vivid picture of the assaults on mind and body that are an integral part of daily life for her and other residents of the Hotel Martinique for homeless families. She, her mother, her sisters ages seven and nine, and her brother age three went to live in the Martinique "because my aunt's house burned down and we didn't have any place to live," she testified. "I don't like the hotel because there is always a lot of trouble there. I don't go down into the street to play because there is no place to play. . . . The streets are dangerous, with all kinds of sick people who are on drugs or crazy. My mother is afraid to let me go downstairs. Only this Saturday, my friend, the security guard at the hotel, Mr. Santiago, was killed on my floor. The blood is still on the walls and on the floor. . . . We can't cook in the apartment. The hotel warned us that if we are caught cooking in the rooms, we could be sent to a shelter."

Adolescent Parents

Teenage pregnancy is both a cause and a consequence of poverty. In recent years a huge new group of children has been added to the list of those with special needs – adolescent parents.

A young woman testified before the House Select Committee about her life: "I would like for you to meet Robin. She is 15 years old and alone, out of school and married at 16. By the age of 21 she has no friends or family, no education, no skills. . . . She is basically alone. I guess Robin never would have been able to have seen the grave mistakes she made, if she had not been seeing her children reliving her own mistakes. . . . I am Robin." She described as eloquently as anyone could the frustrating viciousness of the cycle of teenage pregnancy, poverty, and dependency.

Adolescent pregnancy is a crisis among all races and classes of American youth today. Each day almost 2,700 girls under the age of twenty get pregnant and 1,300 give birth. Every year a million teenage girls – one in ten – get pregnant. Although these statistics include a disproportionate number of poor, minority, and urban teenagers, two-thirds of those who give birth each year are white, two-thirds do not live in big cities, and two-thirds come from families with above-poverty incomes.

Adolescent pregnancy is a crisis not because teenage birthrates are rising, as is widely believed. (In fact, both the proportion and number of adolescents giving birth generally have fallen since 1970.) It is a crisis because the society is changing and young parents are tragically unprepared to deal with the consequences of early birth in contemporary America. Both the number and rate of births to teenagers who are unmarried are rising, thereby increasing the likelihood of poverty for two generations of children – young mothers and their children. In 1950, 15.4 percent of these births were to unmarried teenagers. By 1970, the proportion had doubled. By 1986, it had doubled again – to 60.8 percent.

The costs of adolescent parenthood are enormous, and they are magnified if the mother is unmarried. Forty percent of teenage girls who drop out of school do so because of pregnancy or marriage. Only half of the young women who become parents before the age of eighteen complete high school by the time they reach their midtwenties. Furthermore, the average lifetime earnings of a woman who has dropped out of school are roughly half those of a woman who has graduated from college. In 1986, more than four out of five children living in families headed by young females were poor.

An eighteen- or nineteen-year-old man can no longer earn enough to support a family, and the average single mother of any age has never earned a decent wage in this country. Yet the birth of a child to a teenager often means that the mother will not complete her education and will be unable to secure any employment at all, let alone a job that pays well enough to support the family.

Often the father of a child born to a teenage girl is in his early twenties. As discussed in the previous section, the erosion of employment opportunities and wage levels makes it impossible for even the young men who find work to earn enough to support their families.

This trend is particularly disturbing because earnings losses among young men reduce the likelihood that young Americans will marry and form two-parent families. Research indicates a connection between unemployment or low earnings and marital instability and between joblessness and delayed marriage. The decline in real earnings and the resulting drop in marriage rates have been most severe among high-school dropouts and graduates who do not go on to college—the young people who have tended to marry and bear children earliest. While a reversal of recent earnings losses would not restore marriage rates to their previous levels, more adequate earnings would substantially increase the proportion of young adults who would be willing and able to form stable families.

Children of Adolescent Parents

As Robin suggested in her congressional testimony, the babies born to adolescent parents often seem condemned to repeat the mistakes and suffering of their parents. Shawn Grant, a member of a gang in Philadelphia, grew up in a single-parent household. When he testified before the House Select Committee on Children, Youth and Families, he was on intensive probation for committing a robbery. "My father has had little contact with me since I was one year old," he told the committee. "In my neighborhood, a lot of negative things go on. People sell drugs; a lot of the gang members' parents use drugs and often these guys do not see their parents. . . . When I was young I use [sic] to worry about my father. I also resented his not being involved in my life. Now I do not care. However, I think that I would not have become involved in a gang if I had had a job and if my father had had a relationship with me."

Babies born to adolescent, single parents have two strikes against them. First, they enter life with particularly high risks to their health and well-being. Babies born to single mothers are five times more likely to be poor than those born to two-parent families. Only 53 percent of all infants born to teenagers in 1985 had mothers who began prenatal care in the first three months of pregnancy. More than one in eight—twice the national average—had a mother who received either no prenatal care at all or none until the last trimester. Babies born to women who receive no prenatal care are three times more likely to die in their first year of life than infants whose mothers received comprehensive care. Children born to teenagers are also more likely than other children to grow up in poverty. Young families are two and a half times more likely than the average American family to have incomes below the poverty line.

Children who grow up in persistently poor families are far more likely to face inadequate nutrition, housing, and health care, not to be enrolled in preschool programs, to enter school less prepared than their more advantaged peers, and to be held back one or more grades. They are also more likely to drop out of school with seriously deficient academic skills that prevent them from competing in the labor market and gaining access to postsecondary education and training programs. Like Shawn, children of poor single parents may end up in a gang, committing crimes, feeling that they would prefer another kind of life but having no idea how to find it. In this way the cycle of poverty that begins with limited employment opportunities, low wages, too-early pregnancies, and low marriage rates among today's teenagers and young adults will—if society fails to intervene—be repeated and perhaps amplified in the next generation.

Children with Other Special Needs

While most children grow up safe, secure, and emotionally sound, a sizable minority do not. Millions of American children and adolescents endure abuse or neglect in their parental homes; others are awaiting permanent homes while in foster care; and many have unmet emotional needs. Judicial decisions and federal statutes have given handicapped children a right to education and provided a framework for state efforts to address the complex needs of children who are abused, neglected, emotionally disturbed, or in foster care. Current resources and systems, however, remain grossly inadequate to meet their growing needs.

Reports of child abuse and neglect have increased steadily since 1976, with more than a 90 percent national increase between 1981 and 1986. More than three-fifths of the states reported to the House Select Commitee on Children, Youth, and Families in 1986 that the deteriorating economic conditions faced by many families were a primary contributor to the increases in child abuse and neglect since 1981. While reports of abuse and neglect escalated between 1981 and 1985, federal resources for prevention and treatment fell further and further behind, and child protective service agencies have been overwhelmed.

About 275,000 children and adolescents live in foster-family homes, group homes, residential treatment centers, and other institutions. While some have been abused or neglected, others enter care because their parents are unable to meet the demands of their disabilities or behavior problems. Still others enter because their families are homeless or too poor to support their children.

The group is varied in age and background. About one-half are minority children, who are represented disproportionately in care in many states and who tend to be in care longer, waiting for permanent homes. While youths thirteen and older account for about 46 percent of the children in foster care, very young children are also entering the system in greater numbers in some communities. Moreover, children in foster care are increasingly reported to have more special needs, such as serious medical and emotional problems, compared with the foster-care population in the past.

The foster-care system is severely challenged by increasing poverty and homelessness; the use of crack, which results in births of infants at high risk of medical and development problems; and the spread of acquired immune deficiency syndrome (AIDS), which requires more intensive supports for the children and families who are affected. Although many states report fewer children in foster care, several states — particularly those with large urban centers — report that the number of children in care is going up, not down. And virtually every state and region agrees that children in care today pose greater challenges to the foster-care system's resources. Shortages of foster homes (partly due to inadequate community support and low reimbursement rates) have propelled some states to increase out-of-state placements, a practice that impedes the reuniting of families and hampers the home state's ability to monitor the quality of care. The foster-care system also lacks the necessary resources to help children make a successful transition when they leave care. Of special concern are the tens of thousands of youths who "age out" of the system in their late teens and have no family members or friends to whom they can turn.

An estimated 7.5 million to 9.5 million children in this country have emotional or other problems that require mental-health services. Of this group, 70 to 80 percent do not receive the care they need. Even among the approximately 3 million children who suffer from serious emotional disturbances, the majority go without proper treatment. Today many of these children are being helped in a piecemeal fashion, or not at all.

Various state mental-health systems have cited growing demands and continuing deficiencies similar to those facing child-welfare agencies: the increasing severity of the problems presented by disturbed children and their families, over-reliance on institutional settings and a lack of sufficient in-home and community-based support programs, the transition needs of youths aging out of mental-health programs, and the inadequate number of professionals trained to address the mental-health needs of children and adolescents.

Saving the Children

If it is to save itself, America must save its children. Millions of children are not safe physically, educationally, economically, or spiritually. Many of the special children described in this essay are poor or members of minority groups. On average, they are less safe than their white, more affluent counterparts. But all are at risk spiritually. The common good, truth-telling, and moral example have become devalued commodities in the United States. And all children are in danger of being corrupted by their exposure to the values reflected by the Michael Deavers, Ivan Boeskys, and Jim and Tammy Bakkers of the world. The poor black youths who shoot up drugs on street corners and the rich white youths who do the same thing in their mansions share a common disconnectedness from any hope and purpose, sense of community, and shared strivings. What one social observer has called the bug of "affluenza" has indeed bitten thousands of youths who are growing up in families that offer everything that money can buy but somehow not enough to create a purpose in life. What is done collectively to save this generation will have a major impact on how today's children and youths perform as tomorrow's adults.

Solutions Do Exist

Despite the length and dreariness of the litany of special children and their problems, solutions are at hand. One absolutely essential avenue to pursue to save the next generation — and a generation yet unborn — is to launch a full-scale campaign to prevent teenage pregnancy.

This essay has shown how poverty and lack of education reinforce a cycle that results in underemployment or unemployment and a declining rate of marriage among young people, even when they have children. A society in which growing up with a single parent — and, worse, one who does not have the maturity, education, or resources to cope — is dangerously close to becoming the norm.

The Children's Defense Fund has been engaged since 1983 in a major initiative to prevent adolescent pregnancy. Its top priority is to prevent a teenager's first pregnancy. The second is to ensure that teenagers who have already had a child do not have a second one. The third priority is to make sure that teenage mothers get adequate prenatal care so that prematurity, low birth weight, and birth defects are not added to the hurdles already awaiting their babies as they enter this world. More specifically, it has identified six areas that are extremely important in bolstering the motivation and capacity of teenagers to prevent too-early pregnancy:

1. Education and strong basic skills. Youths who are behind a grade or have poor basic skills or poor attendance are at high risk of early parenthood. Low-income and minority teenagers have higher rates of school failure.

2. Work-related skills and exposure to work. Teenagers who perform poorly in school and become parents often have poor work-related skills and, because of lack of exposure to workplace norms, behave in ways unacceptable to employers.

3. Community service, sports, and other nonacademic opportunities for success. The potential for self-sufficiency is related to self-esteem and self-perception. For youths who are not doing well in school, nonacademic avenues for success are crucial.

4. Family life education and life planning.

5. Comprehensive adolescent health services.

6. A national and community climate that makes the prevention of teenage pregnancy a leading priority.

A decent society cannot condone any increase in child poverty, let alone the increase from 10 million to more than 12 million children between 1979 and 1987. And child poverty is not just a widening problem — it is a rapidly deepening one, as poor children become poorer.

An effective national effort must be launched to address the root cause of child poverty — inadequate family incomes. This effort requires progress on several fronts:

• Restore a strong economic base by continuing to pursue full employment, investing in productivity improvements for young workers, raising the federal minimum wage, and expanding the earned income tax credit.

• Respond more effectively to the new realities of a rapidly changing labor market by enacting the Act for Better Child Care Services, extending basic health-insurance coverage to all low-income families, and strengthening child-support enforcement and safety-net programs for poor families.

• Prepare today's children and youths for productive roles in tomorrow's economy by expanding the successful Head Start, Chapter 1, and Job Corps programs, increasing investments to help youths who are not college-bound enter the job market, and bolstering college enrollments among poor and minority youth. Only these things will provide the strong foundation that will make it possible for any child — no matter how special, no matter how many problems he or she may have — to become a proud, productive member of society.

In the long term, a service system must be established that can respond to the individual needs of children and families, regardless of the label assigned them by particular public agencies. The goal should be to develop a single system that serves vulnerable children and adolescents and has the capacity to assess, mobilize, and utilize all the resources necessary to meet their multiple needs. Such a system must have a staff that is appropriately qualified and compensated. The staff must have a system for fully addressing the needs of children and youths who need help as well as a continuum of services and other resources that can meet needs as they are indentified.

A Call for Action

If current trends continue, a disproportionate number of children will grow up poor, uneducated, and untrained at the very time that society will need all of our young to be healthy, educated, and productive. Despite a national debt of $2.7 trillion (which children did not cause) and despite uncertainties in the national and international economies, now is the time to invest in building healthy children, self-sufficient youth and economically secure families.

Children are poor because the country has lost its moral bearings. Perverse national values, hidden behind profamily, "traditional values" rhetoric, have been manifested in budget decisions that have cut billions of dollars each year since

1980 from survival programs for poor children and families. They are creating a new American apartheid between rich and poor, white and black, old and young, corporation and individual, military and domestic needs — and abandoned millions of poor children to the furies of hunger, homelessness, abuse, and even death.

What has been missing is the moral and political urgency required to make children and families a leading national priority. The willingness to protect children is a moral litmus test of a compassionate society. If the Bush administration joins that battle, it can help make the United States a safe place for children.

The International Year of the Child: Ten Years Later

MICHAEL JUPP

The International Year of the Child, celebrated throughout the world in 1979, was the pinnacle of an international effort to promote the needs and rights of children and to provide an unprecedented level of services and support for the children of the poor. It was the culmination of a century-long struggle for social reform, a struggle that began with such pioneers as Charles Dickens, Bramwell Booth, Sidney and Beatrice Webb, Heinrich Pestalozzi, and Eglantine Jebb.

That the International Year of the Child was a short-term success in establishing a framework for advocacy, one that developed into newer and better standards for the protection of children, is beyond dispute. Never before had the cause of children received so much concentrated attention. Children were studied as they had never been before, playgrounds were constructed where there had been none, and family allowances were introduced in countries that had never had them. Children's needs were included — often for the first time — in long-term national planning, and funding was provided for child-oriented programs at an unprecedented level. Education, health, welfare, social insurance, and overseas-aid budgets were all increased. Postage stamps celebrating childhood were printed. Posters depicting children's issues were produced and widely circulated, and the media, both print and electronic, provided exemplary coverage of children. And, perhaps most important, adults began to pay attention to the children and gave them opportunities to speak for themselves and to influence their own futures.

The question that must be asked, as child advocates and activists prepare to mark the tenth anniversary of the International Year of the Child, is whether this level of advocacy has been sustained, whether better services for children have been provided, and whether the optimistic rhetoric has led to substantive changes. To paraphrase a popular political question, Are children better off than they were ten years ago? There can be no superficial answer. On the positive side of the ledger, far more is known about children today than was known ten years ago — to the extent that the depth of adults' ignorance of the problems of children is obvious.

Some elements of technology have been successfully co-opted to work for the benefit of an enormous number of children. Primary examples of this are the achievements of the "child survival and development revolution" and its use of low-cost appropriate technology to carry out immunization campaigns and provide oral rehydration therapy. Simultaneously, the increased understanding of children's issues, coupled with a revolution in communications technology, has led to more sophisticated monitoring techniques. But with an increased ability to monitor social generalities, there is an ever-present danger of falling into the trap of measuring social progress solely in terms of the quantity and quality of services made available at the statistical mean. Whereas for poor children, those at the bottom of the social pecking order, the only meaningful criteria must be the quality and availability of services to them.

An analysis of the global balance sheet, however, indicates that the situation of children has deteriorated over the past decade. One of the most disappointing realizations is that the stresses brought about by a worldwide recession are most likely to be manifested in the abandonment of the poor in favor of a country's privileged elite. The evidence is overwhelming: children, as a subclass, have experienced a devastating downturn in social mobility. Poor children have become poorer, and many of the children of the lower-middle class have become poor. Even more disappointing is that this development has been greeted with a stunning degree of apathy on the part of some of those responsible for framing social policy. For many others, such developments have been welcomed and deliberately used as a means of social control.

Children and the World Economy

Perhaps the most shattering of trends during the 1980s has been the world economic recession, which, together with an escalating Third World debt, has had a disastrously negative impact on many children. In December 1986, the *Christian Science Monitor* published an interview with President Jimmy Carter, in which he spoke of the growing chasm between the industrialized countries and the developing countries: "I think the greatest problem that we face is the relationship between the advanced nations and the poverty-stricken nations. There are probably fifty nations on earth now that will never repay the principal on their debt and in which it takes a substantial proportion of their earnings just to *service* their debt."[1] An example is Sudan, where in 1985 the debt-servicing charges totaled $790 million—$65 million more than the country's entire export revenue.

In December 1984, the United Nations Children's Fund (UNICEF) first documented this crisis in *The Impact of World Recession on Children*, in which the authors state categorically that the world economy is in recession—the deepest, the most sustained, and the most widespread since the 1930s. The authors argue that for about one-sixth of the world's population, economic growth has ceased, and many of them are even poorer than they were in 1979. Yet, as they point out, "not a single international study has analyzed the recession's impact on the most vulnerable half of the world's population—the children."[2] This report was followed in 1987 by a second volume, *Adjustment with a Human Face*,[3] which confirms the earlier findings and recommends ways to make the world financial system more responsible for the effects of monetary policy on the poor. In the introduction to the first report, the editors argue:

> Typically, the relations between child welfare and world economic conditions have not received much attention, even from those professionals who are closely concerned with child survival and welfare. The children's problems are often approached within narrow perspectives which ignore the deeper causes of their unsatisfactory conditions, which attach individual rather than social symptoms and causes. This often leads therefore to inadequate policy analysis and action. Even when a clear emphasis is put on social causes, it is typically within a *national* frame of political, economic and social conditions, rarely linked to the international.[4]

The Impact of World Recession on Children is the first known attempt to rectify this omission. The document analyzes economic trends in eight countries (Brazil, Chile, Cuba, India, Sri Lanka, South Korea, the United States, and Italy) and two regions (Latin America and Sub-Saharan Africa) and then compares them with a series of objective criteria for measuring the social welfare of children, such as infant mortality rates, household income, health-care delivery, education, and welfare budgets.

Although limited in scope by "the overall inadequacy of the information available and by the almost complete lack—even in the most advanced countries— of an information system capable of timely reporting on child health and welfare," the report was able to conclude:

> It is realistic to note that a very real deterioration has and is taking place in the lives of children around the world. While the initial worsening has been somewhat slowed— particularly in middle income countries—by the existence of resources, experience and facilities accumulated in the past, there are strong reasons to believe that the present crisis could turn into a major setback—particularly for the very poor people and countries—in a matter of a few years. The evidence provided by this report should be considered not only indicative of the *deterioration which has already occurred*, but as a *warning signal*. The condition of children's lives will suffer far greater deterioration within a relatively short time unless *action is taken now*.[5]

The world economic recession has had a direct impact on the welfare of children by reducing household incomes as well as government spending on child-related services; these, in turn, effect detrimental change in the behavior patterns of adults and children. A modest drop in the gross national product (GNP) in the industrialized countries can have a forbidding consequence for large groups of the poor, particularly their children, in trade and financially dependent countries. According to Hans Singer of the Institute of Development Studies in England, for every 1 percent decline in the rate of growth of the GNP in the industrialized countries, there is a decrease of 1.5 percent in the growth of GNP for the developing countries. For developing countries producing primary commodities, the multiplier is even higher, and it is suggested that a drop of 0.3 percent in the GNP of the United States between 1969 and 1970 may have produced a drop in the GNP of 3 percent in copper-dependent Zambia — a multiplier of 1:10. When adjusted for population growth and population size of the developing countries, the multiplier is even larger; and, within developing countries, local situations can cause additional negative multipliers. The effect of all of this is that for the person at the bottom end of the world pecking order — probably the youngest daughter in a large landless peasant family in the Third World — a drop in the rate of growth of the GNP in the industrialized world of 2 to 3 percent means a reduction in nutrition, health services, and education availability in excess of 50 percent of its previous value.

Reduction in Household Income

The UNICEF report demonstrates a clear relationship between household income and the general well-being of children. Almost all of the population in the poorer countries, and many of the poor and the lower-middle class in the developed countries, have been affected. Real household incomes have been reduced — often drastically — in most of the poorer countries surveyed (up to 40 percent in Costa Rica and Zambia) and also among the poor of the industrialized countries.

There has been a rise in unemployment among the poorer classes, particularly in the urban areas, and this has lessened the collective bargaining position of workers, resulting in lower wages. The evidence from at least two countries (the United States and the Philippines) shows a deterioration in income distribution, with the rich getting richer and the poor becoming poorer.

Data from the United States, in particular, confirm that the economic crisis facing children is by no means confined to the less developed countries. To the contrary, ample evidence shows that the gap between children of the poor and the rich is widening in the industrialized countries. According to Emma Rothschild, senior research fellow at King's College, Cambridge, between 1979 and 1984 the income for the richest families increased by 2.4 percent a year, while for the poorest families it fell by 4.7 percent a year. Families headed by young women had incomes that were only 29 percent of the median for elderly families.

As of 1986, according to the U.S. Census Bureau, 13 million American children lived in poverty. Among minorities, 40 percent of black children and almost 40 percent of Hispanic children were poor. In *La Crisis Economica*, Francisco Pilotti draws attention to the fact that while 27.7 million children under six years old in Latin America lived in absolute poverty in 1970, by 1980 the total had risen to 35.5 million, and the projection for the year 2000 is 51 million. Poor children's diets have deteriorated as a direct result of the economic crisis in Mexico, to the extent that poor families spend 63 percent of their income on food. The price of a kilo of beans equaled 8.6 percent of the minimum daily wage in 1977, but rose to 20.8 percent of the minimum daily wage as of 1985.[6]

Reduction in Government Services

The findings indicate that while the richer people manage to remain relatively isolated from the effects of the world economic recession, the children of the poor (and, in some countries, the children of the lower-middle class) have borne the brunt of a significant and global cutback in services. There is a clear correlation between reductions in government spending and a deterioration in children's welfare.

Governments, almost universally, have responded to the recession by decreasing the share of social expenditure as a proportion of total government spending, by stopping the expansion of social services and by dropping the quality of existing services. A worldwide trend is developing to charge for services that had been free — effectively prohibiting the very poor from obtaining services at all.

To give some indication as to how the United States has responded to the recession, it should be noted that while government spending has never been higher, with an increase of 8.6 percent in arms spending for the period 1982 through 1985, income-security programs were cut by 15.3 percent, federal higher-education programs were cut by 18.2 percent, and grants to state and local governments were projected to decline 17.4 percent. In dollar terms, the figures are even more astounding: food stamps cut by $2 billion, with nearly 1 million people terminated, and Aid to Families with Dependent Children (AFDC) cut by $1.5 billion, with 365,000 families terminated and an additional 260,000 families with their benefits reduced. In 1981, Medicaid was reduced by $1 billion, the school health program cut by $1 billion (nearly 30 percent), and the school breakfast program cut by 20 percent — with 200,000 fewer children participating.

In Chile, an economic crisis between 1982 and 1984 resulted in 30 percent unemployment and a 20 percent reduction in the purchasing power of wages. Working-class families experienced extreme dislocation, and the government reduced the amount of milk made available to preschool children. The budget of the Servicio Nacional de Menores was frozen, despite severe inflation. It is known that the breakfast and lunch portions given to school-age children in 1982 were 46 percent less than in 1974.

Impact on the Welfare of Children

There are clear indications that when the fall in earnings or the imposition of government cuts have been particularly severe, infant mortality rates have shown a distinct upward trend. This was the case for the plantation sector in Sri Lanka between 1979 and 1982 and also in the states of Michigan and Alabama, as well as thirty-four cities in the United States during the period 1981–82. In all these areas, unemployment had risen to double-digit figures. These trends are confirmed by similar findings in Costa Rica, Brazil, Bangladesh, and India.

Data from Italy, Costa Rica, and parts of Brazil indicate that in those countries, where infant mortality rates continue to improve, the *rate* of improvement has declined as the result of lower household incomes or government spending cuts. In rural India, the previously declining infant mortality rate has stagnated. Even in countries where the infant mortality rate has continued to decline, the world economic recession has brought about a deterioration in the nutritional indicators.

In Costa Rica, the number of children treated for severe malnutrition doubled over the three-year period ending in 1983. In Brazil, an analysis of the decline in infant mortality rates has shown that the number of deaths due to malnutrition (as opposed to disease) has risen. In South Africa, it is estimated that up to 70 percent of black school-age children are underweight, and up to 66 percent of black preschool children have stunted growth. Data from Brazil, Sri Lanka, and the United States indicate a trend toward low birth weights and a stunting in the growth of poor children. There is also evidence to show that there has been a worldwide stagnation or deterioration in public health services. In Chile, typhoid and hepatitis are on the increase because of cuts in government expenditures on drinking water and sanitation. Brazil, Sri Lanka, and India are still characterized by a high incidence of preventable infectious diseases, and in the United States and South Africa there has been an increase in environmentally linked illnesses, such as tuberculosis. In England, a direct link has been hypothesized between an increase in unemployment in the rust-belt North and a rise in the incidence of mental illness.

If the single most important variable in ensuring an infant's survival is, in fact, the literacy level of the mother, the universal cuts in government expenditure on education are likely to have long-term detrimental effects on the welfare of children. South Korea and Cuba, however, have shown that even in times of economic recession, it is possible to improve the material condition of children if the political will is present. Even a modest increase in investment in the social welfare of children has had a disproportionately beneficial effect; both of these countries have lowered their infant mortality rate and increased the level of literacy.

Changes in Child-Rearing Practices

Rising unemployment rates, an increase in the price of food due to inflation, and cuts in government subsidies of staples, coupled with a reduction in free welfare services and cuts in income-maintenance systems, all contribute to changing patterns in child rearing and an increase in abusive behavior within the family. Generally, people of childbearing age predominate in the migration of the rural poor to the cities, leaving their children behind in the care of the extended family. These children are thus denied access to their parents, while children born to the parents in the city are denied the protection and nurturing of the extended family. The separation of the family becomes inevitable.

The pressures of living in an unfamiliar and hostile urban environment, without the traditional social controls imposed by the extended family, frequently lead to a breakup of the nuclear family and the abandonment of women and children. In some countries, such as the United States, the government welfare system militates in favor of the breakup of the family by denying benefits to families headed by able-bodied men. Children in the United States living with their mothers in a single-parent home are four times more likely to be poor than those in two-parent homes; thus, the feminization of poverty.

The lowering of wages and the threat of unemployment, or the devastation of unemployment, combined with rising prices and cuts in services, create feelings of frustration and anger that give rise to an increased incidence of child abuse. In England and Wales, for example, it has been estimated that physical abuse increased by 70 percent between 1979 and 1984, to a new high of 7,038 cases. In the United States, the American Association for Protecting Children documented reports of 1,712,641 abused and neglected children for 1984 alone, an increase of 16 percent over the figure for the previous year.

The loss of wages through unemployment may drive a family into more crowded accommodations and lower the self-esteem of the father. His involuntary leisure time, together with the absence of the mother, who is forced to seek work, and his physical proximity to a daughter or step-daughter increase the opportunity for incest and sexual abuse. Despite the fact that an adult's sexual violation of children is one of the strongest social taboos, it should be noted that reports of sexual abuse in the United States rose by 54 percent in the period 1983–84.

In extreme cases, the family may sell or indenture one or more of their children for the greater good of the family. The child may work under horrendous conditions as a bonded laborer in the quarries of India, as a slave in the sweatshops of Latin America, or as a prostitute in the brothels of Southeast Asia. According to the International Labor Organization, 88 million children are working under conditions detrimental to their health and welfare. Some commentators, however, argue that this figure is far too low and that as many as 150 million children may be working under unacceptable conditions in Asia.

Child-service professionals everywhere report that child abandonment has increased since the beginning of the recession. Street children are now a common phenomenon throughout the world's cities; estimates vary from 30 million to 100 million, depending on the definition used. Youth unemployment is now an area of major social concern in both Europe and North America. Juvenile-crime rates are perceived to have increased in both developed and developing countries, and governments are adopting more hardened attitudes toward youthful offenders. The world economic recession has perpetuated the conditions that have forced millions of children into prostitution, pornography, and other forms of abuse and exploitation, with countless millions of homeless children and children employed under hazardous and often fatal working conditions.

Hunger and Foreign Policy

In 1984, 5 million children died in Africa from hunger-related causes, and one in five children of the world went hungry. The causes of hunger are complex, and it cannot be denied that poverty is a significant factor. Yet starvation is not brought about because there is a lack of food worldwide or, in many instances, even because of a lack of food in the country concerned. Some countries have so much surplus food that it is burned. War, internal armed conflict, and the foreign-policy dictates of the superpowers play as big a part as drought, pestilence, and inefficient farming methods; and, arguably, the harmful marketing techniques of the multinationals can play as big a part as poor traditional practices. The reality is that despite a surplus of grain among the major Western producers, an introduction of new high-yielding varieties to the Third World, and an improvement in traditional agricultural practices, children continue to die from starvation.

The food emergency in Africa continues to be an issue of major concern to the international relief agencies. Although rains have fallen in some provinces, there is a new threat from locust swarms. Droughts continue in Burkina Faso, Ethiopia, and Sudan. Haiti is experiencing a famine; a June 1987 study by the U.S. Agency for International Development found that 82 percent of children under five years of age are suffering from malnutrition — double the figure for January of the same year.

The current opinion among relief and development experts is that food relief must be viewed as merely a short-term, stop-gap measure to tide people over a critical period, and even then it must be introduced to the country concerned in a way that does not destroy the local economy. Given the resources and the opportunity, it is believed that even the driest of African countries could become self-sufficient; the current emphasis is on long-term development aid. The United Kingdom and the United States have refused, however, to commit long-term aid that would help reconstruct Ethiopia — where children suffered the worst during the emergency — because the country is seen as an ally of the USSR. Yet, at the same time, the United States government has consigned shiploads of arms to the government in Somalia, where government troops have allegedly massacred children. Part of the irony of the situation is that these troops have also cut the roads to the refugee camps in the North, thus curtailing the supply of food to refugees unsympathetic to the Ethiopian government. The United States government has also prohibited Oxfam (America) from shipping farm tools and other humanitarian supplies to Nicaragua. On 5 June 1986, South Africa was accused of using troops to sink a Cuban ship that was carrying United Nations food donated by the United States for the hundreds of thousands of malnourished children on Angola's densely populated high plateau.

Economics and War

An important and devastating side effect of the recession has been to increase the propensity for war, armed conflict, and civil unrest. An analysis of the conduct of both government troops and opposition forces shows that children are being actively recruited and used as soldiers and also singled out as targets for assassination, torture, and imprisonment without trial. Children make up more than 70 percent of the population in many refugee camps. The effects of economic recession are therefore not only a decrease in the standards of welfare, education, health care, housing, and job opportunities offered to the poor — in short, an attack on their social and economic rights — but also an attack on the civil and political rights of this vulnerable group.

There appears to be little doubt that governments become vulnerable to change in times of economic crises, and for many in power the very threat of change is sufficient to prompt a Draconian curtailment of civil liberties. The evidence shows that under many regimes the mere threat of loss of political and economic power is likely to result in a banning of political activity, detention without trial, torture, political assassination, curfews, restrictions on movement, restrictions on the practice of religion, and other infringements of human rights; and these new rules are frequently enforced by violent, unconstitutional police and military activity.

In order to justify the suspension of the constitution and to rationalize the lack of social progress, a government may scapegoat a minority group within its national boundaries — such as "communist agitators," "capitalist reactionaries," and members of a minority race or religion. It then creates a series of mythical beliefs about their conduct that emphasizes their alleged deviancy and delinquency. The many examples of this behavior throughout modern history include blaming Jews for the economic depression in Germany, Asians for the lack of foreign investment in East Africa, and blacks for being criminal and welfare-dependent in the United States.

This artificially created belief system has been used to divert the attention of the "respectable poor" away from the true causes of the economic crisis and to focus their frustrations and anger on the scapegoated minority group. This anger, in turn, leads to even more street violence. In Great Britain, one of the most disturbing aspects of the rise in youth unemployment has been the growth of the neo-Nazi movement among young working-class people and the racist attacks on ethnic minorities — particularly on Asians in small businesses.

Civil violence, however, is not confined to the poor responding to the adverse conditions of urban living. Some governments in power use violence to manipulate people. Some regimes use it as a deliberate means of social control. In extreme cases, a government may declare war on another sovereign nation to divert attention from the economic inequities within its own system.

The role of the former colonial powers and the superpowers in the many existing regional wars that are taking place throughout the world today requires more analysis. Some commentators, however, argue that the rationale for these wars can be understood only if they are seen as an effort of the producing nations to ensure their supply of raw materials and future markets. One reason for the length of the war between Iraq and Iran, it has been suggested, is that neither of the superpowers could decide which side it wanted to win. One of the results of this war is that casualties have numbered in the hundreds of thousands; by one count, more than 90,000 Iranian children have died.

Effect of War on Children

A 1986 report by UNICEF to its executive board claims that only 5 percent of the casualties in World War I were civilians but in World War II, civilians made up 50 percent of the casualties. In Vietnam, the proportion of civilian casualties rose to 80 percent of the total. But in many of the current conflicts, as in Lebanon, more than 90 percent of the victims are women and children.

The deliberate or indiscriminate shooting, shelling, or bombing of children has been reported from Afghanistan, Angola, Chile, El Salvador, Haiti, Guatemala, Lebanon, Libya, Mozambique, Namibia, Nicaragua, Northern Ireland, the Philippines, South Africa, Sudan, Sri Lanka, Thailand, Turkey, and the West Bank (Palestine) Occupied Territories. Attacks on Kurdish children by means of internationally outlawed poison gas were allegedly carried out by the Iraqi Air Force in August and September 1988.

This increase in civilian casualties is due not only to the changing technology of weapons and the polarization of ideologies but also to changes in the ways that wars are fought. Many wars involve popular or unpopular guerilla movements and popular or unpopular counterinsurgency forces. Both sides depend on gaining the support of the people in order to achieve their objectives. If the support of the people cannot be attained, one or more sides in the conflict will often practice a policy of total subjugation and terrorism.

Under these circumstances, women and children are drawn into the conflict and are likely to become the main casualties, and it is precisely because children are held dear and precious that destroying them is clearly the most effective form of terrorism imaginable. In both the Afghanistan and Nicaraguan wars there were allegations that deliberate acts of violence were waged against children.

The experience in South Africa is yet another example of a government's deliberate policy to terrorize and subjugate children, and during the period 21 July 1985 through June 1987 the South African government admitted, during parliamentary questioning, that its police had shot and killed more than 300 children and injured a further 950 by gunfire. During the same period, an estimated 10,000 children were detained without trial.

The effects of war on children, however, go far beyond their direct involvement either as combatants or as victims. According to UNICEF officials, the infant and child mortality rates in Angola and Mozambique are the highest in the world, largely due to the fighting and conflict-related destabilization in the region. Officials say the blame for the high mortality rates can be traced to the economic difficulties caused by the cross-border military strikes and South Africa's support for guerilla groups in the area. In Angola and Mozambique, the mortality rate for children under five years of age is over 325 per 1,000 children. The infant mortality rate (less than one year old) is 200 for each 1,000 live births. The study estimates that 45 percent of the total deaths of children under five in both countries, or 140,000 deaths a year, are caused by war and economic destabilization, and that without these factors, the mortality rate for children under five would be about 185 per 1,000 children. There are more than 10 million child refugees around the world. At least 9 million children have been killed in wars since 1945, and the number maimed and injured is believed to be at least three times the number killed.

Child Recruitment

The recruitment of children into the armed forces (or into armed liberation movements), contrary to international law, has been reported in at least twenty different countries, including Guatemala, El Salvador, Iran, and Uganda. Typical are reports from Peru that allege that the guerrilla organization Sendero Luminoso focuses its recruiting on boys and girls about thirteen years old, because children of that age are more malleable and because an army of child soldiers is harder to infiltrate. The most blatant violation of the provision against recruiting children into the military is believed to have been by Iran, where 90,000 were reported to have died during the war against Iraq. According to the London-based Friends World Committee for Consultation, children under thirteen may be enlisted in the Iranian military. According to a report prepared for the United Nations Human Rights Commission, about 200,000 children are members of the world's armies.

Disappearances and Torture

Since the mid-1970s, there has been a growing concern over the "disappearance" of individuals after their arrest by government agents or their abduction by vigilantes apparently acting with government consent. Some 90,000 people are reported to have "disappeared" in Latin America alone — 38,000 of them in Guatemala.

In Argentina, between 1975 and 1983, 145 to 170 children "disappeared," either kidnaped with their parents by the authorities or born in captivity to imprisoned women and then separated from their mothers. So far, some forty-one children who disappeared under these circumstances have been located, following a diligent search by relatives of the missing children, led by the group called the Grandmothers of the Plaza de Mayo. Many of these children were found with adoptive parents, some of whom have claimed the children as their own. In one case, a child was discovered in the care of a policeman implicated in her parents' "disappearance." The relatives of the child have resorted to genetic testing in an attempt to establish an index of "grandpaternity."

The "disappearance" of children is not confined to Argentina; similar cases have been reported in Chile, Guatemala, and Peru. There have also been allegations of large numbers of children, 300 between fifteen and seventeen years old in one case, being taken from Afghanistan against their parents' wishes, to be educated in the USSR.

The torture of children by government forces and police is becoming an increasingly common allegation. Reports from South Africa of the indiscriminate beating, suffocation, and electrocution of children have been extensively documented over the past two years, both by groups from within South Africa and external organizations. The torture of children has also been alleged in Chile, Guatemala, and Iran. In June 1988, the U.S. House Subcommittee on Africa heard testimony alleging the torture and extrajudicial execution of children in Somalia. Particularly disturbing are allegations from many countries that children are being tortured in front of their parents in order to elicit information from a parent and, conversely, that parents are being tortured in front of their children in order to obtain information.

The Proposed UN Convention on the Rights of the Child

Despite the public rhetoric that extols the sanctity of children with platitudes about the "future of mankind" and "our most precious investment," an analysis of social and foreign policy indicates that the interests of children are almost invariably subordinated to the political and economic interests of adults. The realization that the human rights of children are being increasingly violated worldwide has given rise to the development of a new and growing international children's rights movement. This movement, made up of diplomats, church leaders, international civil servants, private voluntary organizations, lawyers, and other concerned citizens has a twofold agenda: first, the introduction of an international treaty, the proposed UN Convention on the Rights of the Child, which will establish an international consensus on children's rights; and, second, the beginning of a worldwide network of interested adults dedicated to monitoring the condition of children and ensuring that these rights are actualized.

Children should not be dependent on the charity of adults for their protection. Justice demands that as human beings they are entitled to a basic degree of protection as a fundamental human right. A commitment by adults to establish and guarantee the rights of children should be paramount in the agenda for the twenty-first century.

The developing praxis of the rights of the child divides children's essential needs into three categories: (1) the right to survival through the provision of adequate food, shelter, clean water, and primary health care; (2) the right to protection from abuse, neglect, and exploitation, including the right to special protection in times of war; and (3) the right to develop in a safe environment, through formal education, constructive play, advanced health care, and the opportunity to participate in the social, economic, religious, and political life of the culture, free from discrimination.

Generally, the safeguards for children are provided within the environment of a protective and nurturing family, either the nuclear or the extended family, and they are dependent on the presumption that other adults — including governments — offer a second line of protection, acting in the best interest of the child and separating the child from the parents only in exceptional circumstances. One such initiative for an international legal basis for the protection of children is contained in the 1978 proposal to the United Nations by the government of Poland for the drafting of an international treaty. This treaty, the Convention on the Rights of the Child, has already been endorsed by diplomats representing a wide spectrum of governments and is working its way through the UN committee procedure. It is targeted for completion in 1989.

The review and codification of international children's legislation and the adoption of a UN-sponsored, human-rights approach to the protection of the rights of the child have been major platforms of Defense for Children International since its foundation in 1979. This approach is likely to reach fruition in 1989, with support from both the developing and the industrialized countries and also from the Eastern and Western power blocs.

The actual drafting process for the new convention has already been of direct benefit to some children. Several member nations have reviewed their domestic legislation, and some are enacting amendments to ensure that their laws will comply with the new convention. The very fact that member states are discussing children's needs as human rights, internationally between diplomats and domestically as part of a dialogue between elected representatives and civil servants, has in itself begun a process that legitimizes the philosophical concept.

This convention addresses all three basic rights in the child's hierarchy of needs and will give child advocates, often for the first time, a sound legal and philosophical framework in which to work. Human-rights organizations that hold consultative status with the UN will no doubt take advantage of the convention, when it is completed, to raise the issue of the rights of the child at every opportunity. Experience over the past forty years in other human-rights fields indicates that governments, while sometimes denying that a human-rights approach is effective, do respond when this approach is used. If the convention follows other models, it will give these organizations a right of audience before a UN committee. The convention will provide a universally accepted guideline to governments, one that will assist them in developing their priorities for the welfare of children. The convention's provisions will give an additional strength of law to those recommendations contained in the various human-rights declarations.

The proposed Convention on the Rights of the Child has been a catalyst for grassroots activists and nongovernmental organizations. Advocates have seen the convention as a rallying point and have united in the task of mobilizing public opinion to ensure its passage. At the same time, activists are keenly aware of the history of underenforcement of laws at both the national and international levels and are determined to help establish mechanisms to implement the convention as a tool for social change. While a human-rights approach is not a panacea for solving the social, political, and economic problems of all of the world's children, it is an essential first step. There is no doubt that human-rights advocacy mobilizes public opinion, prompts academic research, gives rise to legislative solutions, and results in effective programming.

John Williams, director of information at UNICEF, has stressed that, even with the passage of the convention, "children will not benefit from these rights unless we as adults work for them." Williams emphasized the need to involve the press in monitoring violations of the rights of the child, and to "probe deeper and look for the acts of omission . . . that probably kill and maim more children each day than the acts of commission." The simple but shocking fact is that, worldwide, 38,000 children die each day—more than 13 million a year—from a lack of food, shelter, and primary health care, and many millions more suffer mental and physical damage.

The current thrust of the international children's rights movement, therefore, is twofold: to lobby for passage of the convention and to make sure that the convention will have immediate and concrete application to the daily crises that children face throughout the world. To this end, organizations are already mobilizing public opinion to generate the political will for implementation; activists are also developing monitoring systems to ensure that the standards set in theory by the convention will be respected in practice by subscribing governments. It is expected that the Convention on the Rights of the Child will be submitted to the United Nations General Assembly for adoption in the fall of 1989, ten years after the International Year of the Child.

NOTES

1. *Christian Science Monitor*, 12 Dec. 1986.

2. Richard Jolly and Giovanni Andrea Cornia, eds., *The Impact of World Recession on Children* (Oxford: Pergamon Press, 1984).

3. Giovanni Andrea Cornia, Richard Jolly, and Frances Stewart, *Adjustment with a Human Face* (Oxford: Clarendon Press, 1987).

4. Jolly and Cornia, 1 (emphasis added).

5. Ibid., 221 (emphasis added).

6. Francisco Pilotti, *La Crisis Economica y su Impacto en la Familia*, (Montevideo, Urugay: Instituto Interamericano del Niño, 1987), 11.

The Health of America's Children

P. A. COLÓN
A. R. COLÓN

As the twenty-first century approaches, a sense of crisis over the immediate future confronts the medical profession. This mood diminishes the feeling of achievement of unparalleled advances in pediatric care that have occurred in this century. The dramatically reduced rates of child morbidity and mortality, made possible by widespread public education on nutrition and sanitation, the discovery of antibiotics, and the development of vaccines against once dreaded childhood diseases, have been exchanged for other threats, other concerns.

While pediatric-care practitioners are busy with their current agendas, national goals and agendas are being set for the year 2000. To an unprecedented degree, clinical care necessarily incorporates social, environmental, and behavioral forces that are important to patients' health. The other essays in this book focus on issues that affect child health care: the family, education, child care, poverty, and disabilities. The contemporary, mundane pediatric clinical issues of, say, colds, croups, ear infections, and diarrheas have to be treated in the context of ever-increasing social issues and crises.

In order to deal with this phenomenon, clinical medicine and preventive medicine are in the process of merging to meet future challenges. The clinician, by training and experience, still deals better with biologic ills than with socially rooted dilemmas. Formidable amounts of new scientific information to review and apply to medical practice consume a great deal of time and energy, allowing little time to deal with the psychosocial needs of patients. Some of the data, as with the pronouncements about acquired immune deficiency syndrome (AIDS), are inconclusive and change rapidly as new insights occur and new information is gathered and published. The medical community must also master this changing data in order to remain current in scientific knowledge and its application. Meanwhile, social mores, behaviors, and priorities are determining health issues and the challenges that society faces. The pediatric community, like all of the medical profession, is struggling to prepare for the tasks that lie ahead.

The pediatrician will have to be an educator and counselor, as well as a physician, who must augment parental- and child-guidance services with sex education, prenatal counseling, accident prevention, substance-abuse warnings, and emotional support for the many kinds of depressed states. The management of these concerns is superimposed on an already demanding — and necessary — routine of immunization schedules, developmental charting, screening for and diagnosing of serious diseases, and the treatment of common ailments. The physician needs a lot of help from parents, schools, the community, and government agencies.

The number-one national health-care priority for the year 2000 has to be a system that will ensure access for all children and adolescents. Dr. Richard Narkewicz, president of the American Academy of Pediatrics, recently stated that 7 million children in this country have no medical care, 11 million have no insurance, and millions more have no adequate health-insurance coverage. Moreover, in 1986 some 1,400 counties throughout the United States were underserved by child-health physicians. It will be necessary, therefore, to increase the number of pediatric health-care providers in all rural and inner-city areas.

The public-health goal of universal access to health care by the year 2000 cannot be reached unless government agencies make a genuine effort to provide the means to supply this level of care. The obvious question is how this goal can be achieved in this country when Americans have insistently rejected the concept of a nationally sponsored health-care system. Certainly, increased Medicaid benefits, entitlement programs, and private insurance coverage would help reduce the number of children deprived of health care. The American Academy of Pediatrics, for example, is encouraging legislation that would increase the coverage of children under employer insurance policies.

Education of the adolescent on matters with individual and public-health implications needs to be emphasized. Teenage behavior, for example, is responsible for many identified, discussed, and treated health problems. Educating this group effectively is the key to progress in preventing many national health ills. If we can reach young people — including the poorest of them — and educate them well on health issues, we will have made tremendous strides in ensuring public health by the year 2000.

Teenagers, Pregnancy, and Infant Health Care

Teenage pregnancies are at the root of several child and maternal health problems of national import — infant mortality, low birth weight, and consequent increased risk of physiologic and developmental problems, poor child nutrition, poor parenting, and child abuse.

Of the 130 nations listed in UNICEF's annual report, *State of the World's Children, 1986*, the United States ranks seventeenth in infant mortality. The infant-mortality rate in the United States is 10.4 per 1,000 live births, or 40,000 infant deaths a year. Perinatal diseases, or those developing around the time of birth, account for 25 percent of all first-year infant deaths. Congenital anomalies cause about 21 percent of these deaths. Sudden infant death syndrome (SIDS) is responsible for another 12.6 percent. Nine percent die of respiratory distress syndrome, which is more common among premature infants. Almost 9 percent of infant deaths are associated with low birth weight, which increases infant susceptibility to illness and disease. Fetal alcohol syndrome, narcotic withdrawal syndrome, and, probably most important, the absence of newborn care are additional major factors in infant death and chronic disability.

Most of these conditions are preventable. In 1985, alcohol consumption by pregnant women was responsible for as many as 11,000 cases of fetal alcohol syndrome, which is the third leading cause of birth defects with accompanying mental retardation. Tobacco use during pregnancy is associated with low birth weight. The mother's use of drugs, of course, can cause the narcotic withdrawal syndrome in afflicted infants. Finally, poor maternal nutrition affects the health of the fetus, as does maternal systemic disease.

There is a clear correlation between infant morbidity and mortality, on the one hand, and the absence of both prenatal care and newborn care, on the other. Marital status of the mother has been shown to be a factor, since unmarried women are less likely to seek prenatal and postnatal care than married women, teenagers even less likely, and minority women the least likely to do so. Over 814,000 nonmarital births were reported in the United States in 1986. About 50 percent of those were to unmarried teenagers (in 1985, 22 percent of births to teenagers from the ages of fifteen to seventeen were repeat births). Overall, 21 percent of white mothers and 38 percent of black mothers did not have prenatal care in the first trimester of pregnancy when preventive care is most significant. The majority of these are the so-called high-risk pregnancies that are more likely to result in infant deaths or produce high-risk infants who are highly susceptible to disease and handicapped conditions. There is a dichotomy, moreover, between mortality rates among the middle class and those among the poor. This difference breaks down along racial lines, with mortality rates of black infants twice that of white infants. While there are no reliable statistical data regarding mortality rates for Hispanic infants, great numbers of Hispanics are among the socioeconomically deprived, and they represent the fastest-growing minority group in the United States. Access to and utilization of available facilities that provide direct health-care and counseling services could substantially reduce infant mortality.

It is important to emphasize that the United States has adequate health-care technology and neonatal facilities, but prenatal-care services are inadequately utilized, and preventive perinatology, or medical screening of the neonate, is inadequately applied. In countries with fewer resources than those available in the United States, people generally have a broader awareness of their community health facilities. Education about health-care needs and available delivery systems begins early in school and is reinforced at home and in the community. People understand that it is especially important to use their local health centers during pregnancy and for subsequent infant and child health care. No social or economic barriers prevent access to and use of these facilities. These optimum conditions must be developed for this country to increase public access to health care.

Eliminating barriers and educating the public on how to use health-care facilities are the most important means of reducing infant mortality.

Public education, however, must begin in the schools. The education of young people on matters related to reproduction, contraceptives, and access to medical-care services is essential now; it would provide a sound foundation for responsible parenthood in the future. According to the American Academy of Pediatrics, delayed sexual activity in young people could ideally be achieved through training in decision making, sex education, family-life education, role-model development, and pressure on the media to moderate their depiction of sexuality. The American Academy of Pediatrics believes that successful educational programs could bring about a 20 percent drop in teenage pregnancies and a 12 percent drop in repeat pregnancies by the year 2000.

Although public-health officials are aware of the controversies over sex education in schools and communities, which require sensitivity to family and community values, such education is vital. Parents must be convinced there are positive returns from value-oriented sex education in schools. Such programs could be developed by education authorities working in a cooperative spirit with parent-advocate groups. While some incidences of teenage parenthood may provide opportunities for growth and maturity for the parents and a consequent secure and nurturing environment for the child, such an outcome is not the norm. Parental, school, and community efforts should emphasize delayed sexuality during the teenage years when the most complex maturational processes are in full force, while judgment and foresight are in an embryonic state of development. The sociological and economic costs of adolescent parenthood are staggering. Eighty percent of teenagers who give birth before the age of eighteen do not complete their high-school studies. Forty percent of the male adolescents who become fathers before eighteen are also less likely to graduate from high school. They join the ranks of the least employed and unemployable. The cost to society of each of their children up to the age of eighteen is estimated at $18,000 a year, for a total cost of $16.5 billion. This figure does not include the lost income that could reduce the poverty-level existences of these young parents or the amounts of lost tax revenues.

Finally, genetic counseling might help potential parents of all ages to make more informed family-planning decisions and thus forestall a number of pregnancies that would otherwise produce infants born with congenital malformations and handicapped conditions. Handicapped children and their parents require a more extensive system of assistance and support for the emotional, educational, and health-care challenges they face.

Child Abuse

Whether the rising figures on child abuse reflect a worsening problem or improved data collection, the statistics are appalling. In 1984 the National Center on Child Abuse and Neglect (NCCAN) *estimated* some 1,727,000 incidences of child abuse.

In 1987, 2.3 million cases were *reported* to child-protective-services agencies in the United States, and this figure was thought to represent only half of the actual incidences. Twenty-five percent of reported cases involved physical assault, 20 percent were cases of sexual abuse, and 55 percent fell into an ill-defined area of neglect and emotional maltreatment. The Kempe Center, which compiles these data, reported that between 2,000 and 5,000 deaths occur annually as a result of child abuse.

The Public Health Service acknowledges that issues of stress and violent behavior — which used to be law-enforcement and social-services concerns — have become public-health problems of great magnitude, involving the basic social structure of our society. While more effective preventive intervention programs to reduce violence are clearly needed, the complexities are such that none beyond the traditional kinds of approaches have yet been designed by public-health agencies.

Child abuse is only one aspect of violent behavior in this country. It is perhaps the most complex problem to tackle, since issues of parental rights and child protection are ill defined and pose legal dilemmas for many. Major studies have been funded for a national survey of family violence that will provide more accurate data on the incidences and severity of child abuse. With improved data, public-health agencies will have a better grasp of the factors that lead to child abuse, will be able to identify high-risk families, and patterns of behavior that lead to child abuse. They will be able to assess programs that are most effective in preventing child abuse, devise new and innovative intervention programs, and expand existing programs that provide treatment for abusive parents and abused children.

Neither the Public Health Service nor the American Academy of Pediatrics expects to meet its goal to reduce the number of reported cases of child abuse by 25 percent abuse in the next five years. Nevertheless, they will design public-education campaigns to increase public awareness and concern about the problem and public cooperation in helping to identify abusive parents. Health-care providers, especially primary-care physicians who are more likely first to encounter evidence of child abuse, will be urged to report all suspected incidences of child abuse. Social-services providers will be further trained to identify and treat potentially abusive parents in order to avert harm as well as to treat those who have been identified as child abusers. These aims must be met while ensuring that parental rights are not violated and cultural behaviors that vary from group to group are not misunderstood. These last two are especially delicate issues and, to date, have no clear-cut guidelines.

One benefit of reproductive education, which encourages the delay of pregnancy, would be a reduction in child abuse through decreasing the number of births to inexperienced and immature adolescents who cannot provide a stable family environment for a child. Success in deterring drug and alcohol use, which influences negative behavior, would lessen acting out. Most important, programs that teach parenting skills in an effective manner would enhance the potential for a healthy parent-child relationship.

Young parents who are among the disenfranchised, the hopeless, and the despairing are the major perpetrators of physical and emotional harm to children. Substance abuse, conditions of poverty, family and environmental stress, and indifference to violent behavior all contribute to a climate in which child abuse becomes possible and likely. The willingness or ability to eliminate poverty conditions and the societal crimes that plague the United States are major issues. No civilized society can tolerate "acceptable" levels of child abuse. The current national goal for the year 2000 is to reduce child abuse to no more than 500,000 reported cases annually. While an improvement on current statistics, that figure is woefully high.

AIDS

As of 25 April 1988, there were only 955 reported cases of AIDS in children under eighteen years of age—1.5 percent of all reported cases. Of these, 76 percent were due to *in utero* transmission by the mother, typically as a result of drug use. Eighty percent of the children affected were under six years old, and 6 percent were hemophiliac children. They were among the 12 percent who acquired AIDS through blood transfusions. A recently developed blood screening test to detect the human immunodeficiency virus (HIV), which causes AIDS, should significantly reduce the risk of transmitting HIV infection to noninfected children who require transfusion.

"At risk" groups of children and adolescents are infants of infected mothers, sexually abused children, intravenous drug abusers, and sexually active adolescents, both heterosexual and homosexual. The number of cases of AIDS in infants, children, and adolescents is doubling every year. The statistics projecting the number of cases of AIDS are uncertain, and when the projected numbers are reassessed, the figures escalate. The Centers for Disease Control have estimated that there will be as many as 20,000 cases of AIDS among infants and children by 1991, and as many as 3,000 infants a year will be born HIV-positive. Current data indicate that nearly all HIV-positive individuals will develop active AIDS. Of course, all projections will be influenced by the effectiveness of public-education campaigns, the availability of more effective drugs to treat AIDS, and the development of a vaccine against AIDS. Surely, impressionable young people must be made to understand the doleful consequences of ignoring parental, teacher, counselor, clergy, physician, public-health, and media warnings about AIDS, permissive sexual behavior, drug use, and the possible catastrophic consequences for them, for their associates, and for their children.

Adolescents, normally a high-risk group, are highly vulnerable to HIV infection. They are sexually active, and they use drugs. Altering behavior patterns in society usually takes a long time. This certainly holds true for those on the threshold of adulthood, in the throes of youthful rebellion and experimentation. The combat can begin with very early AIDS education, such as appropriate programs for children from kindergarten through high school that are being suggested. If, as is hoped, these programs elicit more controlled and responsible behavior in young people, the number of cases of AIDS during the 1990s will be far less than current projections.

Dr. Robert Gallo, who is chief of the laboratory of tumor cell biology at the National Cancer Institute and whose work has greatly contributed to the current understanding of AIDS, recently told a group of newly graduated physicians that AIDS will be with them, their children, and their grandchildren until public education responds to public-health advisories about sexual behavior and needle contamination among drug users and until a cure for AIDS or a vaccine against AIDS is developed. When asked if AIDS is like a plague, Dr. Gallo somberly replied, "No. The plague goes away."[1]

Immediate problems of treatment of AIDS already consume a great deal of time and resources for pediatric subspecialists and skilled, highly trained medical staffs. There are multiple medical problems associated with the AIDS infection — bacterial infections, neurologic syndromes, and encephalopathies. These are all forerunners of inevitable death of the immunosuppressed patient. At the present time, the median survival time for infants with AIDS is only four months. For the older child, the average survival time is twenty-two months. The use of the drug AZT, which has been shown to be effective in retarding the advances of AIDS in adults, may be equally effective in extending the survival time of children. The cost of using this drug, however, is from $10,000 to $20,000 a year per person.

Violence

Violence — accidents, homicides, and suicides — accounts for 77 percent of adolescent deaths in this country, having replaced communicable diseases as the major source of morbidity and mortality. Sixty percent of deaths result from motor-vehicle accidents. Alcohol is involved in more than half of the motor accidents ending in fatalities. Now that the minimum age for the consumption of alcohol has been raised to twenty-one throughout the United States, recommendations for motor-vehicle accident prevention among adolescents are to increase community peer-pressure programs, pass more laws requiring the use of seat belts, delay issuing driver's licenses, and, possibly, establish adolescent curfew laws. The American Academy of Pediatrics mentions studies that report an increase in traffic fatalities in those states in which the speed limit has been raised to sixty-five miles per hour. The correlation between accidents and speed thus seems a valid assumption.

Among children, accidents — especially motor-vehicle accidents — cause the most deaths, followed by cancer, heart disease, and homicide. Surgeon General C. Everett Koop has commented, "If a disease were killing our children in the proportions that accidents are, people would demand that this killer be stopped."[2]

Accidents cause 8,000 deaths annually in children up to fourteen years of age. Over 3,400 of these are caused by motor-vehicle accidents. More than 50,000 young children are permanently disabled by accidents every year. A 1987 report cites an annual figure of over 15 million nonfatal injuries in children fourteen years and under. Public perception of possible injuries to their children is very low, and in one study parents expressed far more concern about abduction, crime, and drugs than about their children's vulnerability to injury or death due to accidents.

The American Academy of Pediatrics is responsible for the wide distribution of brochures on child safety—issues like car seats for infants and small children, home child restraints, smoke detectors, safe hot-water temperatures, window and stairway guards, gates to prevent falls, and close supervision of young children, especially around bodies of water. These public-education brochures and public-safety campaigns have been highly effective, reflected by reduced incidences of childhood accidents in recent years. Their collaboration with the National "Safe Kids" Campaign is part of a five-year goal further to reduce accidents involving children.

A notable example of anticipated success of a nationally coordinated, well-structured public-awareness campaign is the recent effort to expose the dangers to children of all-terrain vehicles (ATVs), which in 1985 were responsible for 224 deaths of children ages one through fifteen and 28,633 injuries of children ages five through fourteen. ATV manufacturers have reached an agreement with the Consumer Product Safety Commission and the Department of Justice to ban the sale of three-wheeled ATVs. This campaign will now focus on the sale of four-wheeled ATVs to children under the age of sixteen. The Academy of Pediatrics expects that ATVs will be eliminated by the year 2000.

As many children below the age of fifteen died of accidents caused by firearms as from accidents caused by ATVs. If one includes the number of children and adolescents who died by homicide and suicide with those who died from firearms, it amounts to a national crisis. Homicides in the United States are almost always associated with the use of handguns. The United States ranks first among fourteen developed countries in the use of guns in homicides. The comparison made by Handgun Control, Inc., of the number of deaths by handgun in Canada (6), Sweden (7), Great Britain (8), Australia (10), Switzerland (27), and Japan (35) to the United States (9,014) dramatically illustrates the extent of this problem. Twenty-five percent of all homicides in the United States occur in the age group fifteen to twenty-four years old. More than 55 percent of adolescent suicides involve handguns.

National antihandgun coalitions have not met with the same applaudable success as the anti-ATV campaign. Efforts have been thwarted for the most part by the money and power of the National Rifle Association's lobbying and publicity campaigns.

Suicide is the third leading cause of death among adolescents in the United States, and 20 percent of all suicides in this country occur in adolescence. Only 10 percent of teenage suicide attempts end in death, and the rate of suicide in the youth population has increased fourfold since 1950. With these facts, a more comprehensive appreciation of the problem becomes possible. Adolescent depression has many causes, some of which are biologically rooted. The major contributors to teenage depression, however, are the breakdown of family life, pressure related to school achievement, unrealistic expectations of life stimulated by the media, and the use of alcohol and drugs (which affect thinking and judgment). Efforts to curtail the rising trend of suicide among juveniles rely heavily on educational programs in schools and communities. Family, school, and health-personnel intervention is essential to avert suicide attempts by recognizing behavioral symptoms suggestive of suicide.

Substance Abuse

Drug and alcohol use among young people has changed over the years. Decreasing numbers of adolescents are experimenting with alcohol and marijuana, but the use of crack is rising. Substance abuse remains a major issue for the future health of children. Although alcohol consumption varies geographically, it remains the drug most often abused by the largest number of children and adolescents. One study in New York State reported that over two-thirds of children under the age of nineteen drink alcohol. Thirteen percent are reported to consume alcohol weekly. About 30 percent of high-school seniors use alcohol in any given month. Forty percent of high-school sophomores report intoxication at least once during the school year. Alcoholic hepatitis and pancreatitis, once considered adult diseases, are now found with increasing frequency among adolescents. In large urban areas, alcoholic-adolescent units in hospitals can be found. Chronic alcoholic consumption beginning in adolescence can result in hepatic fibrosis and cirrhosis as early as twenty years old.

The Public Health Service advocates higher taxes on alcoholic beverages, and some states have made the server of alcohol responsible for any accidents in which a patron is subsequently involved. A national drinking age is supported by most informed groups, and a ban on advertising of alcoholic beverages would likely contribute to a decrease in consumption. Education programs on the deleterious effects of alcohol have been effective, but they are countermanded by advertising and image promotion in the media. As parents become more health conscious and reduce their consumption of alcohol, its use by their children is projected also to decline.

Alcohol use in adolescents is closely followed in popularity by use of marijuana and amphetamines, with cocaine use rising. All of these drugs weaken psychosocial judgment and cognitive function, distort the senses, and impair motor skills. They may also produce organic toxic effects. Twenty-six percent of American high-school seniors admit to the use of marijuana at least once a month. Habitual use of marijuana is attended by deterioration of school work, poor interpersonal relationships, lethargy, apathy, moodiness, frustration, intolerance, and deterioration of personal hygiene. The risk of a suicide attempt is increased during marijuana use.

Intranasal use of cocaine (snorting) is favored by 51 percent of its users. It is smoked (freebased) by 36 percent of users, and 13 percent take the drug intravenously. Cocaine is a potent and highly addictive drug, causing cerebral hemorrhage, seizures, respiratory arrest, and heart arrest due to strong vasoconstriction. It can produce rapid mood swings, personality changes, and the physical signs of dysarthria, gait disturbance, and mental confusion.

The social consequences to adolescents who are habitual drug users are widely appreciated — school failure, alienation from family and peers, altered ethical and moral values, and a life-style in which the need for money to support drug habits becomes the principal motivating factor. The prevention of marijuana and amphetamine experimentation in adolescents increases the likelihood that such use will be avoided in adulthood. The exception to this approach appears to be the use of cocaine.

Tobacco has also been targeted for educational programs to reduce its use. Twenty percent of high-school seniors were found to be daily smokers in 1985. Educational efforts, however, are counterbalanced by effective advertising. One study indicates that 40 percent of high-school seniors do not believe there are significant health risks from smoking. A greater number think that smokeless tobacco is harmless, despite evidence that it is associated with oral cancers. It has been difficult, then, to convince adolescents that tobacco harms their health. The short-term harm has been discussed vis-à-vis the association between tobacco use during pregnancy and low birth weight in infants. Long-term use leads to heart disease, cancer, and emphysema. The scientific community has no doubts regarding the link between tobacco use and these life-threatening conditions. It is hoped that, in addition to public education, a recent federal court finding against a tobacco company — considered by all a breakthrough in antitobacco-industry litigation — will convince skeptics, including incredulous youths, that tobacco use can lead to sickness and premature death.

Preventive Nutrition

A growing body of evidence indicates that unhealthful nutritional patterns and habits developed during childhood set the stage for the adult onset of hypertension, atherosclerotic heart disease, cancer, obesity, and behavioral disorders. Preventive nutrition, which establishes healthy nutritional patterns early in life, is viewed as the means significantly to reduce the number of life-threatening diseases.

The major nutritional factors in Americans' diets have included the intake of sodium, fat, and fiber. It is known that a low sodium intake from birth will result in lower blood pressure throughout life, with consequent reductions in the incidences of heart disease. The average American male adolescent consumes 14.6 pounds of sodium chloride every year. Thirty percent of this salt is in baked goods and cereals, 21 percent in prepared meats, fish, and eggs, and 16 percent in dairy products. Condiments that adolescents use liberally, like catsup and mustard, account for an additional 12 percent of salt intake. Their elders, after fifty-five to sixty-five years of such diets, succumb to heart diseases at the rate of 450 per 100,000 population. Forty-five to fifty-five-year-olds die at the rate of 156.7 per 100,000 population. The number of deaths due to heart disease in the age group of forty-five to sixty-five is on the order of 166,000 a year. The figure jumps to 230,000 from ages sixty-five to seventy-five. Fatalities will be dramatically reduced in the next century if current dietary recommendations become standard throughout the country.

Atherosclerosis begins early in life, with aortic fatty streaks evident in three-year-olds and in the coronary arteries of eighteen-year-olds. Cholesterol is one of the major factors in the development of atherosclerosis. It is thought that lowering serum cholesterol levels in children to 110 milligrams daily would almost entirely eliminate coronary-artery disease in this country. Even lowering levels to 140 milligrams daily would decrease the disease by 40 percent. The current pediatric average for cholesterol is 160 milligrams daily. The recommendation is to reduce total fat consumption to 30 percent of calories. Children can improve their dietary habits by decreasing their intake of fatty streaked meats, whole milk, ice cream, cheeses, sour cream, butter, lard, sugared cereals, and fruit drinks in favor of lean meats, 1 percent milk, sorbet and frozen yogurt, polyunsaturated margarine, safflower and sunflower oils, whole grains, bran cereals, and fruit.

Because selected fibers bind bile acids that are necessary for cholesterol absorption, children should also increase their intake of fiber-rich foods, such as legumes, chick peas, navy beans, pinto beans, and oat bran. Moreover, increasing their intake of complex carbohydrates to 55 percent of all calories should be encouraged, with whole grains, fruits, and vegetables providing the enticement.

Dietary recommendations for healthy children more than two years old include decreasing total fat to 30 percent of calories, only 10 percent of which are saturated fats. A limit of two or three eggs a week will lower cholesterol intake. It is recommended that protein consumption be limited to 15 to 20 percent of total calories. Several years ago a cartoon in the *New Yorker* showed a sophisticated, urbane mother admonishing her small children to "finish your protein, dears, before you eat your carbohydrates." The comic depiction of the past is the prototype for the future. The children of today will be the adults of the first decade of the twenty-first century. If these children heed current dietary prescriptions, there might be no coronary heart disease in their future.

Environmental Pollutants

Ecosystem pollutants in the environment are an on-going health concern that should be addressed to prevent future damage. The six major categories of current pollutants are pesticides and herbicides, polyhalogenated biphenyls, heavy metals, gases like carbon dioxide, sulfur oxides, and nitrous oxides, acid rain, and radiation.

Pesticide and herbicide toxicity may be accidental, as in childhood poisonings. Toxicity is also caused by chronic and long-term exposure, as occurs with agricultural and industrial runoff of toxins and a leaching process. Since most pesticides and herbicides have a lipid solubility, a biological magnification factor can be noted occurring through the food chain. In other words, contamination of water will increase contamination of zoo plankton, which is in turn eaten by fish, which is then eaten by water fowl, and so on. At each step, the concentration of the contaminant is magnified. The best-studied example of this phenomenon is DDT, which was banned in this country many years ago. Lead, mercury, and polychlorinated biphenyls (PCBs) are entering the magnification chain now.

This same concern must be directed to the clinical toxicity of the polyhalogenated biphenyls, which include polychlorinated and polybrominated biphenyls. PCBs are used primarily as transformer coolants and hydraulic fluids, while the polybrominated biphenyls are used primarily as flame retardants. These compounds, when contaminating an organism, are degraded and metabolized very slowly, and they can endure for long periods of time. Toxic effects noted in humans have included dermatologic, ocular, and systemic signs and symptoms, including jaundice, hepatotoxicity, and fetal toxicity.

Not all industrial toxins relate directly to organic toxicity. Some will have long-range environmental effects for children. Excess generation of carbon dioxide, the persistence of acid rain, and the degradation of the ozone layer are among the most potentially harmful.

Carbon-dioxide generation, through the burning of fossil fuels, is one of the contributors to the greenhouse effect of the earth's atmosphere, allowing incoming sunlight to reach the earth but trapping radiant heat. The increased overall climate temperature of the planet and raised sea levels would have disastrous effects in the future. The United States, along with the rest of the world, would be adversely affected. This country's agricultural productivity, moreover, would be diminished, and there would be further erosion of beaches and flooding and damage to port facilities. Part of the proposal to forestall these disasters would be to reduce by at least a third the amount of fossil fuels burned yearly.

Acid rain is the term introduced in 1872 for rain contaminated with sulfuric acid from the burning of sulfur-rich coals in industrial areas. Acid-soluble toxic metals that are leached out by acid rainfall produce toxicity to fish due to a decrease in the pH to a range of 4.7 and to an accumulation of aluminum. Mercury, manganese, zinc, nickel, lead, and cadmium are also leached out, but the heavy-metal toxicity implications of these are unknown. The risk to people is that these metal contamination levels affect both surface and ground water. In addition to the aquatic biosystems destroyed by acid rain, widespread deforestation can occur, which in turn reduces the amount of oxygen released to the atmosphere. The reduction in oxygen is followed by an additional accumulation of carbon dioxide in the atmosphere, which, again, aggravates the greenhouse effect.

There are four critical components in the production of acid rain: emission of sulphurous and nitrous oxides; atmospheric pressure of sulphuric and nitric acids; favorable weather conditions; and sensitive areas to act as receptor sites. But the only controllable factor of these is the emission of sulphurous and nitrous oxides.

Another problem of industrial pollution is that of ozone depletion in the atmosphere, which is believed to be related to emissions from nuclear bombs, supersonic transports, and fluorinated sprays. Maintaining the ozone layer is an issue that is considered essential to life on the planet. A large hole in the ozone layer already looms ominously over Antarctica, and another hole is said to be developing there. The ozone layer is vital to controlling cosmic radiation and shielding the earth from excessive ultraviolet rays. The ozone layer's control of these rays is essential to minimizing skin cancers and maximizing crop yields.

Radiation is another source of global contamination that is accumulating yearly. Several sources of radiation are uncontrollable, such as cosmic and terrestrial radiation. Controllable sources of radiation, however, involve the use of diagnostic x-rays, weapons testing, nuclear reactors, and environmental sources, such as televisions, airport metal detectors, and smoke detectors.

Conclusion

Poverty will continue to have a strong effect on the health and well-being of the nation. Other issues that involve millions of Americans are access to health care, the utilization of health-care facilities, and the response to health-education programs. In preparing this essay, the authors asked senior pediatric faculty of several university medical schools to name the major children's health concerns of the future. With little variation, each said that children's health needs could be met only by an intact family unit—whatever its composition. A stable and secure environment in which to grow was thought to be essential to building a foundation for healthy development. Such an environment cannot be cultivated in the midst of economic deprivation.

Dr. John Watkins, professor of pediatric gastroenterology at the Children's Hospital of Philadelphia, Pennsylvania, poignantly remarked that the health issues of the future will be determined by the degree of hope adolescents have about their own futures. With hope they can mature in a nurturing environment, make more responsible decisions governing their behavior and their lives, and respond more willingly and eagerly to parental and community efforts of encouragement and guidance. In a climate of despair, the converse will be the case, and people will opt for destructive behavior, producing further aggravated societal problems. No less than a national referendum is called for in a commitment of all citizens to participate in bequesting a healthy future to our children.

Notes

1. Comments at the commencement, Georgetown University School of Medicine, 28 May 1988.
2. National Coalition to Prevent Childhood Injury (NCPCI) Report, "The National 'Safe Kids' Campaign."

Homeless Children

ROBERT M. HAYES

On 6 March 1986, ten-year-old David Bright testified before the House Select Committee on Hunger and became an emblem of the homeless children of America in the 1980s. David lived in New York City's Hotel Martinique, a festering behemoth that was home to 1,500 homeless children and their families. He had won an essay contest at the hotel, and he flew with me to Washington for the hearing. When it was David's turn to testify, he looked at me and swallowed hard. I sat, as his counsel, with him at the witness table. David's left hand held his testimony; his right hand was under the table, gripping my hand. He spoke flawlessly.

David spoke of the children left alone at the Martinique, his own fear of the dark stairways, and the drug dealers who prowled the corridors. He closed on a note of triumph.

"When I grow up," David said, "I will be the president of the United States. Then everyone will have a little money in their pockets."

"And," David added, "no little boy like me will have to put his head down on his desk at school because it hurts to be hungry."[1]

There was barely a dry eye in the hearing room. David's tale was page-one news across the United States. But now, two years after he testified, 13 million American children live with families that lack the money to pay the rent *and* put food on the table. Hundreds of thousands of American children are homeless, and many more than that are hungry. And the future of American children is blighted as boys and girls sit in classrooms, sigh, and put their heads on their desks because it still hurts to be hungry.

David awoke the next morning a momentary celebrity in New York City. Television crews mingled with crack dealers in the lobby of the Hotel Martinique, seeking to get young David on camera. It was too much, not for David but for the mayor of New York City, Edward I. Koch.

Murray Kempton wrote: "David Bright is a 10-year-old child who can control himself in public. Mayor Edward I. Koch is a 61-year-old man who can't."[2]

If the poignancy of David's words stirred the hearts of Americans, what followed typified the lives of America's poor. Mayor Koch launched a tirade over David's testimony, insisting that the $6,000 annual allowance provided homeless families living in midtown Manhattan hotels was sufficient to feed children. If David was hungry, Koch said, it was clearly the fault of the child's mother.[3]

After releasing the family's budget, Mayor Koch went further. The Social Services Department's spokeswoman (subsequently appointed judge of the New York Family Court) began leaking confidential information from the Bright family's records about the mother's suspected drug abuse. City workers established a vigil to uncover any neglect by David's mother. Weeks later, while the mother shopped, the city took David and his brother into custody. A court ordered the children returned; extraordinarily, the city appealed. The children were finally returned after an appellate court refused to reverse the Family Court's order.

More than David Bright or his counsel ever imagined, David was emblematic of homelessness in America in the 1980s. He suffered greatly in anonymity, the suffering a product of an ill-equipped parent and a neglectful and incompetent public-welfare program. His tale touched the hearts of America, and homeless children more than anyone else have pushed American politics back toward a posture of compassion, or at least a posture that claims compassion. Yet he was undone — as homeless children typically are — as political structures scrambled for protection. Mayor Koch blamed David's mother. More sophisticated politicians find worthier targets. Governors blame presidents, presidents blame mayors, and mayors blame governors and presidents. The bottom line is the same: little responsibility, little hope, little progress.

The extraordinary thing about homelessness among children in America is not just that it happened but that it happened in the 1980s during years of economic prosperity for most of the United States. By the end of the decade, more than 3 million Americans will likely be homeless. By the year 2003, a study published by the Massachusetts Institute of Technology warns, over 18 million Americans will be unable to secure housing.[4] Since the mid-1980s most people becoming homeless in states like Massachusetts were children. And that is no surprise. It is the poor who become homeless, and the poor are children. In California, one-fourth of the children live in poverty; in New York City, two-fifths.

But the misery of a child's poverty cannot compare to the wretchedness of life for a homeless child. As basic as food, shelter, and clothing are for human beings, children who do not know the security of permanence will be harmed, many of them irrevocably. Why do some families become homeless while others live poorly but in housing? There is no single answer that captures the truth.

In 1980, homelessness among children was rare, and in the United States soup kitchens and emergency shelters were not yet common features of the national landscape. But there were increasing numbers of homeless men and — to everyone's surprise — women living on the streets. The accepted understanding of this unpleasantness was that the homeless were mentally ill and "chose" to live on the streets. People who actually spoke with homeless people knew that the consensus was, as usual, wrong. But few people were then heard who linked homelessness with the beginnings of the demise of the low-income housing market.

Two pioneering researchers and advocates, Kim Hopper and Ellen Baxter, spent nearly a year on the streets of New York talking to homeless people. The methodology they developed in their landmark study, *Private Lives, Public Spaces*, explained then why single adults become homeless.[5] Today, it shows why certain families with children hit the streets.

The first step, according to Hopper and Baxter, is to recognize the underlying causes of homelessness. Those causes form the backdrop demanding that some people fall out of the housing market onto the streets. Exactly who becomes homeless is another question. A variety of "precipitating causes" — often idiosyncratic in nature — explains why one impoverished family can cling to housing while another cannot.

The Causes of Family Homelessness: Housing and Poverty

It is almost definitional, but, given the prevalence of camouflage in political debate, it is important to emphasize that the absence of housing is the fundamental cause of homelessness in America. Over the past decade there has been a dramatic decline in the supply of housing affordable to persons with low income. During that time, an estimated 1 million low-income units were lost from the rental market across the United States.

Housing losses are explained in many ways, but two primary causes stand out. First, most cities throughout the country quickly underwent gentrification, beginning in the late 1970s. Affluent Americans, mostly young professionals raised in suburbia, once more saw attractions in urban life. Millions of dollars in public funds helped convert low-cost housing to residences for the more well-to-do. The benefits of gentrification were inarguable: an enhanced tax base, slum clearance, and rejuvenated urban villages. At a point, though, in many cities the pendulum went too far. The supply of housing that poor people and many working people could afford fell below demand. Refugees from the housing market became America's modern homeless.

Another powerful force was conspiring with gentrification to erode the supply of affordable housing. That was the federal government. Since World War II, a broad bipartisan consensus recognized that the private housing market could not create low-income housing without stimulants from government. Republicans and Democrats alike joined in enacting the National Housing Act of 1949, which set forth the often-quoted goal of "a decent home for every American family."[6] For three decades both the White House and Congress supported a panoply of housing programs that helped maintain the equilibrium between the supply of, and demand for, low-cost housing. By 1980 the federal government was approving some $32 billion annually in budget authority to house the poor.

President Ronald Reagan changed that. During his two terms in office, budget authority for low-income housing dropped precipitously. In fiscal year 1988–89 the president sought just $6.9 billion from Congress in new spending, a 79 percent drop from 1980 levels. Each year Congress fought the president to restore some money to the housing budget. By President Reagan's final year in office, thanks in large measure to the public outcry against homelessness, federal budget authority passed by Congress had crept back up to $7.5 billion, still a 77 percent drop from 1980 levels.

Once the supply of housing drops below the need, a Darwinian struggle for that survival commodity is certain to ensue. Housing is a commodity that economists refer to as "inelastic." No matter how much it costs, housing is something people need and no substitute goods can replace it. If one examines the categories of Americans who became homeless as the housing market deteriorated in the 1980s, one sees a totally predictable application of the laws of social Darwinism.

In the early 1980s, the least competitive renters — mentally disabled men and women living in shabby residential hotels and boarding houses — fell out of the housing market. They were disorganized, sometimes disoriented, and almost always poor. As the first wave of fallout from a housing market in decline, mentally ill adults were the vanguard of contemporary homelessness.

By 1983, as housing stock continued to wane, young able-bodied men and women were dubbed "the new homeless" by the media. Displaced from the job market by the recession, these young people — sound of mind and disproportionately black and Hispanic — had comparatively little education or job skills. Yet, by 1985, the depopulation of psychiatric hospitals had ended. And the recession receded along with unemployment rates. Enter homeless families.

The forces eroding the housing supply continued unabated into the mid-1980s. Shelters, soup kitchens, and skid rows experienced the most dramatic shift ever in their clientele. Families were hitting the streets, but only certain families: those that fit the profile of "losers" in a Darwinian contest. Typically, homeless families wore the badges of weak competitors. They were headed by a single parent, usually a woman. The families usually had a number of children, most of them very young. The cutting edge of the housing market decline had crossed the graph to make both mothers and children homeless. The feminization of poverty had become the impoverishment of children. And like the civil rights movement before it, the feminist movement had left behind most of the poor.

The flip side of the unavailability of housing for the poor is, of course, the question of affordability. In older northeastern and midwestern cities, there is an absolute shortage in the supply of housing. Vacancy rates, which should hover around 5 percent in a healthy market, are negligible in these cities. For low-cost housing, the vacancy rates in cities like New York, Washington, and Chicago are virtually zero.

But in a number of cities where homelessness among families is rampant, vacancy rates are high. In some Sunbelt cities, for instance, it is in the double digits, yet families with children sleep in cars. Homelessness in these cities is a function of the affordability of housing.

The major shelter for the homeless in Dallas is an old warehouse in the heart of the city's industrial wasteland. An Episcopal priest, Jerry Hill, runs the shelter, which offers refuge to up to 600 people. Every afternoon two lines begin forming hours before the shelter doors are open for the night. In one line are homeless men. Children, usually with their parents, are in the other line. They have to get in line early because the competition is fierce; the competition is not for a bed, because such amenities do not exist in this Texas shelter. The competition is for space on the warehouse floor. At least it is dry. That is where homeless children sleep in Dallas, the hometown of "America's team" in the National Football League.

As mysterious as homelessness in America seems to be, it seemed unthinkable that so many people — estimates of the homeless in Dallas range up to 15,000 — would be out of the housing market with a 16 percent vacancy rate. Dallas real-estate brokers offer several months free rent to people who sign a lease. Landlords offer free videocassette recorders and health-club memberships to lure tenants. There is no shortage of housing in much of Texas, but there is a shortage of housing that poor families can afford.

The basic supply-demand analysis still fits — there is an imbalance between the demand for housing and the supply. But what antitrust lawyers call the "relevant market" must be defined precisely. The relevant market facing a poor family seeking housing is not the housing market *in toto*. Six-figure condominiums have no relevance to a mother living below subsistence on public assistance. The relevant supply of housing against which demand must be measured is the housing supply affordable to poor people. That market, in every city and town across the United States, is out of balance. Nearly without exception, there is a dramatic shortage of low-income housing, regardless of the overall housing supply in an area.

So what should be done? A pluralistic response to the housing market is needed. Supply must be increased in many parts of the country. But surely the affordability crisis can be met by increasing a poor family's ability to pay for housing. No state leaves a family with children dependent on public assistance in an economic position to compete successfully for housing. Even the working poor — the majority of impoverished families — live at 60 percent of subsistence when the family's wage earner works a forty-hour job at the current federal minimum wage. It is fair to say the major cause of homelessness is the lack of housing for the poor. But it is also correct to say that poverty, the inability to pay the rent demanded by the market, is the primary reason that so many American children face homelessness at the end of the 1980s. Solutions to homelessness may not be complicated after all.

Poverty

It is generally agreed, by liberals and conservatives alike, that it takes a certain amount of income to subsist in the United States. While the cost of living varies in different regions, the federal government defines the poverty line, a euphemism for the amount of money needed to subsist, at $11,629 for a family of four. *Webster's Ninth New Collegiate Dictionary* defines *subsistence* to mean "the minimum (as of food and shelter) necessary to support life." So when the United States government declared that in 1988 some 32.5 million Americans lived below the poverty line, it meant that 32.5 million Americans lack the income to secure food, shelter, and clothing, i.e., to support life. Most of those people do not starve, and most children of poverty are not homeless. Still, it is easy to see how inevitably many families fall out of the housing market when subsistence is beyond the reach of tens of millions of people. By definition, families below the poverty line cannot feed their children and pay the rent.

The reality of poverty in the United States is something very few Americans who are not poor comprehend. There is among the American public a firm conviction that after decades of the New Deal and the Great Society, a secure safety net is in place for the poor. Several summers ago I participated in a week-long study group on law and society at the Aspen Institute for Justice. An illustrious group of thinkers spent the week in the splendor of the Colorado Rockies reading the likes of John Rawls and John Stuart Mill. Leading corporate lawyers were joined by prominent academics and judges, including the chief justice of the Alabama Supreme Court. Discussions were led by U.S. Court of Appeals Judge Jon O. Newman, recently dubbed — correctly, I think — the smartest judge in America by the *National Law Journal*.

We spoke one morning in Aspen of distributive justice. Note was taken that even Adam Smith in *The Wealth of Nations*, his seminal work on free enterprise, acknowledged, "No society can surely be flourishing and happy [when] part of the members are poor and miserable. It is but equity, besides, that they . . . be themselves tolerably well fed, clothed and lodged."[7] And the learned debate in Aspen turned to the familiar question of whether society owed the poor the tools for economic advancement: job training, education, day care, and the like. Implicitly assumed by the group was subsistence: there was no comprehension that the state of Colorado, which ranks twenty-ninth among the states in welfare benefits to poor families with dependent children, provided income and food stamps sufficient to meet just 73 percent of subsistence. A poor family on welfare in Denver could expect to run out of money well before the end of the month.

That is true of every state in America, save Alaska. While Democrats routinely decry — with considerable justification — the social-welfare performance of President Reagan, it is the states that set the amount of assistance provided to a family in need. For fifty years, since Franklin D. Roosevelt was president, the federal government guaranteed to reimburse the states 50 percent of the funds spent in operating income-support programs for poor families with children. Ronald Reagan never changed that, yet by the time he left office, poor families on public assistance in virtually every state had fallen substantially below subsistence. Governors and state legislatures, not the president, were the cause of that.

In Alabama, the state with the lowest welfare benefits, a family of three receives

$118 per month in public assistance. That combined with the maximum amount of food stamps available to the family is equal to an income at 46 percent of subsistence. The twenty-fifth ranking state, Montana, offers $359 per month, or — combined with food stamps — 74 percent of subsistence. Only six states — Alaska, California, Delaware, Minnesota, Vermont, and Wisconsin — offer over 90 percent of subsistence to poor families. Moreover, these benefits are available only to families with dependent children and only for people who obtain the maximum benefit while maintaining eligibility for assistance. That is typically no easy task. Rube Goldberg-like documentation requirements, senseless rote demands, and degrading and useless make-believe work projects characterize the eligibility hurdles poor people face to obtain their meager benefits.

Entrenched poverty, in tandem with the tight housing market for the poor, inevitably leads to homelessness, at least for some children. But one of the vexing puzzles that plague social-policy analysts is why only some families hit the streets. Economic causes alone do not explain homelessness.

Precipitating Causes

In Hopper's and Baxter's 1981 landmark study of homeless adults, the researchers identified idiosyncratic occurrences, which they dubbed "precipitating events," as the propelling cause of a person's homelessness. These "precipitating events," conspiring with the "causes" of homelessness (loss of housing, deinstitutionalization of the mentally ill, and joblessness), explained why a particular man or woman hit the streets. In the early 1980s the precipitating events that cast single adults out of the housing market were fundamentally the same ones that made families and their children homeless by the late 1980s.

Typical of the events that precipitated homelessness for a single woman, Hopper and Baxter found, was the loss of a spouse through death or desertion. For men and women alike, precipitating events included an emotional or mental breakdown, the loss of a job, a bureaucratic error that delayed a benefit check, a disabling illness, or an eviction caused by the conversion of a single-room-occupancy hotel. Judgmental critics of early relief programs for the homeless in the 1980s made distinctions between the "worthy" and the "unworthy": the mentally ill were plainly deserving; not so clear was the social responsibility to aid people who lost their homes when they relapsed into alcohol abuse or failed to find new employment promptly after the loss of a job. But if, as Hopper and Baxter have written, skid row became more democratic in the 1980s as new groups of Americans became homeless, the government response to homelessness was consistent: deserving and undeserving poor were treated alike — little was done for either.

Some different precipitating events now cause homelessness. Psychiatric disturbances are far more common for mothers in families on the brink of homelessness than is commonly believed. And among families that remain homeless for an extended period, the likelihood of serious mental or emotional illness mounts substantially. In the late 1980s a new scourge swept through poor communities. Crack, the potent and cheap cocaine derivative, became the drug of choice for thousands of people living in poverty. It devastates families who live, as most of the poor do, on the precipice of homelessness. Rent payments and a child's needs become secondary to the fierce, uncontrollable craving for the drug. Crack, child abuse, and homelessness often coincide to wreak havoc on the health and safety of a child.

The emergence of drug abuse in conjunction with homelessness among families was employed in some cities as a political vehicle to avoid aid to the homeless. After ten-year-old David Bright shamed Mayor Koch with his testimony on Capitol Hill, the mayor's immediate response was that David's mother must be spending her welfare-payment largesse on illicit drugs. By 1988, when mothers and children begging on New York City streets made some fashionable neighborhoods resemble the streets of Calcutta, Mayor Koch suggested that the children were decoys set up to help fund maternal crack habits. The *New York Times*, whose generally sympathetic reporting helped prod the Koch administration to take some responsible steps to abate homelessness, assigned a metropolitan reporter to the beat who seemed to search for a crack addict behind every homeless mother. There was some, but not much, backlash from the public.

Neither side in the ideological struggle over child-welfare policy has responded meaningfully to the torture of a child living, homeless or otherwise, in a family headed by a drug abuser. Drug treatment is unavailable for most addicts. It is totally unavailable for a parent seeking to keep his or her family together. Fiscal conservatives say these treatment programs cost too much money, so the government does not fund much treatment. At the same time, little effort is made to rescue these children from parents who — without drug treatment — are a clear and present danger to their children. Civil libertarians say a mere threat to a child cannot justifying terminating a parent's rights to that child. So nothing happens until the child is maimed by violence or, more frequently, by deprivation.

In analyzing causes and precipitating events that result in homelessness, the moralist in everyone is tempted to judge. The debate between social responsibility and individual freedom is triggered in the Aspens of America, and of course there is never a satisfactory resolution. A poor, uneducated young mother can do virtually nothing about the housing crisis. Yet, one might argue, the woman could avoid pregnancy and could search for work while organizing child-care cooperatives. At a minimum, she could prudently manage her meager income and certainly avoid drugs. There may be truth, untruth, or shades of truth in all that. There are arguments and counterarguments, some of which even prove interesting. But there is a bottom line. Homeless families always include the incontrovertibly innocent and deserving. No matter what caused or precipitated a child's homelessness, the child deserves better.

A Slow Death

There is no surer way to destroy the beauty of childhood than by rendering a child homeless. It strips a child of the values that create humane adults. It erodes a child's sensitivity, ethics, and ability to love. And it destroys children by a slow death.

The physical torments are well documented. Whether it is infant mortality, developmental disorders — mental retardation, cerebral palsy, and learning disabilities — or the physical abuse of burnings, malnutrition, and lacerations, the story is the same. But the physical torment pales in the face of psychic torture to which homeless children are subjected: a five-year-old who still cannot speak and probably never will; a twelve-year-old whose palate is gnarled and whose front teeth stick straight out because he still sucks his thumb; and children long past that lonely stage when they run into the arms of any stranger — children who do not even look for love anymore and never will.

Photoessayists and news cameras catch the outer beauty of homeless children with regularity. But it does not take very long for homelessness to destroy the inner beauty of a child.

Gretchen Buchenholz is the president of the Association to Benefit Children (ABC), a New York City organization that runs an array of housing and day-care programs for homeless children. She spends her days tending to homeless families, striving to salvage a preschool child here, a family there, by offering interim care for the period that ABC needs to find permanent housing for a family. Mrs. Buchnholz told me about Shariff, a five-year-old homeless boy she met with his mother in a welfare office in 1984. Shariff shook in fear the first time he was taken outside the city to a well-manicured nature preserve. "Yuk! Nature is disgusting," he screamed in terror. But ABC stuck with Shariff and Teresa, his mother. He went to day care; Teresa went back to school. The formula for rescue included the most important and indispensable element: ABC rehabilitated an apartment for the family. With housing, with day care, and with friendliness, a family was rescued from homelessness and the horrors that are caused by it. Teresa has worked as a medical secretary for the past two years. She is putting Shariff (who now likes trees) through a local parochial school, and she has never missed a rent payment. It is a nice story but, in a country without housing, a rare one.

"Who is the saddest homeless child you know?" I asked Mrs. Buchenholz. She described Darla, a three-year-old she met at Manhattan's Terminal Hotel, a rat-infested firetrap on the city's Far West Side. She attended one of ABC's day-care programs.

"Darla never, never showed any facial expression," Mrs. Buchenholz said. "She was totally blanked out. And then, unprovoked, she would bite anyone who held her. She would take flesh off people's arms.

"I don't know where she is now. She had lacerations on her side, and she was taken to Mount Sinai Hospital. She was examined there, this three-year-old, and she had bruises and cuts around her vagina. Mt. Sinai said she was sexually abused.

The Family Court ruled she was injured by being slammed down on a metal potty. People are afraid to use the bathrooms at the hotel. "We were trying to get through to her, somehow, anyhow. The city removed her from her mother. We were the only family Darla had — and, yes, she would bite her teachers. But we thought maybe we could get through. "The city put her in a boarding home. All we know is that she's somewhere in Queens. We can't find out where. They won't tell us."

What is the prognosis?

"It's inevitable that a child like Darla will be angry, isolated, depressed," said Mrs. Buchenholz. "The biting will escalate. She'll grow older and become violent more and more. She'll never trust anymore. She'll never form attachments."

Are these the hollow children?

"They are something scared and they are something wild. Are they hollow inside? I don't know. A child is helpless. All children know that. A parent who can't feed or take care of a child can only scare a child. To a kid, that's terror."

Solutions

Solutions to homelessness are at once complicated and simple. The analytical problem is that it is always treated as a discrete phenomenon. But homelessness is nothing unto itself. It is a symptom of systems, of people, and of policies that have failed. To address homelessness is to address its causes. And its causes are as broad as the range of human needs.

That is no reason for paralysis. Major steps can be taken, as a matter of public policy, to eradicate homelessness as quickly as the mass homelessness of the 1980s was created. First, the housing market must be balanced. Second, the incomes of dependent people — one way or another — must be increased. And third, intelligent administration of publicly funded initiatives — housing, schools, and day care — must be found.

Homelessness, particularly among children, has moved Washington toward a serious shift back to at least considering restoring federal housing programs. During the 1988 presidential campaign both George Bush and Michael Dukakis pledged renewed partnerships — fueled by federal dollars — to build housing for the poor. While neither candidate looked toward the ambitious federal housing programs started in the late 1940s and maintained through the Nixon years, Republicans and Democrats alike moved toward a consensus that the federal role in stimulating the supply of low-income housing was a political necessity. The 101st Congress will consider a host of new bills to create permanent and affordable low-income housing, primarily aimed at rehousing the homeless. Senator Alan Cranston (D.-Calif.) is expected to push for enactment of recommendations made in 1988 by a bipartisan commission chaired by James Rouse, head of the Enterprise Foundation.

One clear gain of the New Federalism promoted by the Reagan administration was the more aggressive involvement of state governments in housing issues. California, Virginia, Pennsylvania, New York, and Massachusetts all made progress toward housing the poor in the 1980s. The Reagan federalism was plainly misplaced ideology — the state could not and would not replace the forty-year tradition of federal housing subsidies. But modest, model programs of considerable efficiency were launched by some states. A positive — if unintended — legacy of the Reagan years will be the establishment of federal supports to fund efficient state housing programs at levels realistic enough to tilt the housing market back into equilibrium.

Reasonable public-assistance benefit levels must also be part of any serious effort to abate homelessness and hunger among children. Obviously, children will go without when they live in households languishing far below subsistence. The focus of welfare reform, apparently, will have to expand to force state houses to increase benefits. The rhetoric, to be sure, will be around workfare, employment, education, and independence, as well it should be. But for those routes to carry poor families anywhere, subsistence benefits must be the floor below which people will not fall. As one homeless mother put it quite correctly: "Hungry kids don't learn. They stay stupid."

It must be admitted that these proposals — an increase in low-income housing stock and subsistence welfare benefits — cost money. But housing children is an investment. And any commercial enterprise that refuses to invest in its future goes bankrupt — quickly.

Gretchen Buchenholz of the Association to Benefit Children travels the trenches where homeless children live and die. Some children die fast in those trenches, some die slowly. A few escape. Matthew, an eight-year-old homeless boy in New York City told Gretchen Buchenholz how he and his siblings marked the slow death of their baby sister, a child whose death was attributed to "a failure to thrive." Matthew's tale, as nightmare or heartbreak, tells why an investment in these children is essential:

When our baby die we start to sit by the window. We just sit an' sit all wrapped up quiet in old shirts an' watch the pigeons. That pigeon she fly so fast, move so fast. She move nice. A real pretty flyer.

She open her mouth and take in the wind. We just spread out crumbs, me and my brother. And we wait. Sit and wait. There under the window sill.

She don't even see us til we slam down the window. And she break. She look with one eye. She don't die right away. We dip her in, over and over, in the water pot we boils on the hot plate.

We wanna see how it be to die slow like our baby die.

NOTES

1. "It Hurts to be Hungry, Homeless Boy Tells Panel," *New York Newsday*, 7 *Mar. 1986*; "Terror in Shelter — Menu of Complaints from a Hungry Boy," *New York Daily News*, 7 Mar. 1986; "'Hotel Kid' Becomes a Symbol for the Homeless," *New York Times*, 16 Mar. 1986.

2. Murray Kempton, "Koch Needs Primer on Behavior," *New York Newsday*, 29 Mar. 1986.

3. See, e.g., "The Mayor vs. the Kid," *New York Newsday*, 8 Mar. 1986 and "Koch: City Isn't Playing Scrooge — 'If Kids Are Hungry, It's Not Our Fault,'" ibid., 9 Mar. 1986.

4. Philip Clay, *At Risk of Loss: The Endangered Future of Low-Income Rental Housing Resources* (Cambridge: Massachusetts Institute of Technology, 1987).

5. Kim Hopper and Ellen Baxter, *Private Lives/Public Spaces: Homeless Adults on the Streets of New York* (New York: Community Services Society, 1981).

6. Public Law 81-171.

7. Adam Smith, *The Wealth of Nations* (1776; University of Chicago Press, 1976), 88.

The Care and Education of America's Young Children: At the Brink of a Paradigm Shift?

SHARON L. KAGAN

In contrast to other social challenges, providing care and education for America's young children should be comparatively simple. After all, the needs of young children are modest. Their care, grounded in decades of research and centuries of practice, is not a highly complex or technologically sophisticated undertaking. Further, rhetorically at least, the United States acknowledges that children are its most vital natural resource. The national press, reflecting this ethos, features front-page articles extolling the need for child care and early education.

Yet American social and political history does not reflect the ease or commitment indicated by such rhetoric. The United States has never had comprehensive child care and early childhood policies or services. Torn asunder by different missions and ideologies, the policies, regulations, and funding patterns that govern the care and education of America's young children have yielded an inequitable, fragmented, and sadly mediocre array of services.

Exploring the implications of this dichotomy—between reality and rhetoric, between what is and what could be—provides the basis for understanding the current status of the field. It also provides the basis for the central proposition of this essay, namely, that the United States may be at the brink of a fundamental paradigm shift in how it conceptualizes and delivers services for youngsters. Not well served by a categorical and fragmented approach to service delivery, the United States is flirting with entitlement as the core of its redefined commitment to young children and their families. How the nation arrived at this critical juncture and what it means for children, families, communities, and government will be examined in this essay.

Policy Parallels

Recalling the history of free public education in the United States and the move to provide kindergartens within public schools, one is immediately struck by the parallels that characterize the national commitment to children, including the very young. In both cases, services were initially provided to those who could afford them at parental expense, so that long before free public education existed, the children of the prosperous received private instruction in their homes or in fashionable academies. Similarly, before public kindergartens became readily available, families who so desired and who could afford the service purchased it.[1] In both cases, a critical justification for the expansion of publicly funded services was the inequity of opportunity afforded by a nonuniversal system and the desire to uplift the poor from the perils of poverty.[2] In both cases, expansion occurred at the state level, with a "movement" emerging only as a result of widespread, though geographically disparate, interests[3] — a situation similar to the current expansion of child care and early education efforts. And in the case of the expansion of American public education in the midnineteenth century, as in the case of the expansion of child care and early education today, religious considerations were powerful influencers in shaping programmatic and policy outcomes.[4]

Such parallels are more than coincidental. One explanation suggests that these early experiences left the unintentional legacy that has shaped the ensuing policy debate. Like family traits that are passed from one generation to the next, the nation's policy stance on children, formed early on, has perpetuated itself, transcending decades and issues. An alternative, more likely proposition suggests that fundamental ethical and moral principles shaped the American ethos, then and now. Rather than reflecting concerns of an era, which, in turn, molded subsequent patterns of debate, the United States's unique (and not always compatible) values of family privacy, the work ethic, and religious freedom formed the bedrock from which all children's policy has been and will continue to be extruded.

In both cases, two points emerge. First, any major effort that fundamentally alters the conceptual orientation to children's service delivery (e.g., from targeted to universal, private to public, categorical to entitlement, federal to state) will become embroiled in value-related controversy, irrespective of the era. Second, and more significant, the greater the degree to which new children's services seek to alter these extant orientations, the more complex the challenge.

In child care and early education, the historic policy stance has been rather unventuresome, barely tackling significant policy reorientations. Lacking political clout and robust empirical data, most initiatives in behalf of young children, until recently, have not sought to alter the basic paradigm but to add programs and services. While legislatively expedient, such a strategy has not built an infrastructure that can diminish inequity and fragmentation; rather, it has yielded a polyglot array of overlapping and competing services. Essentially, American services to young children are characterized in process by an add-on, or "tinkering at the edges," approach and in content by inconsistent services. What has been the real consequence of this approach to children's policy?

Tinkering at the Edges: America's Approach to Improving Quality and Access

Gilbert Steiner, in his well-known volume, *The Futility of Family Policy*, acknowledges the difficulties inherent in establishing and implementing a comprehensive policy: "The design of policies that can positively affect the quality of family life challenges the inventive capacity of any government. Problems of design present only the first difficulty. In a libertarian democracy that prizes privacy and rejects the primacy of the state, further constraints stem from constitutional limits to permissible government action. In addition, good inventions that are within constitutional boundaries may pose insuperable difficulties of delivery."[5] Steiner adds that "organizing on behalf of family policy is not feasible, because it is more like peace, justice, equality, and freedom than it is like higher welfare benefits, or school busing, or medical care for the aged."[6] Although Steiner was writing about family policy, his comments are equally applicable to the development of a comprehensive children's policy. As conceptualized to date, children's policy has been too vague and amorphous to be configured into broad legislation. Paradoxically, by focusing on the specifics of the legislation or on an individual program initiative, child care and early education functions without a policy gestalt, a vision or plan rooted in fundamental principles of developmental and organizational theory.

Within this "tinkering at the edges" modality, two issues that have been addressed are quality and access. Quality embraces all the efforts to enhance the *nature* of services to young children and their families. It includes regulatory, accreditation, and staff-training issues. Access includes efforts that increase the *number* of services available, including their distribution across segments of the population. Lacking a cohesive vision, policy initiatives in the areas of quality and access have made important strides to date but have fallen short of the mark.

Although the "tinkering at the edges" approach has failed to ensure quality in all programs and to provide equitable access to all who need services, some achievements can be noted. In the area of quality, the field of child care and early education continues to debate precise thresholds, but a clear consensus has emerged on variables associated with quality. Drawing from experience and empirical evidence, child developmentalists and early educators agree that quality is intimately related to classroom factors, most notably the adult-child ratio and group size. The experience and training of the caregiver have also been closely linked to quality outcomes for children. Comprehensive programs that meet children's cognitive, social, intellectual, creative, health, nutritional, and social needs are encouraged, as is close involvement of the parent with the child and with the program. Given this knowledge base, it is no wonder that various efforts to foster quality — licensing standards and voluntary accreditation along with staff certification and training — have received policy attention.

One of the most complex legislative attempts to improve quality has focused on the establishment of federal standards or regulations for child care. Not new, these efforts have been largely ineffective. Recently, another attempt to consider child care regulations broadly was reconfigured to address child abuse. The long process and dashed hopes concluded with a congressional appropriation for $25 million that tied state receipt of funding for caregiver training to the addition of criminal-record checks to existing screening procedures for child care personnel. The actual legislation, entitled the "1985 Model Child Care Standards Act — Guidance to States to Prevent Child Abuse in Day Care Facilities," was a far less comprehensive regulatory effort than many had hoped for and raised once again the value conflicts inherent in reaching consensus on federal regulation.

Reeling from a series of unsuccessful attempts, advocates and scholars have chronicled and analyzed these efforts.[7] Such analyses indicate that several factors coalesce to inhibit the development of federal regulation: many policymakers think that, given wide variation in the states, regulation should remain a state prerogative — a reincarnation of one of the arguments that led to state control of education; and excess regulation, because of its associated costs, is thought to limit profit and drive providers out of the industry, thereby reducing the number of services available for youngsters. The point is that, for legitimate reasons, federal efforts to enhance quality via regulation have only tinkered at the edges, never yielding the kind of comprehensive quality assurances that many child advocates consider appropriate.

States and private initiatives have sought to compensate for regulatory gridlock at the federal level. States, assuming responsibility, have enacted standards that, in most cases, define the *minimum* level of service necessary for licensure and hence do not reflect ideal conditions for children. Although these regulations vary considerably from state to state, Gwen Morgan has reported that forty-one states have updated their standards with the most common improvements, including lower child-staff ratios and ongoing training for providers.[8] These improvements are not as far reaching as might have been expected, because in some states church- and school-based programs are exempt from meeting standards. Such uneven application of standards yields program inequities and acrimony among providers, with regulated programs often providing higher quality care.

Dissatisfied with both national and state regulation of child care quality, professional organizations such as the National Association for the Education of Young Children (NAEYC) and the Child Welfare League of America (CWLA) have each developed their own recommendations.[9] Other professional efforts to promote quality include NAEYC's voluntary Center Accreditation Program (CAP); centers voluntarily participate in a self-assessment and validation process that is based on an amalgam of the best state licensing standards, research, and the experience of seasoned practitioners. Several states have developed their own accreditation systems based on the CAP.

Quality efforts that have focused on staff training and credentialing have also suffered as a result of the "tinkering at the edges" approach to policy. Multiple avenues to certification and competence incorporate a blend of theory and practice, with the traditional training ground being the nation's postsecondary institutions: four-year colleges and universities, community and junior colleges, and vocational technical schools. Fairly widespread, there are an estimated 1,650 early childhood training programs located in 49 states and the District of Columbia. In addition, a competency-based program, the Child Development Associate (CDA), provides an alternative avenue for training and credentialing caregivers. Although a variety of training options exist, child care and early education, like teacher education in general, are hampered by a dearth of personnel. Policy has focused on the content of the training and the requirements for credentialing, with less attention paid to global issues of attracting and retaining personnel. Low status and low salaries are major deterrents to attracting individuals to the field, but other factors also complicate the development of a quality teaching cadre. Because so many different agencies fund child care and early education, each with its own requirements and salary standards, there is no salary or benefit comparability. Consequently, once in the field, early educators are tantalized by higher salaries in different programs: it is not at all uncommon for a child care worker to leave her program and move to another where she will be paid twice the salary for the same work. Such differentials add to the tension among child care and early education programs and providers and exacerbate the staff turnover rate. Unpublished figures from the U.S. Bureau of Labor Statistics indicate that 35.2 percent of child care workers leave the field annually. This does not fully reflect all turnover (because those who transfer from one program to another are excluded), but it conveys the severity of the staffing problem.

In sum, while the "tinkering at the edges" approach to quality has yielded some important advances, the strategy has created as many problems as it has solved. Without a comprehensive policy strategy, the government has focused on generating more slots and establishing minimum standards, leaving the profession and the field to devise strategies to facilitate quality. Unfortunately, no matter how well-intentioned, nongovernment efforts, while helpful, often have limited and idiosyncratic impact.

Efforts to enhance access, the second major dimension of the child care and early education challenge, have yielded similar results — inequality and competition. In the absence of broad initiatives, efforts have been disjointed and have had limited success in addressing systemic problems. The resource and referral (R&R) programs provide one example of a piecemeal approach to services because they are not provided in every community. Essentially, R&Rs increase access in three ways: improving the functioning of the child care market by matching supply and demand, maximizing consumer choice by educating consumers about available options, and providing supply and demand data useful for community planning as well as for state and federal purposes. R&Rs have also proved especially valuable for parents because they provide information about parenting skills and about available child care, and they have assisted providers by tracking changes in supply, parent preferences, and distribution as related to demand. Moreover, R&Rs serve as neutral facilitators of collaboration among the many providers of child care and early education services within communities. As a consequence of their vital role, the number of R&Rs has increased dramatically.

With such proliferation of services, new issues relating to the ethics and auspices of R&Rs are emerging. Since R&Rs are most useful in locating heretofore underutilized services provided by unlicensed or underground child care facilities, questions arise about reporting licensing violations to the appropriate authorities and about providing these referrals to clients. Who controls or administers the R&R is another issue. Should R&Rs be run by a government agency or by the private sector? Whose interests are maximized and whose are sacrificed under which auspices? Because there is no major national commitment to R&Rs, communities throughout the country respond to the issues differently. In some communities, R&Rs are considered a necessary component of the child care system and are funded accordingly. Conversely, in other places they are considered ancillary and are forced to scrounge for operational dollars. Some communities may recognize the importance of R&Rs but may be too resource poor to fund them. Sadly, the inequity that characterizes the delivery of services to young children directly ripples further to engulf the child care and early education infrastructure.

Other efforts to increase access have been undertaken by the public schools and have also unwittingly fostered inequity of service. In 1980, eight states had state-supported prekindergarten programs, in contrast to twenty-six in 1987.[10] The unprecedented increase was based on the rationale that schools were well qualified to serve young children because they are ubiquitous, have a known organizational structure, and are able to generate local financial support. There are concerns, however, that schools may not be the ideal providers of services to young children. Many contend that schools already have enough to do without serving a younger cohort of children. Others think that schools, dominated by a white middle-class orientation, are not well suited to serve the needs of minority children unless certain safeguards are taken.[11] Many are concerned that the pedagogy of school will filter into preschool classrooms, pressuring children into academics long before they are ready and long before such structure is developmentally appropriate. Whether public schools are the appropriate vehicle for increasing access is still debated. What is clear is that state public school efforts are not evenly distributed among wealthy and poor states. Further, even within states, the vast majority of efforts have been targeted to at-risk youngsters, with insufficient funding to meet even their needs. The consequence is that more slots are being made available for at-risk and special needs youngsters in programs that separate these children from their mainstream peers.

Other strategies to increase access are receiving attention, but they also affect only segments of the population. One such effort is to increase access by providing financial support to families to offset their child care costs. In this system, the tax credit goes directly to the service purchaser as opposed to a subsidy to the provider. Whereas a supply subsidy limits and segregates services for low-income children, a demand subsidy enables parents to select a child care facility. Already, the largest federal support to child care, the tax-credit strategy, has some weaknesses in that its primary beneficiaries are middle-income families. Since a family's tax credit can be no larger than its tax liability, low-income families are eligible for litle or no credit.

A fourth strategy to increase access is through employer support for child care. This takes a myriad of forms: on-site child care, vouchers to offset purchase costs in community-based child care facilities, parenting education, and resource and referral services. These services can be provided directly by the company or through a contract with an outside service. While the increase in corporate commitment to children and families is important, its impact is limited: of the 6 million employers in the country, only 3,000 provide any type of child care support to families. Employers are often reluctant to enter this arena because they are concerned about liability costs, benefit inequity among employees, and uncertainty regarding the direct benefit of employee supports to the company. Consequently, this strategy, while helpful, benefits only those who are fortunate enough to work for companies that provide such benefits.

Like initiatives to enhance quality, these piecemeal efforts to increase access have had limited effect. In most cases they have yielded some improvement, affecting a subset of services or population. But they have not been sufficiently potent individually or collectively to address large-scale needs or to compensate for the fragmented nonsystem of services.

Optimistically, these add-on efforts could be considered part of an incrementalist approach to policy. Such an interpretation suggests that major policy reform is typically accomplished in a series of small, sequenced steps, implying the existence of a long-range, comprehensive plan toward which these separate efforts are directed. A more realistic interpretation suggests that the absence of such a plan, coupled with the difficulty of implementing a comprehensive child care and early education initiative, forced policymakers to adopt a "capture the moment" policy strategy. A more pessimistic analysis suggests that even though there have been marginal improvements in services, the unintentional consequence of "tinkering at the edges" has produced a jagged array of services, exacerbated tensions in the field, pitted providers against one another, and ultimately eroded the hope of developing a planned and coordinated system of child care and early education. Whichever stance one advocates, there can be little question that the lack of a comprehensive approach to child care and early education policy has left a legacy of fragmentation and inequity.

Fragmentation and Inequity: The Critical Challenges

Historically, child care and early education have represented two distinct service strands. The former, rooted in the social welfare orientation, was established to assist working parents; the latter focused on providing services that emphasized children's cognitive growth and the enhancement of their social competence. In the classroom, this dichotomy between early-childhood education and child care is slowly diminishing because standards of quality that transcend auspices have been developed. But in other important aspects of the field, the dichotomy between child care and early education persists. Because there is no single funding source, salary inequities between systems are dramatic, as are differences in benefits and working conditions. The preservice training required to be a lead teacher may differ, as does the amount of in-service training.

The consequences of the care and education tension are many. Not only do centers compete for staff, with lower-paying centers severely disadvantaged, but they also compete for children. Parents often choose programs with the least-stringent preentry requirements, even though the setting may be of lower quality. Rather than banding together for legislative action, programs are often at cross-purposes, making consensus and legislative passage difficult.

No less serious than the care/education dilemma is the fact that the current system actually segregates youngsters. Children from low-income families attend subsidized programs, while those from middle- and upper-income families attend fee-based services. In many communities, fee-based segregation amounts to racial segregation — a reality that ignores the research findings of the positive effects of integration on children from all economic levels. Such segregation also disregards the spirit, if not the letter, of the law (*Brown v. Board of Education*, 1954). How can one justify the segregation of three- and four-year-olds, when integration is mandated for school-age children, just a year older? The categorical approach to early care and education policy has yielded this inequity.

Not only does the system segregate children, but it also deprives low-income children, who need services most, of the opportunity to obtain them. Head Start serves only 16 percent of the 2.5 million children who are eligible.[12] Further, 54 percent of three-year-olds in families with annual incomes of $35,000 or more attended preschool programs in 1985. In contrast, 17 percent of three-year-olds in families with annual incomes less than $10,000 were enrolled in such programs in the same year. One needs to question how such stratification of youngsters at this early age perpetuates class inequities. Equally important, why have such policies been created and allowed to continue? Why has no comprehensive plan for the care and education of young children been developed, and what will it take for such a plan to emerge?

The Prospects for a Paradigm Shift

Thus far, this essay has suggested that the "tinkering at the edges" approach to child care and early education policy is dysfunctional. The results of such a strategy have made the delivery of services to children inequitable, segregated, and lacking the quality that could and should characterize early education services, particularly given the extant knowledge base. Stated simply, "tinkering at the edges" is an inefficient and insufficient policy strategy. On the surface, the explanation might seem to be the absence of a strategic plan and an action-oriented strategy that would foster its implementation. Such analysis also suggests the lack of sufficient political will and assumes that the controversial issues undergirding the plan have been resolved. In fact, these assumptions are flawed. Far too little attention has been paid to the conceptual issues that form the heart of the debate: Is child care and early education a private right or a public responsibility? If it is a public responsibility, which level—local, state, or federal—should be responsible for what? Should services to young children be targeted to the most in need or conceptualized as an entitlement for all youngsters? Since nearly half the child care slots have been privatized, who pays if they are an entitlement?

While the answers to such questions are not immediately available, they are becoming the subject of current discourse throughout the country, signaling an imminent change in the approach to child care and early education. No longer are isolated interventions or quick-fix solutions the topic of study. Rather, acknowledging the complexity and tenacity of the issues, major national panels, and commissions, including the National Academy of Sciences Panel on Child Care Policy, the Committee for Economic Development, the National Governors' Association, the National Association of State Boards of Education, and the Association for Supervision and Curriculum Development, are grappling with governance and structural issues. Calls for collaboration resound across the states. Partnerships, unheard of a decade ago, have become the common thread in new state preschool programs. A renewed commitment to preventing rather than ameliorating social problems has taken root, and with it an entirely new emphasis on the care and education of young children.

Adding to this groundswell, there is a rekindled political will for politicians to address the child care needs of American families. Members of the 100th Congress introduced over 100 bills related to children and families. Elected officials who just two or three years ago would not have put their names to a piece of child care legislation are fashioning their own. In the executive branch, the National Association of State Budget Officers acknowledged that balancing resources—investments and children—was among their first priorities. The U.S. Department of Education has scheduled a landmark conference on child care and early education. The chief state school officers have also targeted early childhood and parenting education as their top priority, devoting their summer institute to its study.

This revitalized political will and the new infatuation with child care and early education are rooted in two additional factors—changing demographics and a growing body of research that supports the importance of early intervention, particularly for low-income youngsters. The issue of child care only for low-income families moved off the table when middle- and upper-class women joined the paid work force. With half of all married mothers of infants and over 50 percent of mothers of preschool children in the work force, child care is no longer the problem of the isolated few. The deficit orientation that framed early intervention efforts of the 1960s and the stigma long associated with child care have been replaced by a new understanding of the importance of child care as a universal work-force issue. Serendipitously, the nationally recognized need for care collided with the availability of data suggesting that early intervention was not harmful for children, and in some cases it was beneficial. There can be little doubt that the social gains reported in the literature and the media accelerated parents' comfort with using child care and hastened policymakers' attention to it as a national priority.

Julius Richmond and Milton Kotelchuck have offered a helpful theory of policy construction. They suggested that three factors must converge before "we can really talk about the development and implementation of public policy": (1) an appropriate knowledge base, (2) political will, and (3) social strategy.[13] The above discussion suggests that at least the first two conditions have been met. But what of the third? Is there a social strategy that is sufficiently articulated to guide child care and early education policy? An analysis of the extant pieces of legislation in Congress and the nature of the inquiry of numerous commissions indicates that there is not a single strategy emerging, although the proposed Act for Better Child Care (ABC) Services is the most comprehensive approach since the comprehensive child development bill of 1974. ABC, in addition to increasing services, addresses issues of affordability, availability, quality, staff training, coordination, and parental choice: such comprehensiveness indeed reflects a changing national attitude toward service delivery. Clearly, while no one approach has garnered full consensus, dialogue is being generated and new social strategies that transcend incremental advances to what went before are being discussed.

Outside the policy arena, there is even more dramatic evidence that a new ethos — one that addresses the question of social strategy — is taking root. In a dramatic shift from a categorical to an entitlement approach, the Council of Chief State School Officers in the document "Elements of a Model State Statute to Provide Educational Entitlement for At-Risk Students"[14] suggests that each school district make available to all preschool children within its jurisdiction who are at risk of school failure the opportunity to participate in a child development program of at least a half day's duration that is reasonably calculated to provide preparation for successful participation in public schools. While districts have offered preschool programs in the past, they have been at local discretion. And previously, with rare exceptions (New York City's Giant Step program, most notably), there was no stipulation that programs be offered to all preschool children or to all of those at risk. With its emphasis on all at-risk youngsters, this recommendation marks a dramatic change in orientation, a change that has the potential to reduce fragmentation and acrimony among preschool providers and to reduce the extant inequity of services to children and families.

Other inventive proposals reflect a similarly broad reconstruction of conventional approaches to policy. Jule Sugarman, in advancing the proposal to create a children's trust, has shifted the nature of the debate to embrace new approaches to financing services for children.[15] In addition to creating a much-enlarged pool of revenues from which Congress can appropriate funds to improve program quality and expand services, the trust concept would not significantly increase the regressivity of the tax system or impose an unreasonable financial burden on lower income-tax payers.

While a single social strategy has not yet emerged, it is significant that unique approaches are being discussed and debated. Business as usual is being altered;

scholars and practitioners are at the threshold of a new policy era. In conceptualizing the problem differently, in fostering increased articulation about the issues, in beginning to alter the extant constellation of beliefs, values, and techniques that characterize child care and early education, they are anticipating what Thomas Kuhn has termed a "paradigm shift."[16] Kuhn suggested that major scientific advancements come about as a result of a community rejection of time-honored theory or approaches in favor of other alternatives, by a revolution of thinking rather than by gradual accretion. Composed of closely knit social, cultural, economic, and scientific concepts and values, the paradigm shifts when the benefits of new approaches outweigh those of old. Such a shift alters the problems that are available for scrutiny and the standards for inquiry. Further, a paradigm shift transforms scientific imagination in ways that require a reconstruction of a prior theory or strategy.

Child care and early education may well be in a preparadigmatic state. The "tinkering at the edges" approach to policy is being disregarded. New ways of conceptualizing and addressing challenges are being considered. Creativity of thought and resolve of purpose characterize the current zeitgeist and give promise of addressing the fundamental inequities that have plagued the field for decades. That suggestions have been made to move from categorical to entitlement programs, that new roles are being suggested for the public and private sectors, and that inventive financing mechanisms are being debated signal the emergence of a radically different approach to the problems.

Whether such a remarkable transformation will take place in American child care and early education remains a subject of speculation. That such issues are receiving attention from different sources suggests a widespread concern. That such provocative proposals are being given serious consideration signals a ripeness for change that has not existed in child care and early education for nearly two decades. Without question, it is a fertile and creative time when complex values and conventional policy strategies are being challenged. Given the ambiguity associated with being part of a creative and fluid era, what is an appropriate role for communities, states, and the federal government now? What positions should communities and states be taking to ready themselves for such change? In the absence of a clear direction, how can the child care and early education community realistically prepare for imminent change?

Preparing for Change:
Roles for Communities, States, and the Federal Government

Two key issues precipitate the paradigm shift. First, there is a growing sense that what has gone before has been only marginally effective. Second, there is a willingness to learn from the past and to structure a new approach that will address previously intransigent issues. Regardless of the particulars, minimizing fragmentation and inequity will hallmark any paradigm shift.

Such a reorientation will pervasively affect the way services to young children and their families are planned, delivered and funded. To minimize fragmentation of services and to curtail inequity, community and statewide planning that spans agency boundaries and funding streams will need to be undertaken. To that end, communities need to establish mechanisms and engineer partnerships that will foster collaboration among planners, policymakers, and providers of services.

Capitalizing on the current zeitgeist and preparing for a future reorientation can be accomplished by establishing community-based planning councils with representatives from the multiple sectors that constitute the child care and early education community, including the public and private sectors, higher education, and the regulatory agencies. These councils would have multiple functions. First, the local planning teams need to identify sacrosanct principles upon which to base programs. These principles should be grounded in child development theory and should reflect the common values of the community. Second, each planning team needs to identify what it regards as the array of desirable services for children and families. The list should include all services that are deemed appropriate. Third, planning teams need to take the lead in ensuring that a community-needs assessment is conducted. Such an assessment must consider what constitutes need and must distinguish need from desire. In addition, such an assessment should chronicle available services, including their utilization rates, and current and anticipated population. Fourth, the team should map extant services against needed ones and then enumerate and prioritize those that are not already being offered in the community. Finally, the team should be charged with identifying sources and resources to assist with program expansion and modification. With consensus on the priorities and with this analysis complete, municipalities will have the basis for action plans.

Because states control licensing, set standards, establish monitoring procedures, and have the ability to enjoin parties and agencies, they can be catalytic in preparing for change. Mirroring local-level efforts, states also need to develop cross-agency comprehensive plans. In so doing, states need to look at the comparability of regulations across systems and understand which services are exempt, which are not, and how such exemption affects service delivery in the state. States need to seed staff. Via support for teacher-training institutions, incentives to potential teachers, or other mechanisms, states must increase the supply of trained personnel. States need to assist municipalities as they craft their plans and as they assess long-term needs. Finally, states need to reexamine their guidelines for preschool and early childhood programs to ensure flexible programming at the local level.

States without an office to coordinate these functions should consider establishing one. To be successful, such an office would need to have sufficient funding and cross-agency authority to carry out program planning and development. One variation might be to establish an interagency office within an existing agency, but it must be perceived as neutral and must have resources and clout.

Although this strategy places a heavy burden on communities and states, there are important roles for the federal government. The federal government should take on the role of generating and disseminating information. Research that fortifies the knowledge base should be federally funded, as should information about how to evaluate programs. The federal government should set up demonstration communities where new ideas will be tried out, with the goal of adapting successful strategies or efforts in other locales; such demonstrations should focus on structural alternatives to the current piecemeal delivery system. It should create inducements to expand the supply of services and personnel. It should swiftly take the leadership role in helping to alleviate crises in the field—for example, the insurance crisis that forced many child care programs to close in the 1980s. Finally, working with the states, the federal government should reexamine its policies and procedures, including regulations and program-performance standards, to ensure that quality and cross-program collaboration are facilitated.

The nature of a paradigm shift is such that its occurrence is somewhat unpredictable. Indications point the way, signaling discontent with the past and a readiness to alter previous modes of thinking and doing. In child care and early education, the time seems ripe. Whether such a change takes root and what its consequences will be are uncertain. What is certain is that the field needs and welcomes such a transformation of the imagination.

NOTES

1. Elizabeth D. Ross, *The Kindergarten Crusade: The Establishment of Preschool Education in the United States* (Athens, Ohio: Ohio University Press, 1976).

2. S. Alexander Rippa, *Education in a Free Society: An American History* (New York: David McKay Company, Inc., 1967).

3. Robert L. Church and Michael W. Sedlack, *Education in the United States* (New York: The Free Press, 1976).

4. Ibid.; Lawrence A. Cremin, *The Genius of American Education* (New York: Vintage Books, 1965).

5. Gilbert Y. Steiner, *The Futility of Family Policy* (Washington, D.C.: Brookings Institution, 1981), 8.

6. Ibid., 215.

7. Donald J. Cohen and Edward Zigler, "Federal Day Care Standards: Rationale and Recommendations," *American Journal of Orthopsychiatry* 47, no. 3 (1977): 456–65; Deborah Phillips and Edward Zigler, "The Checkered History of Federal Child Care Regulation," in *Review of Research in Education*, vol. 14, ed. Ernest Z. Rothkopf (Washington, D.C.: American Educational Research Association, 1987); and John R. Nelson, Jr., "The Federal Interagency Day Care Requirements," in *Making Policies for Children: A Study of the Federal Process*, ed. Cheryl D. Hayes (Washington, D.C.: National Academy Press, 1982).

8. Gwen Morgan, *The National State of Child Care Regulation, 1986* (Watertown, Mass.: Work/Family Directions, Inc., 1986).

9. National Association for the Education of Young Children, "NAEYC Position Statement on Licensing and Other Forms of Regulation of Early Childhood Programs in Centers and Family Day Care Homes," *Young Children* (1987), 64–68.

10. Fern Marx and Michelle Seligson, *The Public School Early Childhood Study: The State Survey* (New York: Bank Street College of Education, 1988).

11. National Black Child Development Institute, Inc., *Safeguards: Guidelines for Establishing Programs for Four-year-olds in the Public Schools* (Washington, D.C., 1987).

12. Children's Defense Fund, *A Call for Action to Make Our Nation Safe for Children: A Briefing Book on the Status of American Children in 1988* (Washington, D.C., 1988).

13. Julius Richmond and Milton Kotelchuck, "Commentary on Changed Lives," in *Changed Lives: The Effects of the Perry Preschool Program on Youths through Age 19*, ed. John R. Berrueta-Clement, et al. (Ypsilanti, Mich.: High/Scope Educational Research Foundation, 1984).

14. Council of Chief State School Officers, *Elements of a Model State Statute to Provide Educational Entitlements for At-Risk Students* (Washington, D.C., 1987).

15. Jule Sugarman, "Financing Children's Services: A Proposal to Create the Children's Trust" (Olympia, Wash.: Washington Department of Social and Health Services, June 1988).

16. Thomas S. Kuhn, *The Structure of Scientific Revolutions* (Chicago: University of Chicago Press, 1962).

The Possibilities for
Child and Family Policy:
A Cross-National Perspective

SHEILA B. KAMERMAN
ALFRED J. KAHN

There are many anomalies in American child policy. The United States is one of the richest countries in the world, yet it has one of the highest child-poverty rates among industrialized societies. Its data collection, reporting, and child-development research have exposed problems and suggested potential solutions, yet child policy remains low on the national agenda. Despite a new level of awareness among the political right and left, no general agreement has emerged on the issues to be debated.

In this essay the results of research in the United States and Europe will be employed to offer perspectives on these issues and to present a variety of child-policy opportunities.

Child Poverty in the United States

About one in five children in the United States was poor in 1986, according to the U.S. Bureau of the Census. Except for a slightly higher rate in the early 1980s, this proportion is greater than at any other time since 1965. Moreover, after declining steadily during the 1960s and remaining stable in the 1970s, the child-poverty rate increased in the 1980s. Clearly, child poverty has become one of the most intractable social problems.

Child poverty is unusual in the industrialized world outside the United States. The most systematic international comparisons to date show that by either a relative or an absolute measure of poverty, the United States had a higher proportion of poor children in 1979–80 than any of seven other countries: Australia, Canada, West Germany, Norway, Sweden, Switzerland, or the United Kingdom.[1] Indeed, with the exceptions of Canada and Australia, the United States had more than twice the percentage of poor children than any of the five other countries. The absolute child poverty rate in the United States is slightly greater than Australia's but more than 60 percent higher than the next two closest countries, the United Kingdom and Canada.

Convincing explanations are not readily found. In the United States, as in the other countries, the economic well-being of children is closely tied to the wealth and income of their parents and to the earnings, labor-force status, and number of wage earners in their families. Demographic factors are also of major importance. In comparing countries, however, it is clear that the United States is not unique with regard to any of these variables or to other usually offered explanatory factors.

For example, labor-force participation rates for males in the prime labor-force years (as well as the prime parenting years) are high and relatively comparable in the industrialized countries. While labor-force participation rates for women vary from country to country, they have risen dramatically in all industrialized countries over the past twenty-five years. Among the Western countries, female labor-force participation rates are highest in the Nordic countries; in Sweden, for example, they are about 85 percent for women with children and more than 80 percent for women with preschool-age children. (These women are largely part-time workers.) They are at not quite so high a level in the United States, Canada, and Norway; in these countries, the rates are about 65 percent for women with children and 55 percent for women with preschool-age children. (In the United States and Canada, these are largely full-time workers.) And rates are somewhat lower in many other countries, such as Britain, France, and West Germany, where they are about 50 percent for women with children and still lower for women with young children. Labor-force participation rates for women with very young children are among the lowest in Britain (about 27 percent) and heavily part-time. The labor-force rates for single mothers are higher than for married mothers in most of these countries but not in Britain, Norway, and the Netherlands.

The United States is not exceptional in its birthrate or in the number of children per family. The proportion of single-parent families is also comparable to that of other countries with high rates, such as Sweden and Denmark. There is nothing unique in these demographic characteristics or in the family situation of children in the United States that by itself would fully explain the United States's distinctly poorer economic status of children. This observation, of course, does not rule out multifactorial or multivariable analyses that might in the future provide new insights into some interrelationships.

Child poverty in the United States is closely tied to family structure. Fifty-four percent of all children in families headed by a woman were poor in 1985, and more than 20 percent of all children lived in such families that year. Yet even the situation of children in single-parent families, increasingly the major poverty group in the United States, is worse in this country than elsewhere. Because of the large number of children in single-parent families, the United States has the highest child-poverty rate among the eight countries compared. Only Australia has a higher poverty rate for children in single-parent families, but it has a far lower proportion of children in such families.

Black child poverty in the United States is almost three times as common as white child poverty. Nonetheless, the poverty rate among white children in the United States is higher than either the overall minority or the majority poverty rates for children in all other countries but Australia. Race and ethnicity, as well as family structure, clearly affect the rates of child poverty, but there are obviously other issues that increase United States child-poverty rates.

We have explored these matters historically, politically, and with regard to public-policy impacts in an effort to account for the more positive outcomes elsewhere. We have concluded that a large component of the difference between the United States and European countries is the system of income transfer for families with children. To one degree or another, European countries have established far more generous income-transfer systems that benefit children in general and poor children in particular. In contrast, the United States provides benefits to only some poor children (and at nonuniform levels). In addition, social-insurance benefits for children in Europe are more generous and more extensive than in the United States. Furthermore, while European countries stress the use of income transfers to supplement earnings and family income, especially for families with children, the United States has largely maintained a separation between earned income and transfer income.

More specifically, when parents' earnings are absent, irregular, or inadequate, the economic well-being of children depends on such public income transfers. For children in poverty — or in families with modest incomes — these transfers play a critical role. Public family benefits usually account for a very small portion of family income, but these benefits can make a significant difference to the families in which children are most likely to be at economic risk — single-parent families and large families.

This fact is well documented by an analysis that draws on the Luxembourg Income Study (LIS) data for nine countries (covering only the early 1980s). The United States has a higher pretax and pretransfer poverty rate (that is, before the receipt of any benefits) for families with children than any other country except Australia. Even after tax-and-transfer programs, it still has a higher proportion of poor families than every other country besides Australia. Furthermore, United States programs reduced the number of poor families less than any other country that had pretransfer poverty above 8 percent, again with the exception of Australia. Of the six countries with pretax and pretransfer rates above 10 percent, the United States and Australia had a reduction rate of 15 to 17 percent; the other four countries had an average reduction rate of 45 percent. The conclusion emphasized by the authors is startling: "U.S. transfer policy reduced the poverty gap of our poor families with children less than in any other country."[2]

United States Income Supports for Children

The United States has neither a policy of providing cash benefits for all children nor a national policy regarding standardized benefits for all poor children. Apart from a modest earned-income tax credit, tax exemptions in the United States aid only those with incomes above the tax threshold and benefit those with higher incomes more. Children who are dependents of recipients of social-insurance benefits or their survivors are eligible for benefits as they are in other countries. These benefits are greater than public-assistance grants but are available only to a relatively small group. Some states also make dependents' benefits available under unemployment insurance (UI), but UI is far less generous in the United States than in many other countries. Most important, no safety-net program ensures adequate sustenance for poor children in the United States, except for the federalized guaranteed minimum income for food for all poor people, including children and their families.

The major cash-benefit program for poor children is Aid to Families with Dependent Children (AFDC). It varies greatly among the states in eligibility criteria and benefit levels, as well as in coverage of poor children in husband and wife families. AFDC benefits are not indexed, and as a result there has been considerable erosion of benefits since 1970.

In January 1988 the maximum monthly AFDC benefit for a family of three (the typical AFDC family) ranged from $118 in Alabama to $779 in Alaska. Family benefits are about $600 in high-benefit states other than Alaska (California, Connecticut, and Vermont) and between $118 and $160 in low-benefit states (Tennessee, Alabama, and Mississippi). Although "average" means little here, the median 1988 AFDC family benefit was equal on an annual basis to about 25 percent of the weekly wage for a full-time production worker in the private sector and about 60 percent of the minimum wage for a full-time worker.

Food stamps go to 83 percent of AFDC families, who accounted for less than 40 percent of the monthly average of 21 million food-stamp recipients in 1985. In many parts of the country this is the only financial aid available to intact poor families and their children. Nonetheless, Patricia Ruggles reported that not many intact families with young children were among the recipients in 1983.

Not surprisingly, the combination of modest food-stamp benefits and eroded AFDC benefits still leaves most families that receive the maximum AFDC grant below the poverty threshold. In more than half the states, these combined benefits brought recipients up to somewhere between 65 and 90 percent of the poverty threshold. All of this is inevitably reflected in the comparative international poverty statistics.

Of particular importance in understanding this policy outcome is the fact that during the Reagan years the United States has stressed a sharp distinction between work and receipt of benefits. Except for food stamps and a modest earned-income tax credit for families, no benefits are designed to supplement low wages and family income. The proportion of AFDC recipients who are working and receiving grants, earnings "disregards," and child-care "disregards" to supplement their income has declined markedly since 1981 to a historically low point. Further, except for a small amount of public housing and a modest program of housing assistance to some poor households, there is no national program of housing-allowance entitlements available to subsidize the rental costs for low-income families with children. Despite public belief, there are indeed major "holes in the safety nets."[3]

Finally, unlike the situation for pensions, health care, disability, and sickness, where the private sector may be said to be particularly important in the United States in compensating for government inaction, there is no private (fringe benefit) provision of family benefits. Moreover, except in minuscule amounts, employers do not provide any supportive services, such as child care for families with children.

The Roots of United States Child Policy

A brief history of AFDC (Aid to Dependent Children [ADC] until 1962) may offer some insight into why this primary cash benefit for children has been so ungenerous.[4] The cornerstone of United States social policy, the Social Security Act of 1935, focused on unemployment insurance and old-age pensions. Modest child-health and child-welfare measures as well as ADC were added, but with relatively little attention. ADC did not even provide cash support to caretaker mothers until 1950. The federal matching-grant levels to states for ADC were far below the levels for old-age assistance. By 1939, the social-insurance benefits for widows and dependent-child survivors had been added to the original Social Security Act with the expectation that this group of single mothers (widows) would eventually have no need for ADC.

For the other children of single mothers, ADC retained some of the racial and moral exclusions of an earlier era by offering an opportunity for labeling the homes of some single mothers "unsuitable." Winifred Bell's *Aid to Families with Dependent Children* documented the many campaigns against allegedly unsuitable homes in the 1950s.[5] Blacks, unwed mothers, and women considered "immoral" because they were involved with men either found it hard to get aid or could be dropped from the rolls. Some unwed single mothers had their babies in maternity homes, which also offered a hiding place for middle-class unwed mothers. Their babies were usually adopted. Moreover, although reformers spoke of ADC as offering the opportunity for single mothers to maintain a home for their children, in most places the grants were too low even after the caretaker grant was added to the budget. Budget levels and relief availability throughout the 1940s and 1950s were said to reflect local labor-market needs in a number of parts of the country for field labor, laundresses, and domestics.

Federal and state administrative reforms increased equity concerns, and the civil rights movement eventually generated progress toward expanding benefits. The fights over "suitable homes" and "man in the house" rules went on for a long time, but AFDC caseloads did grow and become more representative over the 1960s, especially outside the South. Blacks and unwed mothers appeared on the caseloads in large numbers. Finally, after a major confrontation in 1961 in Louisiana, federal authorities enunciated a coherent policy stating that a home could not be called unsuitable and children left in it. If assistance was denied because of unsuitability, it had to be followed by child removal for neglect. The states did not resist openly. For them, the sharing of financing for a low-level, means-tested benefit by the federal government was more attractive than full state assumption of the costs of a much-expanded system of foster homes and institutions.

In other words, despite the enthusiastic pronouncements of 1935 and 1939, it was only in the 1960s that AFDC actually covered both poor children and their caretakers and was potentially available to children in all kinds of single-parent homes. Then, in the context of economic growth, higher eligibility ceilings, the civil rights movement, and other developments, the welfare rolls exploded. Just as the battle for equity seemed to be progressing, however, concern over the large and rapidly growing caseloads, especially of blacks, and fear of stimulating out-of-wedlock childbirth created renewed hesitation and reactions. A degree of fraud and inefficiency was exposed and attacked by opponents as well. At that point, those who always felt that work should supersede cash relief joined others who observed that labor-force dynamics had in fact brought large numbers of married mothers from all groups into the work force. This observation challenged the idea of supporting single mothers at home. AFDC was given work incentive and work program add-ons, even as it won more objective administration and improved benefits and as its enrollment burgeoned.

In sum, AFDC had begun on the assumption that some single mothers might be supported without work. By the end of the 1960s the whole gamut of poor single mothers could qualify, but some were compelled to register and either encouraged or required to work. Those who worked were to be encouraged by "disregards" and expense considerations.

But those advocates who had fought for greater equity in AFDC programs and protection of AFDC rights and who had worked to increase budgets and to simplify eligibility procedures had also generated enthusiasm for larger reforms. These reform movements spawned campaigns for the negative income tax and child allowance, both addressed to family and child poverty. The 1964 War on Poverty had not resulted in significant income-transfer reform. While some authorities imposed caveats, requirements, and restrictions for AFDC, there were also significant groups discussing an expanded and improved welfare program.

Family (child) allowances were proposed in the 1950s and 1960s in the United States but with no success. Daniel P. Moynihan advocated a family allowance as early as 1966. He took child poverty at a time of national prosperity as his point of departure, but he noted that the discussion was already dominated by the negative income tax. Citing poverty in large families, he commented both on the attractiveness of the family allowance as a well-targeted benefit and on the concern that the allotment would encourage the economically disadvantaged to have children. Moynihan concluded that on account of the issues of race and ethnicity in the United States, the possible pronatalist effect of a family allowance was a negative factor, not a positive one, as it was in Europe.

The proposal of family allowances was first attacked as a measure favored by Catholics (in the context of their opposition to birth control), and then the plan was opposed because it would possibly increase birthrates among poor blacks. Even the liberals who had opposed the arguments that these measures should be rejected because they were favored by the Catholic church were not able to discuss openly and counter the fears of those who alleged that family allowances could encourage poor blacks to have more children.

Many economists favoring the negative income tax spoke of family allowances as economically inefficient: in order to have a program that would reach the smaller poor groups, middle-class families would collect substantial benefits — and much money would need to be collected and paid out unnecessarily in order to do so. In response, Moynihan spoke of the urgency of unifying, universal measures, not divisive income-tested ones, following the assassination of Martin Luther King, Jr., and the riots in black ghettos. He urged a serious review of the options. Tax-recoupment devices could cope with alleged inefficiency. Several proposals were made in Congress, and a leading child-advocacy organization launched a campaign in support.

Child allowances won very limited backing. The Heineman Commission of 1969 chose the new negative income-tax strategy that had attracted both "liberal" economists like Milton Friedman and the reformers identified with the Office of Economic Opportunity and the Treasury Department. The latter groups were followed by a large, progressive constituency attracted to the guaranteed-minimum-income concept. Moynihan designed what became the Family Assistance Plan (FAP) of former President Richard Nixon, an attempt to provide aid to all poor families with children, including intact families. While it would appear that the universal family allowance was less attractive than the targeted income-tested guaranteed income, it is unclear that this is why family allowances were not adopted. After all, there was to be no negative income tax, either. Food stamps, backed by a strong coalition of farm interests and urban antipoverty advocates, became the American guaranteed income and soon had a larger budget than the one estimated for the Nixon FAP. Thus, the issues remained unresolved, and United States incrementalism prevailed.

In considering why the United States did not pursue alternative child-policy strategies, we hypothesize that: the United States began the development of its national income-transfer programs much later than most European countries; the country's complex pluralism led it to avoid, wherever possible, inevitably controversial national child or family policies; policy developments were inhibited by the need to deal, first, with the problem of race and unequal access to social benefits by blacks. Finally, in contrast to the situation in several European countries, children's economic well-being has never been high on the agenda of the major political parties in the United States, nor has any one party chosen a role as a special champion of children.

The Experiences of Other Countries

Public income transfers for families and children have been shown to account for major poverty differences among countries. A child- or family-policy agenda for the United States could begin by assessing the provisions of other countries and their experiences. A "family benefit system" seems to be emerging that includes a cluster of child and family-related income transfers, both universal and income-tested, with generously set income criteria.[6] As used here, public "family benefits" include universal (nonincome-tested) cash benefits, income-tested cash benefits, means-tested cash benefits (both income- and asset-tested benefits), cash equivalents or near-cash benefits, and tax benefits (tax credits or allowances). By and large, these measures are distinguishable from social-insurance systems primarily because their benefits supplement earned income rather than substitute for it. In their greater uniformity and consistency of provision, widespread acceptance, and avoidance of demeaning investigations of personal assets, these family benefits also differ from public assistance, even when they are income-tested. Moreover, they rarely provide income sufficient to support a family without an earned wage.

The program components of the system include universal and income-tested child allowances or child tax credits; child-support or advanced maintenance payments; maternity and parental benefits (both cash and job-protected leaves) housing allowances; paid sick leaves to care for ill children; and so forth. In addition, there are important service elements—child care, in particular.

Thus, for example, almost all industrialized countries provide a universal child benefit as either a direct cash benefit or a refundable tax credit based on the number of children in a family. Since single-mother families constitute an increasingly large proportion of families with children in the industrialized countries and since these families run a high risk of poverty everywhere, an important growing trend among the Western European countries is to provide a special income transfer in the form of a guaranteed child-support payment. Benefits that take account of the rising cost of housing are a standard part of child and family policy as well. All the European countries, as well as Canada and many others, provide special cash benefits to replace income forgone at the time of childbirth and to offer job-protected leaves. Almost all the industrialized countries except the United States provide statutory short-term disability or sickness benefits through their social-insurance system. Of the countries mentioned thus far only the United States does not provide universal health insurance or health services for children and their families.

Child or Family Allowances

Cash benefits or payments to families with children are the core of the family benefit system in most countries; they fit into the category of "demogrants," universal benefits to population categories. They are usually provided as flat-rate benefits, with a specific amount paid for each child in the family. In some countries the amounts vary by age, ordinal position, or number of children. In contrast to other cash benefits, in most countries family allowances are universal, tax free, not indexed, and available regardless of parental labor-force status. They are usually awarded while a child is of compulsory school age. In some countries the benefit can be extended for some years if the child is a full-time student. The benefits range in Western European countries from 5 to 10 percent of median wage (for one child), but they are often higher for larger families.

Family allowances are usually financed out of general revenues or through the contributions of employers and are administered as part of a country's social-security system. These benefits are almost always popular wherever they are provided, and all who can qualify take advantage of them. About sixty-seven countries (including all European countries) and every industrialized country except the United States provide such benefits today.

Family allowances became an alternative to more general wage increases, when society recognized that salaries and family obligations are unrelated. They were subsequently viewed by some as a strategy aimed at encouraging parents to have more children (even though there is no evidence of long-term effectiveness for such a plan). These benefits are now widely seen as a policy strategy or device in which society shares in the economic costs of rearing children, just as it shares ultimately in the economic benefits of a healthy, productive adult, nurturant parent, and good citizen. No country comes close to fully compensating for the economic costs of children through family allowances. However, just as social-security or social-insurance benefits have extended the range of risks protected and the proportion of the population covered, family allowances have also extended support. The allowance is generally a supplement to family income and of particular value to those with low or modest income or with several children. A few countries, such as France, Denmark, and West Germany, have introduced some element of income testing for these benefits or for their supplementary family allowances. Others, like Canada, have included them as part of taxable income. But most countries continue to provide such allowances, regardless of income, employment, or family structure.

A more recent alternative to family allowances or direct cash transfers is to provide a child benefit through the tax system. Unlike the tax exemption for dependents in the United States, a plan shared by many countries that is of value only to those who pay taxes and favors those with higher incomes, the child-benefit tax credit is a fixed amount available to families at all income levels. Furthermore, it is refundable to those whose incomes are so low as to preclude any tax obligations. Some countries, such as Britain, Israel, and the Netherlands, have in fact moved to integrate both tax benefits and transfer benefits for children by eliminating the tax exemption for children (which benefited higher-income families more than low-income families) and substituting larger tax credits or direct payments. The trend is not completely unidirectional: West Germany, which enacted a tax credit in 1975, has partly reverted to child tax exemptions and now also uses income tests of family allowances at higher income levels.

Rigorous analyses of the effects of income-transfer policies in several countries indicate that family allowances are effective in redistributing income from those with more income to those with less, as well as from households with no children to those with children. Low child-poverty rates and the absence of child poverty as a policy issue in countries with child-related income transfers are largely attributable to these measures.

A refundable child tax credit in place of current tax exemptions for dependents would be an extraordinarily effective child benefit for the United States. Several policy experts have offered analyses of distributional impacts and costs of different schemes.[7]

Housing Allowances

Cash supplements to aid in the payment of rent, property taxes, or other costs of home rental or ownership are usually income tested and often specifically directed at families with children. Combined with family allowances, they are an important income component in several countries. The availability of the allowance as an entitlement makes it significant, whatever its specific administrative ties and philosophical base.

The core idea of the housing allowance is well-known and shared in a number of countries: if families make a responsible contribution to meeting their own housing costs and if they rent or own standard and reasonable housing, the government will meet a share of the excess costs. Thus, the contribution will usually be based on family size, income, housing costs, a fair share of income to be assigned to housing, a fair cost for housing, and some minimum requirements as to the housing quality and amenities. All of this is separate from what government provides on the supply side to help fill housing needs, including public housing construction. Neither does it include the efforts to facilitate home purchase, ranging from the United States tax deductions for taxes on homes, taxes on mortgage interest, and federal mortgage guarantees (which largely benefit those at middle- and upper-income levels) to Israel's highly subsidized mortgages, which facilitate widespread home ownership.

In several countries, housing allowances constitute a significant income-tested supplement for families with children. In Sweden, a country with an extensive and generous family policy, housing allowances cover more than one-third of all families with children, down from about one-half in the late 1970s, and constitute 15 to 20 percent of family incomes for "vulnerable" families (low- and modest-income families, single-mother families, large families, and families with an unemployed or underemployed head). More than half of all single-mother families qualify for housing allowances. In France, about one-quarter of the families with children received the benefit at the end of the 1970s (and a higher proportion in the 1980s), and the benefit was worth 10 to 20 percent of family income for these same family types.

Of special importance to income-maintenance policy is that even though it is income tested, a housing allowance can reach far into the income distribution, cover a large part of the population, and thus serve as a nonstigmatized benefit. If one considers the high costs of housing in the United States and the contribution of housing inflation to the problem of family homelessness, a housing allowance could be an important component of a family benefit system designed to supplement income so as to reduce the use of public assistance.

Child Health Care or Insurance

A universal child health program, either a health-service or a social-insurance benefit, is high on any child- and family-policy agenda. Despite the long-standing presence of such programs in almost all other major countries, there has never been enough support in the United States to pass legislation. Recent expansion of Medicaid eligibility for poor children under age five and for poor pregnant women, as well as proposals to mandate coverage by employers, may signify a gradual approach to such provision.

Child Support

The term *child support* describes payments by parents for support of their children who live in other households. Parents are legally responsible for the maintenance of their children in all countries. One major cause of child poverty is the absence of a parent's support (overwhelmingly the father's) following separation, divorce, or unwed parenting. When noncustodial parents fail to provide payment for child support or when payments are irregular or inadequate, authorities in a growing number of countries find it necessary to intervene. Intervention may take place to enforce payment obligations, to guarantee support, or to substitute for support payments. The methods for implementing these interventions, as well as the goals, may vary, but the trend among the advanced industrialized countries is toward a greater involvement of public authorities, particularly the social-security agencies, child-welfare boards, and the courts in ensuring income to those who are rearing children of divorced or separated parents.

In many countries, public assistance has increasingly assumed primary responsibility for providing child support involving low-income families. In recent years, however, there has been growing dissatisfaction with such social assistance and a conviction that an alternative method of providing financial help should be developed.

There have been two developments in those countries implementing new policies. In the first, a public authority, often the social-security agency, guarantees a specified level of child support by advancing support payments to the custodial parent if payment is made irregularly, at a very low level, or not at all by the absent parent. In addition, the same or another public agency assumes responsibility for the collection of child support from the absent parent, crediting what is collected against the payments advanced. Within this framework, policies depend on whether the public authority acts for all single parents or only low-income women, whether a court order is required for the process to be initiated, whether the support is for mother and child or only the child, or whether the primary concern is with reducing the burden on the public purse or ensuring adequate support for the child.

Among the countries with such guaranteed advances of child support or child maintenance are Denmark, Sweden, Austria, West Germany, France, and Israel. While all of these countries share the objective of ensuring more adequate provision of child support, several also exemplify a trend observed in many countries, the use of transfers to provide a supplement, rather than a substitute, for earned income or other benefits. Thus, they incorporate a work incentive into the income-transfer system.

While the United States has not yet established such a program nationally, several states are clearly moving in this direction, Wisconsin having taken the lead. Recent welfare-reform legislation also builds on the concept but does not include the guarantee. No proposal for a child-policy agenda today would be complete without such a component.

Maternity and Parenting Policies

There are two key parallel policies to protect income in families with working mothers at the time of childbirth. First, there is a guarantee of a right to leave work with assurance of full job protection, seniority, and pension entitlements. The leave varies from a minimum of three months — the "standard" pattern — to a maximum of three years (in Hungary). The typical pattern among European countries is five to six months. In Sweden, this right can be shared equally by both parents. In several other countries, such as Finland and Norway, fathers may share in a portion of this parental benefit.

The second, parallel policy is the provision of a cash benefit that replaces the full wage covered under social security or a significant portion of it. Or there may be some combination of full wages followed by a smaller flat-rate benefit. These benefits are available to almost all employed women and, under certain circumstances — or in certain countries, such as the Nordic countries — to their husbands also. The benefits may be tax free or considered as taxable income. In some countries an unpaid, job-protected parenting leave supplements the right to a paid maternity, or parenting, leave.

These benefits are contingent on prior work and represent an attempt to replace earnings at childbirth and for some period thereafter, during which, it is assumed, a parent needs to be at home to provide critical child care. There is an increasing tendency to extend these rights to adoptive parents as well as to biological parents.

Cash maternity benefits for employed women, as a social-insurance benefit, were first established by Otto Bismarck in Germany more than 100 years ago. By World War I several European countries, including France, Italy, and Britain, had already legislated some form of national maternity insurance for working women. In addition to overall concern with the health and well-being of mother and child, the development of a cash-benefit program within the overall social-insurance system reflects a view of maternity as contributing to the needs of the society as well as those of individuals and a view of income loss at childbirth as a social risk against which society should provide protection. In other words, maternity is a circumstance, like old age, retirement, disability, illness, and unemployment, that leads to some loss of income through no "fault" of the individual. The most rapid expansion of benefits was during the 1960s and 1970s, decades that experienced an extraordinary growth in the proportion of women entering — and remaining — in the labor force.

Cash maternity benefits are available in more than 100 countries today, including almost all industrialized countries and many developing countries. In the United States, there are proposals being discussed for an unpaid, job-protected parenting leave but not for a paid leave. This may be a modest item on a long agenda, but it is nonetheless important.

Child-Care Services

If women are to enter the paid labor market, affordable, accessible, and decent quality child-care services are essential. Although all Western European countries permit unpaid, job-protected leaves, in addition to maternity leaves, few women avail themselves of this benefit, for obvious reasons. As a result, most working families in Europe need some form of out-of-home child-care service, beginning when a child is about six to nine months of age. Compulsory school attendance usually begins at age six, as it does in the United States; but in Britain five is the age of entry, while in some Nordic countries and some Eastern European countries, it is seven. Most continental European countries provide free public or publicly financed preschool for all children aged two and one-half or three to age six, available to all parents, regardless of whether the mother works. Countries assume that children of this age will attend preschool because the experience is good for them. Thus, for most working families in Europe, child care is available for children age three and older, at least through the normal school day — which is a half day in some places, such as West Germany, and a full day elsewhere, as in France.

Infant and toddler care is nowhere as extensive as care for children older than two years. Indeed, no country offers nearly enough services to meet the needs of working parents with infants and toddlers, but in a few countries new policy thrusts are focused on the younger age groups. Care for preschool and primary-school children before and after school hours when they do not coincide with work schedules is recognized as a universal need. Few countries, however, provide adequate coverage, and most even lack systematic data indicating how children of this age are cared for now.

Clearly, parenting benefits in the United States, which would offer a paid and job-protected leave for up to six months, would seem to be a reasonable policy, given the developments in many countries, including Canada. But, in addition, the supply of accessible, affordable, good quality child-care services needs expansion as well. Encouraging a larger role for the schools in delivering preschool services, after-school services, and a variety of options for care of those less than three years old, is an essential aspect of making paid employment viable for women with young children and improving family income while ensuring good child care.

Conclusion

Government has played an increasingly important role in providing income support to families with children in all the industrialized countries. Countries vary in the scope of government benefits, the goals they seek to achieve, and the special strategies they use. Because the resources of the market and of the extended family network are too limited to improve the economic status of low-income families with children, it is unlikely that the United States alone will achieve much progress without a larger measure of direct or indirect public income transfers and related policies, whether along the lines of European programs or by unique American adaptations. The agenda suggested in this essay is only an illustration of how the discussion might proceed.

What are the prospects for improving child and family policy? Recent "welfare reform" legislation was very modest, the claims and alarms to the contrary. Nonetheless, it did establish the important principle that many AFDC mothers should be helped into the mainstream with training, education, job-search stipends, child care, a period of medical coverage, and related supports. But only about one-fifth of the AFDC load will be served, there is no improvement for the mothers of infants, and there are no provisions to supplement low wages. The latter is important, since most mothers who relinquish AFDC following welfare-reform initiatives will remain in poverty because of the low minimum wage and modest prospects for increases. Neither child allowances nor child tax credits are under active discussion. Other major supplementation, such as an upgraded earned-income tax credit, is discussed but lacks visible constituencies.

The recent welfare "reform" legislation (P.L. 100–485) requires child-support wage withholding, more adequate support standards, and a major effort to establish each child's paternity. There is no provision for maintenance advances or guarantees in the absence of support payments, although a few states will move in this direction. After two years of consideration and public debate, parental-leave legislation failed to reach a vote in the 100th Congress, even though the proposed bill offered job protection only, without income replacement. A federal child-care initiative, much discussed and debated, failed as well. Modest state improvements — mostly connected to welfare reform — continue, and the late 1988 welfare "reform" makes more federal funds available for child care tied to work and training. Both parental leave and more comprehensive child-care legislation are likely to be addressed in the 101st Congress, but it is unclear with what success.

But there is also the considerable state-level interest in early childhood education and child health. Much of the discussion and legislative advocacy has connected these issues to state economic development. Concern over the birthrate decline and the quality of the potential labor force represented by the large numbers of minority and poor children has already affected public commitments somewhat. The scale and effectiveness of the response have not yet been fully assessed. Neither is it known whether the alternative solution, importing more of the needed labor force from other countries, will prevail. "Need" does not necessarily predict the response.

The needs of poor and minority children have become more visible, and the discussions are better informed. Perhaps this is a beginning. The 1988 presidential campaign included more speeches and editorials about the need for a "child-policy decade" than has been evident in the United States since the period between the 1890s and World War I. While one cannot know whether all of this will translate into major federal initiatives and public support, the subject is on the table — and there are Americans who do not wish it ignored.

Notes

1. Timothy Smeeding, Barbara Boyle Torrey, and Martin Rein, "Patterns of Income and Poverty: The Economic Status of the Young and Old in Eight Countries," in *The Vulnerable: America's Young and Old in the Industrial World*, ed. John Palmer, Timothy Smeeding, and Barbara Boyle Torrey (Washington, D.C.: The Urban Press, 1988): 351–80.

2. Barbara Boyle Torrey and Timothy Smeeding, "Poor Children in Rich Countries," *Science* 242 (November 1988): 873–77.

3. Issaac Shapiro and Robert Greenstein, *Holes in the Safety Nets* (Washington, D.C.: Center on Budget and Policy, 1988).

4. Sheila B. Kamerman and Alfred J. Kahn, *Mothers Alone: Strategies for a Time of Change* (Dover, Mass.: Auburn House, 1988).

5. Winifred Bell, *Aid to Families with Dependent Children* (New York: Columbia University Press, 1965).

6. Sheila B. Kamerman and Alfred J. Kahn, *Child Care, Family Benefits and Working Parents* (New York: Columbia University Press, 1981).

7. Irwin Garfinkel, ed., *Income-Tested Transfer Programs: The Case for and Against* (New York: Academic Press, 1983); Alvin Schorr, *Common Decency* (New Haven, Conn.: Yale University Press, 1987).

Federal Support Revisited

JULE M. SUGARMAN

The end of the Reagan administration affords a splendid opportunity to reexamine the federal role with respect to education, health, and social programs for children, youth, and families. This essay presents a brief history of federal support and then addresses the purposes of federal support, levels and processes of funding, and federal administrative mandates. The recommendations call for strong leaders at the federal level, substantial funding increases, and a modest rebuilding of the federal capacity to administer programs but with considerable flexibility granted to states that perform well.

The United States has a fifty-year legacy of federal programs, especially those enacted in the 1960s and 1970s, premised on a strong federal role in policy, funding, and administration. But the Reagan administration, for the most part, denied federal responsibility for education, health, and social issues and emphasized substantial reductions in regulations and administrative capacity to formulate and enforce federal policy. The reductions were often welcomed by governors and some state and local officials but deplored by national advocacy groups. There has also been a hiatus in creative thinking and leadership by federal officials about new program needs and program improvements. Most of their energy has been devoted to cost containment, often with inadequate attention to the impact on program effectiveness.

The Reagan adminstration also sought to reduce federal spending dramatically for these programs. After some initial successes in 1981, congressional opposition to the president's policies led to the rejection of reductions in many areas and even allowed modest increases in a few selected programs (e.g., special education, Head Start). Nevertheless, most programs lost ground because of inflation, and some programs, such as youth employment and student aid, suffered drastic reductions. The author has calculated that since 1979 the overall constant-dollar increase in sixty-seven federal programs serving children, youth, and families was 13.7 percent. This contrasted with increases of 46.3 percent in defense and 36.4 percent overall.

During this period the administration exhibited a hands-off policy toward state administration of programs, except when it sought to enforce a particular ideology (e.g., prolife) or to save money. It consistently sought to reduce reporting and analysis, rejected proposed regulations as overintrusive, and reduced staffing to the point that there was little capacity to enforce policy, much less assist grantees. The situation at the end of these eight years can be characterized as a legislative framework premised on strong federal policy, financing, and administrative capacity but in terms of operating realities characterized by an emasculated federal bureaucracy with extremely weak policy, financing, and administrative capacity. It is these ambiguities that this essay addresses.

The Purposes of Federal Participation

It must be understood that federal participation in education, health, and social-service programs does not follow any grand design. The federal role is not specifically described in the Constitution. Congress and the courts have permitted the federal role to grow because of their dynamic interpretation of the public-welfare and interstate-commerce clauses of the Constitution, as well as its prohibitions against discrimination. Each new program was designed independently to satisfy different constituencies, and relatively little attention has been given to the relationship among programs.

Before the 1960s, the federal role in serving children, youth, and families was extremely modest. A public-assistance program for mothers and children was enacted in 1935 following the implementation of several state programs. Later, federal funds were provided for maternal- and child-health services, and a nominal budget became available for child-welfare services. Leadership on children's issues was originally vested primarily in a small agency, part of the U.S. Department of Labor, which was headed by a presidential appointee, the chief of the Children's Bureau. Her principal concerns were the enactment of child-labor laws and then the establishment of maternal- and child-health services.

One of the strategies of the early programs was to use small amounts of federal money as incentives to states to expand and improve the quality of their services. That strategy was often successful in encouraging greater state funding as well as sound (in the view of the federal government) policies. Many state officials depended on the force of federal regulations and the threatened loss of federal funds to persuade a reluctant governor or legislature to do "the right thing." At the same time, some observers thought federal policies or standards were sometimes overly uniform and barriers to effective state and local programs.

The enormous growth in federal programs and funding during the 1960s and 1970s had numerous and diverse causes. Among these were the public alarm over deficiencies in American education when the Soviet Union achieved a major scientific goal by launching Sputnik; the civil rights struggles and the War on Poverty, which increased public recognition that many children, youth, and families were not equal beneficiaries of the American dream; the growing conviction that access to health care, while not a constitutional right, represented a moral imperative; the interaction between public concern about hunger and the agricultural community's desire to increase farm income; the emergence of vigorous advocates for specific populations (e.g., the developmentally disabled, the mentally ill, the abused child, the bilingual family); and the recognition of the federal government's superior fiscal capacity to assist states that had very limited financial resources.

The Current Federal Programs

The remainder of this essay will not touch on programs that are for the most part operated by the federal government. These include the Social Security retirement and disability programs, the Medicare program for the aged and disabled, and the supplementary security-income programs providing cash assistance to elderly and disabled persons. While the Reagan administration toyed with the idea of privatizing Social Security, no serious proposals were made, and the degree of federal responsibility remains unchanged.

The largest set of federal programs in terms of dollars are those in which there is a "partnership" between the federal and state governments or other public organizations. In the aggregate the federal-state partnerships involve about $75 billion in federal funding. The major ones receiving federal funds are indicated in table 1. The characteristics of these ten programs vary significantly. Medicaid and AFDC have substantial matching requirements, whereas the remainder have modest or essentially no federal matching requirements. Adult and Vocational Education and Social Services have very general or no requirements on eligibility, whereas food stamps and child nutrition have stringent criteria for eligibility. Medicaid and AFDC have some specific limitations on eligibility and benefit levels but give considerable discretion to each state on the levels thereof.

In addition to these programs, many smaller programs make grants to state agen-

TABLE 1

Federal-State Partnerships
(in billions of dollars, FY 1989 levels)

Medicaid**	$32.7*
Food stamps**	12.5*
Aid to Families with Dependent Children (AFDC)**	10.7
Child nutrition***	4.8
Compensatory education***	4.5
Social Services Block Grants**	2.7
Training and Employment***	2.7
Supplemental Feeding Program**	1.9
Education for the Handicapped***	1.8
Vocational and Adult Education***	4.5

Source: Budget of the United States: 1989.
*Large portions of these funds are used solely for the benefit of adults.
**Some states pass funds through to county or city governments.
***Funds are passed through to local governments or local education agencies.

cies (including state boards of education), usually for rather specific purposes. These "categorical" programs characteristically have highly restrictive eligibility definitions, program-policy specifications, community and consumer participation, and detailed reporting requirements. In the aggregate, these programs provide about $10 billion in federal funds for fiscal year 1989.

Finally, a number of smaller programs make federal grants directly to local governments, local educational agencies, and nonprofit agencies, thus bypassing state legislators and state bureaucracies. These highly categorical programs probably have aggregate funding of less than $3 billion. The largest of them is Head Start, which has a 1989 budget of $1.2 billion. Most of these programs have been created in response to the requests of specific constituencies. The statutes tend to be highly prescriptive and proscriptive as to eligibility, program content, staffing standards, and community participation.

Some 100 federal programs now serve children, youth, and families. Taken together, they cover virtually the full range of types of services that may be needed. Nevertheless, Congress, when it becomes interested in an activity, frequently enacts a new program rather than increasing funds for or modifying existing programs. By way of example, at this writing four overlapping types of early-childhood programs could require substantial federal funding. These are preschool programs targeted to low-income four-year-olds; Head Start, which services a similar group but is not limited to education agencies; day care, which is targeted to children of working parents; and child development, which would provide health, education, and social services for children from birth through age seven. Logic would argue for a single comprehensive bill to provide a coherent system of services. However, the conflicts in philosophy, congressional-committee jurisdictions, advocacy organizations, and administering agencies at state and local levels make such a result unlikely. More probable, legislation will pass in each area and will be followed by a demand for a new organization to coordinate these programs.

State officials and others are often critical of these direct-grant programs because of the lack of state control and monitoring. Furthermore, some funded activities, such as community action, legal services, and mental health, have very frequently attacked state agencies. In many such programs this was an intended consequence as the federal government sought to empower women, as well as minority, handicapped, and disadvantaged persons.

Federal Administrative Mandates

All of the programs have a great many federal mandates and proscriptions on administration. In fact, an informal survey by the author indicates that more than three-quarters of the content of legislation is administrative in nature as distinct from programmatic. These provisions specify how services should be provided. During the 1960s and 1970s, state program administration aroused considerable skepticism with respect to equity and nondiscrimination. In addition, there was great concern regarding the quality of education, social, and health services being provided. Critics, especially a newly emerging corps of program evaluators and journalists, were devastating in their criticism of rigidities, cultural insensitivities, estrangement from clients, bureaucratic obfuscation, and harassment as well as plain incompetence and lack of motivation on the part of the traditional bureaucracies. Not infrequently, social, health, and education programs were characterized as so bad that any change had to be for the better. *Creativity* and *innovation* were perhaps the strongest buzzwords of the time.

These feelings underlay the emergence of strong federal mandates on administration — as to how a program would be carried out. A major factor in the new programs was the strong interest in consumer and community participation in program decisions. Much later, staff participation was also acknowledged as a major factor. It was thought that each group chosen was closest to the problem and the solution; parents knew best what was good for their children, and the neighborhood knew best how to develop its community. The federal prescription varied as to how to involve consumer and community representatives as well as staff. Some programs simply called for public hearings, others for advisory committees, and still others for actual approval of administrative decisions. For example, Head Start required that the parent advisory committee approve the selection of a program director and the submission of a budget to the federal government.

The interest in empowering new groups and eliminating discrimination had several consequences. Almost all legislation specifically prohibited discrimination against women, minorities, and the handicapped. At the same time, much of the legislation granted a high priority for services to women, minorities, and the handicapped, thereby discriminating against other parts of the population. The term *poor* became in some people's minds the surrogate for minorities, and the poor among majority populations sometimes received little attention. An emphasis on the use of paraprofessionals and the evolution of new careers was characteristic of most programs. At the higher-skill levels the focus was on developing minority professionals in health care, teaching higher education, social services, corrections, and many other fields.

The federal interest as expressed in law and regulation also extended to the organizational arrangements for providing services and the process for delivering them. For example, at one point federal law mandated separate organizational units for providing income assistance and social services. Similarly, vocational rehabilitation had to be a separate organizational unit. Frequently, federal rules effectively prohibited an organization from delivering a service because its staff was not certificated in a particular specialty. Many provisions of law were designed to protect program and fiscal integrity. Congressional and agency officials — often in response to the entreaties of a particular constituency, advocacy and professional groups — narrowly compartmentalized funds. Although Congress sometimes enacted statutes aimed at joint funding and simplified administration, they were almost never successfully translated into practice.

During the 1960–80 period a great deal of interest emerged in planning, reporting, analysis, and evaluation. The volume of such activity rose dramatically and sorely taxed the human resources available to carry out these tasks. Many plans became paperwork exercises, rather than true guidelines to what an organization actually intended to do. The enthusiasm for evaluation clearly outran the state of the art and the availability of skilled evaluators. Few changes in programs at the national level have been based on valid studies of their value or deficiencies. Evaluators have had some success in identifying populations in greater need as well as the need for additional services. They have had little success in influencing the discontinuance of programs or making changes in policies affecting services. They have had remarkably little influence on individuals who actually deliver services.

The emergence of a large human-services bureaucracy at both federal and state levels was of great importance. These bureaucracies played key roles, including formulating legislative proposals, interpreting laws through federal regulations, making funding decisions, and auditing funded activities for conformance to program and financial roles. In addition, a set of federal activities developed that can be classified as the provision of leadership. These include catalyzing the development of new program ideas and services; advocating the provision of and funding of services; creating training and technical-assistance resources; establishing networks of service providers and consumers; organizing meetings of interested parties; and developing media, elected official, and public support. Many federal officials became known throughout the country because of their leadership.

It is in the balance among legal, fiscal, and leadership activities that profound changes have taken place at both the state and federal levels. During the 1960s there was enormous growth in the number of federal and state employees who oversaw programs as distinct from actually providing services. Large numbers of officials who were hired had little or no prior public service and sometimes little experience in a program area. Most of them clearly preferred leadership roles. Some rejected or scorned the legal responsibilities of bureaucracy. Thus budgets, performance standards, financial controls, personnel regulations, travel limitations, contracting processes, and the enforcement of program regulations were of little interest in the early days of many new programs. The emphasis was on creativity, empowerment, building advocacy groups, putting new services in place, and overcoming discrimination. In their zeal to achieve these objectives, the new federal leaders were quite prepared to run over or ignore the established state leadership, as well as the traditional state, local, and private service-delivery organizations. They often intervened on service-delivery issues at an extraordinary level of administrative detail. Some clearly thought that being a federal official was a mark of superiority and that state and local officials, as well as private providers, should readily defer to their views.

Many of the officials and providers initially reacted with a combination of enthusiasm that federal financial assistance was becoming available and guilt at their own program inadequacies. Later, a deep resentment developed at the attitudes of federal officials, the perceived arbitrary nature of federal policies and standards, the extraordinary paperwork requirements, and the refusal to recognize differences among states and local areas. This resentment was greatly exacerbated by repeated delays in federal appropriations, uncertainties about the levels of funding, and extreme complexities in many application processes.

In the mid-1970s and early 1980s, the balance began to alter as federal staff increasingly concentrated on budgetary management and, to a more limited extent, the application of performance standards. The reductions in levels of new funds made federal advocacy tougher and reduced the opportunities for other types of leadership. Moreover, state political leadership and bureaucracies were changing and building strength. Many states were able to modify federal policies of the 1960s to suit the needs of their particular states. Others went beyond federal thinking to introduce additional innovations. Some states remained mired in the past, but the balance of bureaucratic leadership was perceptibly shifting toward the states.

The arrival of the Reagan administration spelled the death knell for leadership at the federal level. As Edwin Meese III said, "We have not come to Washington to tinker with the government, but rather to change it." As for the federal bureaucracy, this meant decreased staffing, greatly reduced regulation, and substantial abandonment of other leadership responsibilities. Staff reductions were so sharp that even many mandatory activities could not be performed in an effective fashion. Collection and analysis of data was a particular victim.

The feelings about state agencies have moderated over the years, particularly when new governors have provided leadership and state agencies have changed their leadership and behavior. However, there is a strong residual of mistrust, most prominently found among the advocacy groups in Washington, D.C., that work closely with congressional staff and individual members. These groups retain a strong preference for empowering local—particularly private, nonprofit—organizations. Alternatively, they seek to continue or expand in law the prescriptions and proscriptions that control how programs are carried out.

Despite the reservations about the federal administrative mandates described above, their use clearly produced many direct and indirect benefits. Education, health, and social-service agencies were forced to reexamine themselves and make many important changes. Discrimination was reduced. Minorities and women did find new opportunities and were significantly empowered. Services were more equitably distributed, and those most in need received greater attention. Perhaps most important, improved performance by many public and private agencies resulted in greater acceptance of state financial responsibility for the provision of services. These improvements, however, are not so universal or so firmly embedded in state policy that federal responsibility can be abandoned, as the Reagan administration believed. What is needed is a rebalancing between the autocratic, arbitrary nature of federal support in the 1960s and 1970s and the laissez-faire policies of the 1980s.

Federal Funding

Federal funding of child, youth, and family services skyrocketed in the 1960s and 1970s as the United States undertook more programs and strove to serve more children. By 1988 there were some 100 federal programs, involving more than $40 billion in federal funds. Despite that significant level of effort, child advocates think that multibillion-dollar increases are essential to the welfare of society.

Advocates of increased spending have pointed out that federal funds for children in constant dollars increased only 13.7 percent during the past ten years, whereas other federal spending increased 46.3 percent for defense and 36.4 percent overall. Children appear to be the neglected constituency in America. Yet the needs for services to children, youth, and families, as documented in other essays in this volume, leave no doubt about the urgency of such funding.

The levels of federal deficits remain very high, particularly if one excludes the surpluses generated by the Social Security, airport, and highway trust funds. Similarly, many consider the public debt to be a serious threat to the American economy. These circumstances do not augur well for the financing of additional children's services through general-fund revenues. It is unlikely that they can successfully compete in the normal budgetary processes. A realistic evaluation of the situation argues strongly for new approaches to financing children's services.

This analysis led the author to propose in a 1988 concept paper the creation of a Children's Trust. It would provide by means of a 0.3 percent tax on employers and employees about $20 billion of additional funding annually for education, health, and social-service programs benefiting children, youth, and families. This would supplement a guaranteed current level of $28 billion of appropriations, thus providing a 70 percent increase in funding. Other individuals were advancing other ideas for dramatically improving funding.

Ideas abound as to the form in which federal funding should be provided. General revenue sharing and community-development block grants are examples of approaches that provide federal funds with few directions on how the funds are to be used. Experience indicates that congressional and presidential support for continued funding is weak when the federal government has little to say about how the funds are to be used.

President Reagan advocated the consolidation of categorical (i.e., specific purpose) grants into block grants. Some consolidation did occur in 1981, but the effort stalled, and Congress has enhanced the categorical nature of federal programs. Within those block-granted programs there are significant differences. The Social Services Block Grant (Title XX of the Social Security Act of 1935) allows great flexibility to a state, including permitting use of funds for all income levels. The Maternal and Child Health Block Grant continues to allocate funds in accordance with congressionally determined priorities. All factors considered, the block-grant approach had little effect on the relative roles of federal and state governments. Both this situation and the experience described above suggest that Congress will not lightly surrender its role in deciding how federal funds are to be spent.

The president, the National Governors' Association, and a detailed study by Alan Pifer and Forest Chisholm have all suggested a realignment of responsibilities between the federal and state governments. For example, the states might assume responsibility for all education activities and acute-care medical services if the federal government took total responsibility for public assistance and long-term care. There are many variations on this theme, but none of them has attracted significant political support. It appears unlikely that there will be any major change in the allocation of responsibilities between the federal and state governments or in the level of congressional control.

The point worth noting here is that congressional judgments about who needed what services were interwoven with a wide range of federal decisions as to how services would be provided. For many professional and advocacy organizations, the *how* became even more important than the *what*.

Opportunities for Change

The federal government should continue to play a major role in determining not only what but also how funds will be provided. During the Reagan years, that role was considerably eroded because of the administration's dislike of both regulation and the programs themselves.

The question for child and family advocates today is what improvements they should concentrate on as a new administration takes office. Several criteria suggest themselves for pursuing change. First and foremost, will the change actually make a significant difference in the quality or quantity of available services? Second, will the change make it easier to deliver services? Finally, can public political and bureaucratic support be developed to overcome the natural resistance to change? New administrations almost always look to agency reorganization as a means of improving programs. But many observers now believe the costs of change, both financial and nonfinancial, are generally greater than the advantages gained. The author sees no potential reorganization that would produce substantial gains in children's services.

Most administrations also seek to rationalize the basis for the federal role and to define a "correct" balance between public and private as well as among federal, state, and local responsibilities. Understanding the inconsistencies and irrationalities of the present role, the author does not believe that a political consensus can be developed around any grand scheme for realignment of responsibilities. Similarly, it is difficult to find convincing evidence that a realignment of responsibilities will produce significant gains in quantity or quality of services.

The opportunity to appoint new leadership for children, youth, and family programs does offer an enormous opportunity in terms of the criteria outlined above. The need here is not only to find exceptional people but also to empower them to act as leaders. An administration's selection of leadership and the charge that it gives that leadership may be the single most important statement of its commitment to children. Strong federal leaders will understand that one cannot depend on law, regulation, and grant or plan approvals alone if one seeks to achieve major improvements. Rather, a leader needs to work with and in support of state and local organizations that actually deliver service. Only rarely does the weight and authority of the federal government need to be exercised.

Even the best of leaders will not be able to accomplish much without a quantum increase in federal funding. There is no question that there are substantial political obstacles to raising additional revenues and serious disputes among children's advocates as to where funds can be most efficiently used. Nevertheless, political, business, and public leaders are overwhelmingly sympathetic to meeting the needs of children. It is necessary to mobilize supporters around legislation that can produce a much higher aggregate level of funds committed to children's services. Decisions as to how these funds might best be allocated should be deferred until adequate overall funding is available.   The bureaucratic ambiguities described earlier must be decisively resolved, but that need not mean a return to the bureaucratic relationship of the 1960s and 1970s. What follows is a description of significant bureaucratic changes that would improve the delivery of services.

There is widespread concern among service providers about the validity of congressional and agency standards. This includes issues of why standards should be uniform in different geographic areas where client needs, facilities, available professional personnel, and community resources vary widely. The development and application of program and staffing standards need to be rooted more solidly in objective evidence. Two changes would contribute to that objective. First, Congress should refrain from incorporating detailed program standards in legislation. To some extent, it should obtain judgments and recommendations not only from professional and advocacy groups but also from independent organizations that have assessed the evidence justifying the need for a program or personnel standard.

Second, agencies should be required to submit their proposed program and staffing standards to independent panels of experts. These panels could be constituted by an organization like the National Academy of Sciences. Each panel would review a proposed standard to determine whether there is reasonable evidence that a standard is needed at all, that the particular standard chosen has an adequate basis in fact, and whether a less restrictive standard could be applied in communities with lesser resources. The membership of each panel should be chosen so that the majority of members are not representative of advocacy or professional groups but selected for their ability to assess the evidence presented in support of a program or personnel standard.

Many programs fail because the program operators do not have access to the kind of expert help they need. The federal government should increase the level of technical assistance and training to all grantees and program operators. In doing so it should make heavy use of educational and consulting contractors (professional groups and individual experts) rather than expanding its own staffs. Wherever possible, the grantee should have a choice among contractors as to who will provide it with technical assistance or training. Technical assistance and training should generally be available to interested grantees but mandated by federal officials when programs are seriously deficient.

Some states or other grantees clearly perform their functions well and should enjoy more freedom to modify programs on their own initiative. Similarly, they need not be audited as frequently as less proficient organizations. The federal government should create a category of meritorious-performance grantee organizations. Grantees with a meritorious performance over two or three years would be placed in that category. A meritorious grantee would have the frequency of its program and financial audits reduced. It would also be authorized to develop program variations, waive certain standards or regulations if it determines that doing so would increase or improve services, and reprogram funds within the available grant on its own volition. Waivers would be subject to review three years after they were instituted.

The federal government should consistently encourage networking among grantees and support the costs of related meetings and publications. Networking should facilitate communication among federal, state, local, and private agencies, as well as professional, staff, consumer, and community organizations. Congress should expand the use of advanced funding so that grantees will know the likely level of funding a year before program operations begin.

States and local agencies and other grantees should have access to mediation within thirty days in cases of disputes among grantors, grantees, and subgrantees as to refusal to fund, terms and conditions of funding, and results of audits. Federal agencies should put a premium on selecting supervisory employees who have or obtain experience in state, local, or private agencies.

A major effort should be made at both federal and state levels to remove nonessential barriers to program integration and coordination, including unreasonable professional qualification requirements, prohibitions on merger of funding as well as uncoordinated application and funding requirements. The federal government and states should make a major effort to facilitate program coordination at local levels so as to ensure continuity of care and the most efficient use of resources. This planning should be interdisciplinary in nature and should include consumers, private providers, and community representatives. The federal government should strongly support health, educational, and social-psychological epidemiology data collection and analysis and should require grantees to cooperate. It should also strongly support consumer and community participation in decision making but should take steps to make sure that participants are indeed representative of those for whom they speak. Finally, the federal government should continue to support the strengthening of evaluation skills and techniques. It should put great emphasis on the practical utility of evaluation to both program operators and policymakers.

With these modest but important changes, the advantages of federal involvement in administration can be maintained and enhanced. Federal officials can exercise real leadership while recognizing differences in geographic areas and providing ample opportunity for creative leadership by state and local organizations.

Urban Governance and the Idea of a Service Community

JOSEPH P. VITERITTI

There are generally two aspects to the notion of governance within the public sector. One aspect is political. It concerns the structural arrangements through which institutions are held accountable by the public they are supposed to serve. The other aspect is managerial. It concerns the capacity of government organizations to deliver public services efficiently and effectively. Conceivably, the political and managerial aspects of governance are intertwined. It is reasonable to assume that sound management practice is one of the goals for which political leaders will be held accountable by the electorate. Most astute observers would agree that the larger managerial strategies formulated by government officials are to some extent the product of political decision making. The high-level coordination needed among multiple-service organizations in order to implement complex programs successfully is often facilitated by the existence of a political mandate.

Both good politics and good management require a certain level of citizen participation. With regard to good politics, the need for public involvement is quite clear. According to the most fundamental democratic principles, government works well when it is responsive to the will of the people. With regard to good management, the appropriate public role is not so apparent, but it can be equally significant. The involvement of citizens in service delivery through cooperative efforts with service providers can have a positive impact on the quality and effectiveness of service. For example, modern approaches to community policing are built around the idea that police officers can more effectively prevent crime, apprehend criminals, and improve the general quality of city life when they establish networks of communication between themselves and the communities in which they work. It has been known for some time that fire-department personnel would devote fewer resources and less energy to fighting dangerous fires if they were to expand their efforts instructing the public on how to prevent such catastrophes. In no place, however, is the relevance of citizen involvement to the effectiveness of local services so profound as in the area of children's services, particularly education.

A substantial body of educational research as well as common sense indicates that the formation of cooperative partnerships among school administrators, teachers, and parents is one of the most constructive ways to create a positive learning environment for the child. It is an unfortunate fact of the last century of American educational history, however, that most discourse on the subject of school governance has focused more on the politics of accountability than on the management of service. One of the mean ironies of that history is that it resulted in the creation of institutions, particularly in the city, that are neither politically accountable nor managerially effective. While the connection between politics and public management is well established, there are significant differences in the kind of activity each encompasses with regard to citizen participation. Meaningful participation in the political process involves the exercise of power or influence in a conflictual arena where there are differences over issues of policy. Conflict in the political arena is most intense when policy debates emerge from a fundamental disagreement over social values, such as school prayer, sex education, and racial integration. Meaningful participation in the delivery of services usually involves cooperative action among people who agree on basic policy objectives and whose fundamental values are either consistent with one another or irrelevant to their common activities. Most institutional reform over the last two decades has been preoccupied with affording individuals open channels for conflict, but it has offered little opportunity for meaningful cooperation. This is true with regard to urban governance in general and school governance in particular.

What is often called the "community revolution" of the 1960s was a predictable and necessary reaction to a century-old governance model that was irrelevant and counterproductive to the needs of an urban environment. Demands for community control gave access to many groups that had been excluded from participation in the political process. The increased politicization of local-government administration created a forum in which various groups could ventilate their differences, articulate their distinct values, and pursue what they believed to be their self-interests. But the emphasis on conflict and competition overshadowed the need for urban dwellers to form a viable service community. The term *service community* is used here to define a group of people who, despite possible differences on the larger issues of politics, share a common active interest in the value of service quality. Individual and group activity within a service community is more likely to be of a cooperative than of a conflictual nature. It is directed at the street-level bureaucrat who is immediately involved in service delivery rather than at the middle-level manager or political executive who makes policy decisions.[1]

The absence of a service community while inner cities were experiencing the birth and growth of newly active political communities contributed to a dilemma of urban governance I have described elsewhere as "the dichotomy between constituent and client."[2] Constituents are individuals or groups to whom public organizations are politically accountable; clients are individuals or groups who depend on public organizations for the delivery of tangible services. When the identities of these two groups differ, as they do in American cities, the result is a serious problem of governance that affects the accountability, responsiveness, and representativeness of public bodies. Since the fundamental causes of this dichotomy are not institutional, the solution to the problem cannot be achieved through institutional reform. However, it is possible and certainly desirable to design institutions that not only provide avenues for serious political debate and discourse about major public priorities but also offer opportunities for cooperative public action at the street level that can result in more effective delivery of public services to all clients, including children. The development of such institutions is the subject of this essay. Before proposing a plan for improvement, however, it is first necessary to explain more fully the origin and nature of the existing problem.

The Original Model as the Original Problem

The present-day institutional arrangement in most large American cities is a product of another era. That period, which began in the late nineteenth century, brought forward a reform movement that was distinctly antipolitics in nature. The Progressive movement, as it is known, was a reaction to bad government characterized by patronage, incompetence, and corruption. It was an attempt to undo the excesses and the shame of the Jacksonian spoils system. Several external influences contributed to the emergence of the reform model of government. One, adopted from the private sector, was scientific management. In the true Taylorist sense, scientific management was an attempt to rationalize the productive process. Adherents to the principles of scientific management assumed that by observing, analyzing, and experimenting with the productive and administrative process, it is possible to define rules of management that would determine the "one best way" of accomplishing tasks. Of course, the criterion for determining the "one best way" was to discover that which was the most efficient. The prescription of sound rules for conducting business also had the benefit of reducing personal discretion, a major contributing factor to the abuses of the spoils system.

A second element of the reform model was the European civil-service system. It required that individuals be recruited to public service on the basis of merit, as determined by written examinations. Once a candidate qualified for a position, he or she was granted life tenure. Several presumed benefits were to be derived from the civil-service system. It would promote competence in administration, further curtail the discretion of political leaders who habitually hired and fired individuals on the basis of patronage, and perhaps lead to the development of a professional corps of government administrators.

Conceptually, one of the great hallmarks of the reform model was the proposition that it is both possible and desirable to separate administration from politics. Few students of public administration today believe in the dichotomy as a practical reality. But the idea is an important clue to understanding contemporary institutions. On the one hand, it was antipolitics because it sought to limit political interference in the business of government. As one might say, there is no Democratic or Republican way to remove the garbage or clean the streets. On the other hand, the notion of a politics-administration dichotomy recognized the important role that the political process plays in a democratic form of government. As Woodrow Wilson explained it in his now-famous essay, the existence of political executives who are either popularly elected or appointed at the upper ranks of the administrative hierarchy permits accountability.[3]

Notwithstanding its possible excesses, politics remained the only vehicle for keeping government responsive to the people in a free society. Turn-of-the-century reformers spent enormous energy and creativity in attempting to devise methods for popular election that would allow local government to be representative. A good deal of attention was devoted to reforming the local legislature. But the net effect of the changes made in most cities led to a transfer of authority from the council, where corruption had been most entrenched, to the mayor. A strong, responsible executive would provide the electorate with a central focus of attention through which it could monitor the performance of government and achieve accountability. The existence of a strong executive was also consistent with the concept of hierarchy that was paramount in the classical Weberian model of bureaucracy espoused by reformers. This model did not define a particular role for the client of the government agency other than as a passive recipient of service. According to the rules prescribed, this service would be provided efficiently, but administrators would not even engage the thought that involving clients in the service-delivery process might actually improve quality or effectiveness. This is not surprising, for the hierarchic, procedural, and rigid system of doing business left little room for discretion or imagination even among lower-level administrators or service providers.

The reform model of urban governance would prove to have a peculiar relevance to education, not through imitation but through modification. Its adaptation by school administrators had a lasting impact on the larger service-delivery system that has been created and perpetuated for children. The ideal of professionalism within the public service had a natural appeal to educators, who advanced through their own careers by means of a formal system of training and certification. The hierarchic structure of the reform model easily fit the organizational intricacies of the school system, where administrators (most of whom were men) made policy and teachers (most of whom were women) provided services to the client. Since the teachers themselves enjoyed little discretion, the prospects for developing a service community built on cooperative partnerships between teachers, parents, and children were remote. Educational administrators took the ideals of professionalism to an extreme and invoked prerogatives that allowed little opportunity for public input at any level.

In the larger realm of governance, school professionals not only wanted to limit the role of politics in educational affairs but actually sought to remove it. They did so by maintaining separate structures for policy making, administration, and service delivery. While the school budget absorbs a larger portion of local resources than any other service in most cities, schools stand alone, outside the municipality, with their own system of governance. This ideology of separatism has become a generally accepted American educational tradition, and it has serious political and managerial consequences.

Politically, this arrangement makes it more difficult to hold schools accountable to the public. While many school systems did indeed have elected school boards, the school board of the early twentieth century was conceived more as a public trust than as a representative body. It was assumed that members of the school board would generally reflect the community of families whose children attended the schools. Despite the presence of a school board, most important educational decisions were left in the hands of the professionals. The institutional design was based on three great misperceptions that would not withstand the test of history. The first misperception is that educational policy can be separated from the larger social issues that belong within the political realm of decision making. One needs only a passing familiarity with the present-day rhetoric of presidential politics to judge the validity of such a naive assumption. The second misperception is an exalted notion of educational professionalism that implies more certainty and unanimity on questions of effective instruction than actually exists. Education is at best a soft science characterized by much debate and division on the numerous questions that need to be resolved in determining how best to provide instructional services to children. The third misperception is what Robert Salisbury has labeled the "myth of the unitary community," which suggests that all people within the larger political constituency share the same wants, needs, and values with regard to education.[4] While such unanimity exists in many school districts, it is highly improbable in the pluralist environment of the city.

With these misperceptions, cultivated in a sanctuary of professional chauvinism, educators adopted a model of governance that not only deemed all politics undesirable but dismissed politics as irrelevant and unnecessary. The entire framework was so antipolitics that it was fundamentally elitist and undemocratic.[5] While few educators today would subscribe to its original underlying assumptions, this poor interpretation and application of the municipal-reform model continues to shape the structure of school systems and has had a serious impact on the way services are delivered to children.

From a managerial perspective, the separatism of schools has meant that public institutions where children spend most of their time are not part of the formal network of agencies that are capable of providing a variety of important services. Thus, cooperation and coordination among service providers becomes difficult. If city children relied on government for only instructional services, as perhaps was more the case a century ago, then the present institutional arrangement would not be as problematic. But since inner-city children rely on local government for health, recreational, social, and protective services, the stubborn isolation of the school system becomes a serious obstacle to the effective delivery of essential services to children.

The Limits of Community Politics

One outcome of the events that characterized the 1960s is that they decisively proved the connection between politics and education. Through the flow of government grants-in-aid came a larger federal and state presence at the local school-district level. As a result of increased litigation brought by civil-rights groups, the process of educational policy making began to move from the school house to the court house. Larger social issues, such as racial integration, poverty, nutrition, health care, and bilingualism, became intricately enmeshed with pedagogical issues of policy and strategy. But no issue of the 1960s had a more lasting influence on the future of urban governance than the demand for decentralization and community control.

As originally conceived, decentralization was meant to address both the political and the managerial dimensions of governance. Social scientists distinguish between political decentralization and administrative decentralization. The purpose of the former was to transfer authority and power from professionals within government bureaucracies to clients. The goal of the latter was to delegate discretion from superior to subordinate officials within the bureaucracy. Both forms of decentralization were intended to focus more decision making at the subjurisdictional level of the community district. The two approaches were complementary, for if community participation at the district level was to be meaningful in a political sense, midlevel administrators had to be empowered to respond to citizen demands. As an organizational innovation, decentralization would disassemble the large, unwieldy service bureaucracy into a number of subdivisions that are more manageable in size; as a political innovation, decentralization was expected to increase the access points for newly mobilized community groups.

The demands for decentralization and community control were a manifestation of the political turbulence of the era, when blacks, Hispanics, and other minorities began to question the legitimacy of governmental institutions. While the movement was very much an urban phenomenon, it received great impetus from the federal government with the creation of the Community Action Program (CAP). An innovation that was part of Lyndon B. Johnson's "Great Society," CAP was created in 1964 to establish a direct channel for federal aid between Washington and local communities. This program would circumvent the traditional institutions of urban government that many critics claimed were not responsive to the needs of minorities. It called for "maximum feasible participation" of the poor in community-level decision making. The federal initiative was a source of encouragement and political education for groups that had been historically excluded from local government and politics. It created opportunities and incentives for local experimentation in which many large cities began to develop their own plans for decentralization and citizen participation. And the movement would have a special significance in education.

If the responsiveness of urban government was at issue among minorities, the situation of public education was particularly critical. Given the politically abstruse character of school-system organization, it was questionable whether educational institutions were accountable to anyone. They were certainly not responding to the wants and needs of the changing population that were becoming the clientele of the school system. By the late 1960s, black and Hispanic children were occupying a majority of the seats in inner-city schools, yet policy was still being determined by white administrators who controlled the educational bureaucracies and were remote from the schools. In no other local service was the dichotomy between constituent and client greater than it was in education. The demand for community control of the schools was a manifestation of both frustration and hope — frustration born from the failure of desegregation efforts, hope instilled by the pride and determination of the black-power movement.

Between 1965 and 1971, decentralized structures were implemented in the school systems of New York City, Los Angeles, Chicago, Philadelphia, Detroit, Dade County (Florida), and Houston. By 1980, twenty out of twenty-two school systems enrolling 100,000 or more students had become decentralized.[6] Given the intense political turmoil of the period, it is not difficult to understand why most debates on the governance issue focused on politics and conflict. Whether the political goals of decentralization were achieved by the institutional changes that were brought about is a subject for another essay. However, as a result of political preoccupations, the far-reaching structural reforms of the 1960s also represent a missed opportunity to enhance services.

To begin with, efforts at decentralization and community control moved along two separate tracks in most cities — one involving the municipality, the other the school system. While critics of the traditional system were raising fundamental questions about the legitimacy and efficacy of urban institutions, the preservation of the school system as a separate entity was never challenged by the most radical of reformers. Educational separatism had become so much a part of the political ethos that people simply assumed the system would remain so. In the meantime, the population attending public schools was becoming dominated by children who, because of family structure, economics, and other social determinants discussed in this volume, were more dependent on public services.

By the mid-1960s, educators had come to recognize that the child must be physically and psychologically healthy in order for effective instruction to take place. Thus the efficient delivery of health, nutritional, and social services to the child would not only be valued as an end in itself but as a prerequisite for a good education. At the time, many of these supportive services were provided through federal resources channeled directly to schools, reinforcing the idea that schools could function and thrive without any formal institutional connection to other local institutions. Now federal support has begun to diminish. Schools and their clients are relying more on state and local resources. Nevertheless, schools remain part of a separate institutional structure that inhibits their capacity to draw on locally generated services in the most effective manner.

The principal organizational result of school decentralization was a significant addition to the middle level of the bureaucracy, the community school district.

In most cities, school decentralization was implemented along the lines of the administrative rather than the political model. Some decision-making power was delegated to district administrators; citizens were enabled and encouraged to interact with these midlevel personnel in order to articulate their wants and needs. But only in New York City and Detroit did full political decentralization take place that would allow clients to choose district-board members and make policy decisions. Today, full political decentralization exists only in New York City, where it remains a highly controversial issue of debate. Plans for significant structural reforms are under consideration, however, in Chicago and Dade County.

Advocates of decentralization, determined to empower the poor, argued that the enhancement of district-level administration would make access to decision makers easier and result in more political accountability, even though in most cases the public had no effective way to remove district-level administrators or the school officials who appointed them. Proponents of decentralization had hoped that they could overcome the political impotence of the poor through institutional change, despite a generation of political-science research demonstrating the relationship between socioeconomic variables and political efficacy. They had assumed that people wanted the opportunity to become more politically active, despite substantial evidence indicating that Americans by and large are apolitical. They mistakenly limited the definition of "meaningful citizen participation" to political action.

The promise of decentralization was to move decision making closer to the point of service delivery. In most cities the opposite occurred. District-level authority was enhanced through a transfer of power in two directions. A modicum of discretion was passed down from the top of the educational bureaucracy, where most power emanated from and remained. A certain amount of discretion was moved upward from the school, further eroding the ability of street-level administrators and teachers to make important decisions on a day-to-day basis. Now school personnel would have another level of the bureaucracy to which they answered. Viewing the process from the street level, the new line of accountability would flow upward, not downward or outward as originally intended.

For parents, the message was quite unambiguous. Issues that could and should be resolved at the street level would now go to the district. Getting district administrators to respond to parental concerns would require political and organizational mobilization that would not be needed for involvement at the school level. Politics became a prerequisite for meaningful interaction between citizen and professional. Participation, in order to be effective, would become more of a group process and less personal on an individual level. History has shown that most parents lack either the skill or the willingness to get involved in the new community politics.

In the end, important decisions would remain at the top of the bureaucracy, and little of significance would be allowed to happen at the school level. Perhaps the most revealing development of the period was the politicization of teachers' organizations. Astute leaders in the union movement, enjoying their recently aggrandized power, directed their energies toward influencing policy at the top and middle tiers of bureaucracy. At the same time, teachers at the school level remained powerless to make even the most rudimentary decisions. Given the circumstances, any meaningful cooperation and interaction between teachers and parents would be entirely fortuitous and would occur despite the system rather than because of it.

The School as Service Community

The 1970s and 1980s have been a time of great contradictions in American education. While the Reagan administration acted as a strong vocal advocate of educational excellence, it simultaneously strived to decrease important federal support for school programs. Although many states like Tennessee, Florida, and New Jersey responded to the New Federalism by assuming a more assertive role in educational matters, the most significant reforms brought about in education occurred at the school level.

By the mid-1970s, the effective schools movement had demonstrated through both research and practice that the key variables for achieving successful instruction are determined within the school building. Efforts at reform began to focus on such factors as the leadership, climate, values, and standards of the school organization at the street level.[7] On the frontier of school governance, a quiet revolution was beginning to take place in a few select areas like Rochester, New York, and Miami, Florida, under the programmatic label called "school-based management." As an institutional innovation, school-based management would achieve in practice what decentralization had articulated in principle: it would locate a greater portion of decision-making authority at the point of service delivery, the school. Where instituted, school-based management would provide greater discretion to principals, teachers, and other school-level personnel. Managerially, the school would become a responsibility center, accountable at the outcome stage of service delivery with more flexibility on matters of process and method. From a community or client perspective, the school building would emerge a more viable resource for constructive interaction.

The next decade can be one of great hope and progress in education. As Chester Finn has wisely observed, there is an emergent national consensus supporting an agenda for excellence in education.[8] This populist outcry for reform that demands higher standards, sound management, competent teachers, and an orderly school environment crosses all class, racial, gender, geographic, and political lines. This consensus for change is results oriented, and it is generated by a common understanding that schools must produce a generation of young people who at a minimum have mastered the basic skills. The consensus for instructional effectiveness will never overshadow or eliminate some of the fundamental policy and value differences that make Americans a pluralist people who require political institutions that allow them to confront differences vigorously. But as a people with a common interest in the welfare of their children, encompassed by a larger vision of the general good, they also need institutions that allow them to engage one another cooperatively.

In order for the urban school system to be responsive on all levels, institutional reform must proceed on the basis of both political and managerial premises. First, it must be recognized that the urban school system is a political body shaped by public priorities and financed by public funding. As a public body the school system must be subject to public scrutiny and accountability. It must be headed by an individual who, one might say, is within calling distance of the people. That is, the head of the school, if not chosen directly by the electorate (which is not advocated here), must be appointed by someone who is. Second, the urban school system must be seen as an integral part of a complex network of services designed to accommodate the greater needs of children. Moreover, as will be explained shortly, the school building must function as the focal point of that service network.

In most large urban centers, the appropriate way to address the political and managerial dimensions of school governance on a citywide level is through the incorporation of a commissioner plan. Under this plan, the chief executive officer of the school system is appointed by and serves at the pleasure of the mayor. As such, the mayor, a popularly elected official, is ultimately accountable for the performance of the schools. It is also the ultimate responsibility of the mayor to ensure that school services are coordinated with other child-related services. This coordinative function would be greatly facilitated by including the education commissioner as part of the city-hall cabinet of agency executives who are also mayoral appointees.

Under the commissioner plan, major issues of policy and public priorities in education are debated at the mayoral level of the political arena. This has the effect of removing the school commissioner a step further from the political process, an outcome that even turn-of-the-century reformers would have applauded. While some educators would be alarmed at the thought of conceding pedagogical ground to a politician, policy issues like desegregation, school prayer, sex education, and pledging allegiance to the flag are not entirely pedagogical in nature. Moreover, decisions on such matters are already being made by judges, legislators, and elected executives.

Because most urban school systems are by definition large, some form of decentralization will be required even under a commissioner plan. However, having the school system operate as a mayoral agency facilitates, or in many cases introduces, a new coordinating role for district-level administrators through the development of service network at the community level. Service integration at the community level is enhanced when the boundaries of administrative districts from the various service agencies are coterminous. Since some form of district-level governance exists, there must be suitable channels for interaction between citizens and service administrators. Here it is important to make an analytic distinction between "citizen" and "client." Since no service is actually delivered at the district-level, individuals do not have a client relationship with district-level officials. Since district-level officials have the authority to make governmental decisions, community residents have a citizen relationship with such officials that entitles them to accountability. One can speculate that citizen interaction at the district level will vary in nature from conflictual to cooperative. While most larger political issues will be debated at the mayoral level, some discourse on such matters is likely to trickle down. Moreover, there are likely to be disagreements between administrator and citizen or among citizens over such issues as resource allocations and service priorities.

The school-level organization envisioned under the proposed system of governance would draw on the advantages of the commissioner plan and school-based management to make the school the center for all child-related services. As a mayoral agency, the school would be the optimal place for the integration of children's services, because it is located at the street level where services are actually delivered and because it is the place where children are. The goal here is to bring health, social, recreational, and even employment programs to the child. In light of the serious dropout problem that affects inner-city adolescents, making the school a neighborhood resource for young people provides an extraordinary incentive for attending school.

In order for the school-based service center to operate at a maximum level of effectiveness, professionals who provide services at the street level must be given adequate discretion. Professionalism must be understood as a capacity for service providers to develop meaningful cooperative relationships with clients, rather than as a lame excuse through which bureaucrats removed from the street level exert authority and avoid accountability. The true empowerment of street-level service providers will not only enable professionals to perform their jobs better, but it will also increase the capacity of clients, in this case children and their parents, to assume a more meaningful participative role. An important objective achieved through the creation of a service community is to decrease the opportunity costs for meaningful client participation. Constructive interaction at the street level does not require the kind of political mobilization that is a prerequisite for effective district-level or citywide participation, which most parents do not have the skill, energy, or interest to pursue. Moreover, client interaction at the street level with service providers who have real discretion increases the benefits of such participation and provides a greater incentive for its continuance.

As explained at the beginning of this essay, client participation within a service community is designed to be cooperative rather than conflictual; it is focused on service rather than politics or power. Many individuals would be skeptical at the prospects for designing such an idealistic type of community. But some evidence attests to the viability of the idea. It exists in private schools. There has been much speculation as to why private schools are often more instructionally effective than public schools. Researchers have focused on resources, socioeconomic conditions, and a number of other explanatory variables, all of which make perfectly good sense. However, one factor that truly distinguishes the learning environment of private schools is the existence of cooperative relationships between parents, children, and professionals, who come together for the common purpose of making the educational process successful and are not encumbered by politics. Religious schools have a peculiar advantage because they are often anchored on a fundamental consensus regarding questions of morals and values. But the experience of nondenominational private schools is particularly relevant because they often represent a community of people who can work together, despite possible disagreements over the larger social issues. At the level of the service community, such differences are kept irrelevant so that individuals can focus on the immediate issue at hand, quality instruction.

In advancing the idea of a service community for children, much hope is placed here on the power of the emerging social consensus to which Chester Finn has called attention. Even beyond the great issues of politics that divide people, it is reasonable to assume that there will be honest differences among educators and parents about the efficacy of different approaches to the learning process. In order to overcome such dissension, the marketplace of public schools, like that of the private sector, will need to become more pluralistic in approach. Freeing up school organizations from unnecessary and nonproductive bureaucratic dictates will allow such diversity to flourish. It will provide parents with real choices that allow them to become part of a service community of professionals and clients where agreement over educational issues outweighs other differences that might otherwise keep people apart.

The prospect for the development of service communities within city school systems will depend on the willingness and ability of urban activists to expand their notion of participation. Social action need not always be contentious. While political conflict may be beneficial to the health of the democracy, cooperation and consensus form the social fabric of the overall community and enable the body politic to endure the strains of diversity.

NOTES

1. Michael Lipsky, *Street-Level Bureaucracy* (New York: Russell Sage Foundation, 1980).

2. See Joseph P. Viteritti, *Across the River: Politics and Education in the City* (New York: Holmes & Meier, 1983); idem., "Public Organization Environments: Constituents, Clients and Urban Governance," *Administration and Society* 20 (August 1989).

3. Woodrow Wilson, "The Study of Public Administration," *Political Science Quarterly* 2 (June 1887): 197–222.

4. Robert H. Salisbury, "Schools and Politics in the Big City," *Harvard Educational Review* 67 (Summer 1967): 408–24.

5. This theme is developed further in Joseph P. Viteritti, "The Urban School District: Towards an Open System Approach to Leadership and Governance," *Urban Education* 21 (October 1986): 228–53.

6. Alan C. Ornstein, "Administrative/Community Organization of Metropolitan Schools," *Phi Delta Kappan* 54 (June 1973): 668–74; idem., "Decentralization and Community Participation Policy of Big City School Systems," *Phi Delta Kappan* 62 (December 1980): 255–57.

7. Ronald Edmonds, "Effective Schools for the Urban Poor," *Educational Leadership* 37 (October 1979): 15–27.

8. Chester E. Finn, Jr., "Moving Toward a Public Consensus: The Drive for Educational Excellence," *Change* 15 (April 1983): 14–22.

Delivering Children's Services: The Experience of Ulster County

GERALD BENJAMIN
STEPHEN MORRIS
AZRA FARRELL

In mid-1984 there were alarming signs that the capacity of Ulster County, New York, to deal with child-related problems would soon be overwhelmed. The number of cases was skyrocketing. In the Department of Social Services, reported child-abuse and neglect cases were expected to be up 45 percent for the year, reaching a total of 1,700. In the Family Court, actions involving persons in need of supervision (PINS) were headed for an increase of more than two-thirds. Costs were also rising. Most dramatically, expenses for educating handicapped children were projected to increase from a 1983 base of $1.6 million to $2.4 million in 1984. This was especially compelling for the county. Under the New York State Family Court Act of 1976, it was responsible for paying half the cost of programming for handicapped preschool-age children year round and school-age children during the summer months. Expenses for this program alone would consume more than a tenth of the revenues projected from the property-tax levy for county purposes. Clearly, something had to be done.

Ulster is a semirural county in New York's Hudson Valley, one of the United States's fastest-growing regions. About equidistant from New York City and Albany, it is bordered by Dutchess and Orange counties. Influenced by a number of metropolitan areas, it is apart from all of them, both in fact and in the way it sees itself. Ulster, with 158,158 inhabitants, ranked nineteenth in population among New York counties in 1980. Excluding New York City's boroughs, all larger counties were in the environs of the state's five large cities or within metropolitan areas. Indeed, Ulster County's population places it within the top 10 percent of counties in the United States.

Big Blue, the IBM Corporation, is the principal employer in Ulster County. Tourism and fruit farming are the other major industries. Also, many people are employed by government at the state college in New Paltz, state prisons at Wallkill and Napanoch, nine school districts, twenty towns, three villages, and one city — the county seat, Kingston. Some 1,550 of these local-government employees worked for the county in 1984, about 50 fewer than today. Unemployment is low and has been for a long time. But per-capita personal income is considerably lower than in the state's metropolitan areas; Ulster ranked eighteenth among New York State counties outside New York City in 1984.

The county's politics are Republican-dominated, and its leadership is fiscally conservative. Of the thirty-three members of the county legislature, twenty-eight were Republicans in 1988, compared with twenty-four in 1984. The legislature is the governing body; there is no separately elected executive. Departments are overseen by fourteen legislative committees, all majority-dominated. In particular policy areas the roles of committee chairmen are significant and may be decisive if individuals in the positions are interested and energetic. The chief political and policy-making post, filled by a majority caucus, is chairman of the legislature. A county administrator, appointed by the legislature for a fixed term, is responsible for day-to-day management.

In 1987 the annual county budget totaled $115,183,488; in 1984 it was $88,237,752. These funds come from a variety of sources, and their disparate origins are critically important for understanding the political and governmental dynamics of the county. The principal local sources of revenue are the property tax and a retail sales tax of 3 percent. In 1984, 41.5 percent of the budget was funded from these local sources, about a fourth of it from the property tax.

A consistent policy goal of the Republican legislative majority has been to control the growth of the property tax, which in addition to its use by the county is the sole source of discretionary revenue for towns and school districts. One way of doing this is to maximize state assistance and attempting to avoid additional mandated local costs. In short, programs are assessed not only by their cost but also by who will pay for them.

About a fourth of Ulster's largely white and predominantly middle-class population is concentrated in the city of Kingston and three villages — New Paltz, Saugerties, and Ellenville. The minority population, 6 percent in 1980, is located largely in Kingston and Ellenville as well, though there is a substantial concentration of Hispanics in the southern Ulster town of Plattekill. The remainder of the county's population is scattered across an area slightly larger than the state of Rhode Island.

In 1980, 30.5 percent of Ulster County's population were under the age of twenty. Of these, 3,510 were in families receiving Aid to Families with Dependent Children (AFDC) in 1982. High-school dropout rates are among the highest in the state. According to a county study completed in 1984, in that year there were about 2,000 "high risk" children in the community. These youngsters were actually or potentially in need of long-term care services: the severely emotionally disturbed, the physically abused or neglected, the educationally handicapped, and those already involved with the criminal-justice system.

The State-Local Service System

In Ulster, as in all other New York counties, the system for responding to the needs of high-risk children was extremely complicated. It consisted of many different agencies and organizations operating with limited coordination.

The Family Court was centrally involved in decision making concerning foster care, child abuse, and child custody. It approved petitions for funding programs for handicapped children and made determinations concerning criminal or anti-social behavior by young people. The discretion of the Family Court judge, a state official who is locally elected, was extraordinarily broad, but he or she relied on county agencies for case evaluations and treatment recommendations.

The schools were purposefully separated from other services in the organization of state and local government. Most of the county's children were served by one of nine separately organized and financed school districts or by the Board of Cooperative Educational Services (BOCES). On Ulster's periphery, however, six school districts in neighboring counties enrolled some children, and other residents attended private or parochial schools. High-risk children were often first identified by teachers, and referrals were made. Additionally, each district was required by state law to maintain a committee on the handicapped to assess needs and develop a plan for remedial action. BOCES provided special-education classes for contracting school districts and a day treatment program in cooperation with the Rockland Psychiatric Hospital.

A wide array of county government agencies offered significant services to children. Some, like the Health Department and Youth Board, did not focus on high-risk children but made referrals based on observations during the delivery of preventive services to the broader population. Others were more directly involved. The Department of Social Services (DSS) administered Aid to Families with Dependent Children (AFDC), investigated child abuse and neglect complaints, was responsible for foster-care placement, and located residential placements for the "emotionally disturbed." The Probation Department provided precourt screening and predisposition investigative services for the Family Court, with an eye toward diversion from institutionalization. Finally, the Ulster County Community Mental Health Services offered crisis intervention and regular outpatient care for children and families, as well as evaluations for the family courts and DSS.

Responsibility for inpatient psychiatric care for children was shared by a state facility, Rockland County Psychiatric Center (largely for those under the age of thirteen), and Benedictine Hospital, a voluntary institution (for those between the ages of thirteen and nineteen). A number of other not-for-profit voluntary organizations provided programming for children who were retarded, physically handicapped, emotionally handicapped, or educationally handicapped.

In fact, high-risk children were often served by or affected by the activities of more than one of these agencies. Alternatively, entirely different agencies served children with similar problems and needs. And when jurisdictions overlapped or cooperation seemed logical, government was ill organized to act efficiently and effectively. Thus, for example, DSS would receive referrals from the Family Court or its sister agencies for foster placement even though its preventive services had never been used. The matter would have escalated to a crisis; a place was needed for the child. Alternatives would not have been considered. Agencies offered competing case plans, in which their staffs were heavily invested. Often, the ensuing rivalries resulted in suboptimal outcomes for the child, angry interdepartmental relationships, and higher costs for the county government.

Oversight by state agencies did little to mitigate these realities. New York is a decentralized state for service delivery; generally, it does not act directly but through its local governments. The state regularly spends more than three-fifths of its annual budget on local assistance. This money flows in many streams from state agencies to the local level in accord with the requirements of state law and the implementing agency's regulations.

The system is designed hierarchically within areas of functional responsibility. Requirements for local interagency coordination were traditionally not a high state priority. In fact, shortages of time and resources, and the practical imperatives of intergovernmental operating requirements, discouraged effective interagency cooperation at the local level.

Most local agencies in New York providing services to children must respond to detailed planning, budget, and program guidelines imposed by state agencies. But timetables for the submission of plans are inconsistent, reimbursement formulas for programs serving similar populations differ, and even data must be collected in frustratingly close but still different categories. In this environment, lip service is paid to planning. Service providers attend meetings at one another's agencies to assist in drafting acceptable plans to the state. But there is no real planning, no real coordination. Within discrete and self-contained hierarchies, children and youth are labeled —"dropout," "drug abuser," or "probationer"— and served within that rubric.

From Cost Control to Interdepartmental Service Delivery

After staff initiatives revealed the enormous sums they were spending in aggregate on children's programming, in 1983 county political and governmental leaders sought to launch a cooperative effort with school districts to reduce busing costs and deliver some agency services in the schools. Though it gained a hearing from school leaders, this effort ultimately failed. Under pressure from a number of not-for-profits and county agencies, and with some support from them, Ulster BOCES had earlier launched an alternative education program to serve high-risk youth. But in general the leadership it provided to the local school districts was not innovative. Moreover, school superintendents were concerned that the county government effort was a precursor of attempts to pass responsibility for some expensive programs, such as those serving handicapped children, to the school districts. In light of the position of the New York State Association of Counties on this matter, these fears were not unreasonable.

Despite its failure to generate cooperative programming, this county initiative did leave an important legacy. In order to develop ideas with which to approach the schools, there was created within the county government a Task Force on County/School Cooperation, composed of a number of department heads and chaired by an ambitious, relatively junior legislator. This elected official saw human-services providers as a potential countywide constituency without a clear champion within the Republican majority. Under his chairmanship, this task force was continued as a means for communication and liaison with the schools. Later, it became the vehicle for the development and promotion of the High Risk Children's Project (later the Coordinated Children's Program).

Without cooperation from the schools, the county attempted to control costs on its own. For several reasons, the initial focus of attention was the preschool educationally handicapped children's program. The operation of the program appeared embedded with conflicts of role and interest. As noted above, costs were rising rapidly. And since it was operated out of the County Administrator's Office, with a separate line item in the budget of the legislature itself, the program was highly visible.

As the program then operated, a voluntary agency would evaluate children as being "educationally handicapped," advocate in Family Court for treatment placements, and then suggest itself as the agency to administer the treatment. With no real authority to intercede under state law, the county government could not legitimately review agency evaluations of these children or proposed treatment plans. Accordingly, the Family Court often relied heavily or solely on these evaluations in its decision making.

These circumstances left agencies open to suggestions that treatment plans were sometimes tailored to meet agency rather than client needs, that proposed levels of service were perhaps excessive, and that alternative sources were not explored. This was particularly true of the agencies that advertised free testing and free transportation to testing. In fact, once services were mandated, costs for transportation, often provided by these agencies or associated companies, were borne by the county and the state.

Because they were so obviously excessive and did not directly involve the level of services actually received by the children, these transportation costs were an obvious first target for cost-control efforts. The County Administrator's Office developed a system of contracting for busing. After mild resistance, the providers acceded to it. Apparently, they recognized that they had been enjoying a situation that was too good to be true.

Following this initial success, discussions were opened with Ulster's two Family Court judges to allow the county to play a role in decisions to order special programming, though such a role was not provided for in state law. Although the judges are state officials, they are locally elected and therefore sensitive to the need to control costs and prevent improper practices. They agreed.

Provider agencies resented implications that they might be engaging in improper practices. They were also fearful of threats to their client base. Initial discussions with them were therefore distinctly unfriendly. But though they could not be legally required to cooperate with the county, it became clear that with the Family Court judges aboard they would have to cooperate to stay in business.

With the need to reduce costs the driving rationale, a fragile basis was thus laid for cooperation among several of the actors in the county dealing with children at risk. But the basis for more comprehensive thinking was provided as a result of opportunities presented in the New York State Child Welfare Reform Act of 1979 and by the State Council on Children and Families.

One objective of the Child Welfare Reform Act was to reduce the financial incentives for localities to place children in temporary foster care. Through enriched funding of mandated preventive and adoptive services, the state sought to keep children with their biological parents or to encourage adoption. The State Department of Social Services allowed local agencies to provide these mandated services directly or to purchase them from private providers. But research by the Council on Children and Families, the advocate for this constituency within the state government, revealed that there were few private providers from which services might be purchased in rural areas. The council therefore recommended that the regulations be changed to allow other public agencies to contract with local social-services agencies to provide mandated preventive services.

This was done in 1982, but guidelines for public purchase of services were not written, nor were regulatory changes distributed to localities. (Though written, they still had not been distributed in late 1988.) This was because the State Division of the Budget and Department of Social Services feared that entrepreneurial county governments might seek entirely to refinance local probation and mental health services through this "loophole."

The Ulster County probation director discovered public purchase of services through a contact in the State Department of Social Services. Over his years of working with state agencies on programs for children and families, the director had developed relationships of mutual respect and trust with a number of his professional counterparts in state government committed to improving human-services delivery in New York. Some of these advanced to top staff and planning jobs in Albany and became valuable sources of information and encouragement. This state official was one such contact. Since the law allowed Ulster County to purchase services publicly, he suggested, why not do it? So it did.

The High Risk Children's Project

"What we are proposing," the Task Force on County/School Cooperation told the Ulster County Legislature in 1984, "is a bold new thrust, consisting of a four pronged County program which will emphasize department cooperation, focus on prevention and early intervention, and adequately coordinate the wide range of services within Ulster County. Additionally, it will provide a prominent County role in the review and monitoring of requests with Family Court funding of the educationally handicapped and will give the County access to a system of independent child assessment and evaluation."

The four program elements were designed to address a wide array of problems (see figure 1). The largest element, the Foster Care Prevention and Intervention Service (FPI), funded under the Child Welfare Reform Act, sought to use teams of workers from Probation, DSS, and Mental Health rapidly to deliver a comprehensive range of services in order to divert the highest of the high-risk population from costly institutional care. These services included case screening and planning, intensive supervision and field services, crisis intervention, respite care, family services, parent education, and purchase of professional services to meet special needs.

The Child Intake and Coordination Service, a joint effort of DSS and Mental Health, centralized intake for all high-risk children in the early stages of their contact with provider agencies. It sought to ensure than an appropriate referral was made and that a comprehensive intervention program got under way. Its premise was that early intervention would reduce the later likelihood of residential or institutional placement.

The Handicapped Children's Coordination and Review Service, staffed by a Department of Mental Health psychologist, sought to work with the Family Court to review applications for handicapped-education funding and to monitor the progress of children already being funded.

Finally, the Child Assessment Service was a means of contracting with physicians and other professionals when evaluations and assessments of high-risk children were beyond the capacity of in-house staff. Thus, evaluations while children were in residence at distant facilities outside the county might be avoided.

In designing the program, there were ongoing compromises among key players. The county administrator and the legislative chairman of the task force were concerned with control and accountability. They wanted a free-standing agency so that the initiative would be visible and accountable and would not be co-opted by established departments or lost in their budgets and programs. Department heads, in contrast, were concerned that they retain a significant role, if their personnel and resources were to be heavily committed. The result was a free-standing agency, with an Administrative Review Team prominently situated in its organizational structure (see figure 1). But, ultimately, to get the benefits of the program, the participating departments had to give way significantly on the question of control.

The total cost of the program as initially proposed was $462,098, more than three-fourths of which came from the state. Of the $97,170 that it cost the county, $77,832 represented an additional expenditure of local funds. This could be more than recovered, the proposal argued, if the rate of increase of residential placements of persons in need of supervision (PINS) and education costs for handicapped children could be reduced by one-third.

Later, with both total and county costs revised, a table was prepared to demonstrate that if one child could be diverted in each of seven categories, the program would pay for itself (see table 1). Again, the key fiscal selling point was not overall savings but local savings. Under the revised design, though total costs went up (from $462,098 to $577,620), local costs dropped slightly (from $97,170 to $96,302). County officials might be convinced to spend to save, but it helped a good deal that much of what they were spending was state money.

Ulster's costs were actually a smaller proportion of the total than projected in

FIGURE 1

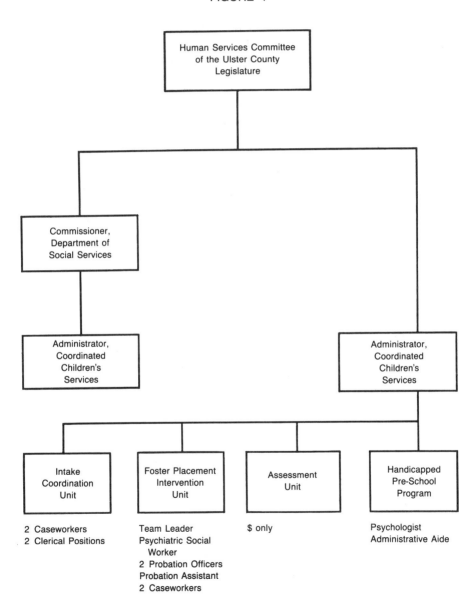

the first year, amounting to less than 10 percent of a total budget of $446,311. But in later years, when the planned level of operation was reached, the county share was closer to a third of the total, rather than a fifth as originally envisioned (see table 2). But over the past three years the local commitment, some of which would have been spent even without the creation of a new agency, has remained relatively constant. And once operations were fully under way, as noted below, substantial savings could be identified that more than justified this level of local effort.

TABLE 1

Possible Cost Savings if High Risk Children's Project Diverted One Child in Each of Seven Categories

Category	Total	County
Juvenile delinquent (JD) placed in Division of Youth (DFY) secure facility by Family Court for a year	$100,375	$50,188
JD placed in residential, nonsecure facility for a year	39,785	18,989
JD placed in residential care by DSS	24,090	12,045
Handicapped child placed in residential care by DSS	24,090	12,045
Handicapped-child assessment (one month out of county)	3,000	1,500
Preschool child placed in special education program for one year	16,000	8,000
School age child placed in special-education program for the summer	3,000	1,500
Total	$210,340	$104,267
Cost for High-risk Children's Project	$577,620	$96,302

Source: High-Risk Children's Project Proposal, Ulster County Task Force on County/School District Cooperation, 1985.

TABLE 2

Projected and Actual Costs of Coordinated Children's Services

Year	Total	County	% County
First projection	$462,098	$97,170	21.1
Second projection	577,620	96,302	16.7
1985	446,311	42,000	9.4
1986	437,499	159,405	36.4
1987	502,244	155,652	31.0
1988	526,243	164,882	31.3

Source: Ulster County, County Administrator's Office, Budget of Ulster County (various years).

Selling the Idea

With a plan in place, the Task Force on County/School Coordination sought a private meeting with the chairman of the county legislature and the chairmen of the committees to which the agencies participating in the project reported. In effect, much of the ordinary political process of the county government was short-circuited. The legislative presence on the task force lent its work legitimacy and provided a rationale for bypassing the committee system. The meeting was granted.

Then luck played a role. The meeting with key leaders was set for the day after the legislature's regularly monthly meeting. The timing could not have been better. As it happened, at that monthly meeting the legislature was required to appropriate an additional $750,000 to cover a shortfall in the appropriation for preschool handicapped-children programming, a graphic illustration of the reality of rapidly escalating costs.

The Coordinated Children's Program package was presented as an integrated whole, the product of months of work. Drawing on experience with the legislature, the presentation relied minimally on written material. Its focus was on a succinct oral briefing, built on a dramatic graphic presentation of cost increases and how they might be controlled.

It worked. Legislative leaders came away with the conviction that a new system was needed. One member asked if a part of the program might be implemented, to "phase it in to see if it worked." Somewhat surprisingly, one of his more conservative colleagues overrode the objection, pointing out that the elements were interrelated. "It's better to do it all," he said, "or not at all."

Walking down the corridor of the county office building after this meeting, the county administrator remarked to the task force's legislative chairman, "That was a big win for you." Another presentation was scheduled to the whole legislature, but with support of the leadership the local battle was won.

But now the idea had to be sold to the State Department of Social Services, and public contracting for services had never been tried. Drawing again on his informal network of contacts in Albany, the probation director was able to generate letters of support for this aspect of Ulster County's new idea from the head of every state agency except DSS involved with children and families. These carried great weight, for DSS would later have to turn to these agencies for comment and review on the formal proposal.

Again, the timing was good. The county's proposal anticipated a major state initiative focused on diverting persons in need of supervision (PINS) from the Family Court. The prospect of having a model on line ahead of time was attractive to the State Department of Social Services. It was also attractive to the Council on Children and Families, which had recently issued a policy document highlighting the importance of interagency coordination and cooperation.

The approach to state managers was far different from the one to local political leaders. In view of the unusual nature of the proposal and of the fact that no one had yet sought public purchase of service funds, the county asked for a high-profile, face-to-face presentation to top DSS administrators. A meeting was arranged — an indication that the state was really interested.

Multiple copies of the detailed proposal were sent to Albany weeks in advance. At the meeting in the capitol, the legislative chairman of the task force made a presentation, but it was largely symbolic, demonstrating to state officials the degree of local political commitment. The real work followed, in a full day of meetings between the other task force members from Ulster County and agency personnel, in which participants from the state proved thoroughly conversant with the county proposal.

At this meeting, the Coordinated Children's Program was accepted in principle. Agency officials determined that the risks of funding the proposal — the inevitable difficulties in starting a new enterprise, the use of an as yet untried funding mechanism, and the possibilities of failure, with all the implications it held for future programming elsewhere in the state — were worth the potential benefits for the development of a model of coordinated children's service programming in the state.

But there were details to be worked out. One in particular was important. The county's desire that the Coordinated Children's Program be a free-standing department conflicted with the state DSS's insistence that jurisdiction and control remain with the local commissioner of social services. Finally, an accommodation was reached. Formal control was assigned to the local commissioner to satisfy the state, while the department remained a separate entity in the local budget for local purposes.

Ulster County department heads expected that the program analyst in the County Administrator's Office who helped create the Coordinated Children's Program would become its head. (She did, in August 1985.) This informal resolution of conflicting state and local organizational requirements was only achievable because of the relationship of mutual trust that developed among them as they worked to create and sell the program.

Staffing and Related Issues

Despite positive relationships among agency leaders, difficulties arose as Coordinated Children's Services (CCS) took shape. With professional jobs in county government increasingly hard to fill, the departments of Mental Health and Social Services were loath to give up experienced personnel to the new program, despite early commitments to do so. Also, department heads insisted on a substantial role in selecting staff to be reassigned or hiring new staff for CCS.

Thus the administrator had to struggle from the beginning to establish herself as the "real boss," a management problem that seems to be endemic to interagency efforts. Moreover, she found herself having to launch an innovative effort with a largely inexperienced staff and a less than full commitment from established county agencies, especially the Department of Social Services, the agency through which she formally reported. Finally, though she was able to recruit a highly experienced social worker as clinical team leader, this person did not begin work until late fall, after referrals had begun to come to the program. Thus procedures for making, assessing, and accepting referrals were not in place in a timely way.

In fact, almost three years into the effort, maintaining the interagency identity of CCS remains a problem. After working closely together for a while, the tendency for staff drawn from different agencies is to identify more with the program than with their home departments. Workers assigned from Probation, for example, begin to chafe at performing probation officer duties, such as filing Violation of Probation Orders with the Family Court. They begin to think of themselves as counselors or therapists and to view their specific duties as interfering with their relationships with clients. It takes persistent effort to remind people working in an interagency program that unless the roles and functions of the agencies from which they were drawn continue to operate, the program loses its special character and becomes simply another department, duplicating rather than coordinating the services to children of the established departments.

Service Delivery — Issues and Achievements.

At the outset, the local Department of Social Services referred few cases to Coordinated Children's Services for Foster Care Prevention/Intervention. DSS workers were hostile to the new program's option to reject referrals and its requirement for additional assessment, which seemed to question their professional judgment. In general, there was a fear that CCS would skim the most manageable cases to improve its success-rate statistics and leave the most intractable to those in the established department. From the point of view of Coordinated Children's Services, in contrast, it made little sense to invest in those clearly unwilling or unable to make gains as the result of intensive efforts.

Resolution of these differences was achieved only after a number of meetings facilitated by a consultant provided by the State Department of Social Services. As a consequence of these meetings, and others chaired by the majority leader of the county legislature, differences were aired and expectations and limits defined. As the contract agency, the new program ultimately agreed to accept referrals from the local DSS without an additional assessment and to give up its authority to screen out potential failures. Dramatic increases in the level of referrals from DSS followed soon after.

In 1986 the Foster Care Prevention and Intervention Program worked with 51 families and 91 children, averting 7,624 potential client days of care in out-of-home settings. Savings to the county totaled about $500,000. In 1987, 14,835 days of out-of-home placement were averted, with the saving estimated at more than $1 million. Also, in 1986 and 1987 the program worked with a total of seventy-three children on the verge of formally entering the juvenile-justice system as a result of approaches to the Family Court by parents or school officials. More than 60 percent of these children were successfully diverted.

The Intake and Coordination unit of CCS faced similar difficulties. It functions to tie together educational, court-related, mental-health, and social-services records and to assess children using a uniform assessment instrument. Although Probation, Mental Health, and DSS participated in designing its intake assessment instrument, they resisted the rejection of cases by the agency based on its use. There were also differences concerning turnaround time on the assessment of cases referred for intensive services and the locus of responsibility for these cases while the assessment was being done. Much time and experience were needed before a realistic set of mutual expectations in these areas was established.

In 1986, 175 cases were assessed by the two caseworkers in this unit; in 1987 there were 191. If the family needs long-term intensive services, referrals are made to the FPI or to other public or private service providers. The unit often becomes an advocate for alternative school placements for children or a service provider for those who might otherwise fall between the cracks of the system.

In one case, for example, a teenager being released from the hospital and not welcome at home was helped to find a room and a job. The agency continues to provide oversight and backing while he supports himself and continues to live in the community. To cite another example, the mother of an emotionally disturbed preschool boy claimed she could not deal with him around the clock during the three-week period between summer school and the beginning of the school year. It appeared that she would sign him voluntarily into care. The agency acted immediately to contract with three teacher aides from the child's special school for assistance. The rate paid was significantly higher than the approved day-care rate, but the mother kept custody of the child.

The Pre-School Handicapped Children's Program of CCS faced the fewest start-up difficulties. The mandate from the county legislature was clear: ensure that the children receiving services were indeed eligible for them.

In consultation with providing agencies, eligibility criteria that met the requirements of federal law were established. The psychologist in charge developed procedural guidelines and a uniform design for the submission of evaluative material. A Committee on Pre-School Special Education (CPSE) was established, modeled on similar committees used in the public schools, and twelve site visits to schools were made. Finally, in response to the concern that once children were placed in the system they became "lost" in it, even if services were no longer needed or alternative approaches were appropriate in new circumstances, procedures were devised for the yearly review of children petitioning to continue in special education.

Between July 1986 and February 1987, the CPSE reviewed evaluations and made recommendations to Family Court concerning eighty-nine children, marking the first time a county agency had taken any role in determining the access of children for services. For the 1987–88 school year, 129 new applicants for services were assessed, and the records of 98 children continuing in preschool were examined under the new annual review process.

A major innovation in 1988 was the establishment of a pilot demonstration project, fully funded locally, to provide low-cost services for young children who were not found to be educationally handicapped but who were at great risk of developing learning or emotional problems as a consequence of their family situations. The county again responded to the argument that spending small sums now—up to $50,000 in 1988—would avoid much larger costs later.

Close monitoring seems to have led to a leveling of the demand in Ulster County for preschool handicapped children's services, while ensuring that those truly in need are well served. As in every area, however, more remains to be done—and not all decision making is likely to be consensual. There appear to be major battles ahead, for example, concerning standardization of fee schedules for services. The assessment component allows Coordinated Children's Services to hire a speech therapist, a pediatric nurse, a psychiatric social worker, and a special educator to review preschool children for special education and related services, providing a source of expertise outside the provider agencies without incurring the cost of full-time staff. It also permits the purchase of comprehensive examinations of children when they are necessary for diagnoses and treatment planning, sometimes avoiding the cost of having these children placed in temporary residence outside the county. Neurological, medical, psychological, and educational examinations have been done with assessment funds. In the first six months of 1988, four children were assessed, up from three in 1987 and one in 1986.

The Continuing Effort

In early 1988, representatives of the state DSS met with Ulster's CCS administrator, program staff, social-services staff, and the county Probation and Mental Health directors to review the first two years' achievements, discuss formal evaluation, and revise goals in light of experience. As a result of these meetings, the New York Council on Children and Families was asked to conduct a comprehensive program evaluation, based on methods developed to analyze other prevention programs in the state. But even before this evaluation is undertaken, the state DSS has formally expressed considerable satisfaction with Ulster's effort to date, and the council has begun to hold out the county's cooperative effort in service delivery and planning as a model to other counties across the state.

Interdepartmental cooperative efforts to serve children have continued and have been extended to include private not-for-profits and public schools. In 1988, with Ulster United Way as the lead agency and with public and private agencies cooperating in preparing the grant application, the county secured three years of funding from the state DSS for a program addressing family violence. In that same year, with the support of county and voluntary agencies, Ulster BOCES and the county's school districts received maximum funding from the State Education Department in three categories of competitive funding for dropout prevention programs. One of these, the School Community Partnership, was to develop and fund a system for human-services agencies that would serve both school children at risk of dropping out and their families. That had been an early goal of the Task Force on County/School Cooperation.

Success bred success. And these successes had the cumulative effect of raising the consciousness of all agencies serving children — that they were involved in a single enterprise. Goals were common and interrelated, and working together had a synergistic effect.

With this lesson in mind, the public agencies in Ulster County with state-mandated planning responsibilities, encouraged by Governor Mario M. Cuomo's declaration of the "Decade of the Child," decided to put together a comprehensive plan for children and youth. Waivers were sought from state oversight agencies to allow the county to assemble a single plan, based on common sets of data, that would meet all their requirements.

The county's reputation as an innovator in cooperative planning and action helped it obtain these waivers. Further innovation followed. Widespread informal involvement of community leaders in the county planning process was achieved when, under the aegis of the Council on Children and Families, Ulster United Way became one of ten United Way organizations in the state to host a two-day round table on children's issues in October 1988. The United Way director, a former county administrator, used his ties to department heads to link this meeting to their comprehensive planning effort.

While the local planning process was getting under way, the governor appointed a statewide Task Force on Children and Youth to determine how services to children and families could be provided more effectively. The county probation director contacted this task force, both to learn what it had planned and to report on Ulster's initiatives. A visit by the cochairs of that group to the Advisory Board of Coordinated Children's Services followed. As a result, Ulster County was again identified as a leader. It now appears that one of the recommendations of the governor's task force will be that all jurisdictions in the state have a single multiagency plan for children and families.

After a few years, Ulster County's approach has become a model for cooperative planning and cooperative service delivery for children and families. This is important, not because it generates another impressive line on a few professional résumés but because it is another resource that promises to offer additional opportunities for the friends of children in Ulster County better to serve them now and in the future.

Anonymous Children/
Diminished Adults

NAT HENTOFF

In the spring of 1988, a teacher asked me to speak to his class on medical ethics at the Clara Barton High School in Brooklyn, New York. It is a public school, and the student body is predominantly black and Hispanic, with some Asians. I was to concentrate on euthanasia, the treatment — or denial of treatment — to severely handicapped infants, and abortion. "Don't simplify," the teacher said. "Talk to them the way you do to your readers."

Clara Barton is a "theme school." As its name indicates, it has long prepared many of its students for the nursing profession. Others take courses related to different kinds of health services. But all must pass standard high school courses.

What first struck me about the school was the way most of the students carried themselves and spoke, particularly in relation to their teachers. Two months before, I had spent a week in some almost entirely white suburban and rural schools in Pennsylvania. Most of the students there were not so much subdued as detached from their teachers. I had the sense that whatever they really thought about something was communicated only to their peers. To their teachers, most of those students supplied rehearsed responses.

At Clara Barton, however, the students looked directly at the teachers when they talked, and whether they were joking or in serious negotiation about an assignment, they were fully involved in the conversation. Their bearing showed considerable self-respect, not arrogance. They were comfortable with themselves, and so they were with others, including adults.

The teachers knew the names of not only the students in their own classes (which is not always the case in large schools), but they knew the names of many of the other kids as well. I talked to a number of the faculty, and while there were the customary grumblings about bizarrely misrouted supplies and other tales of surreal behavior by the apparatchiks at the board of education, they liked being at Clara Barton. They were actually teaching, not just trying to keep order.

In the class of medical ethics, I did not simplify. Then came the questions and rebuttals. I've talked on Baby Does, euthanasia, and abortion to a wide range of groups around the country, and the questions from those high school students were, in many instances, the most challenging I have dealt with. And they wanted more dialogue. Even after the bell rang, the students continued asking questions until we had to make room for the next class.

When I left the school, I noticed four cops and a squad car across the street, where another public high school — Prospect Heights — is located. By contrast with Clara Barton, where the attendance rate is in the high 90s, Prospect Heights is a prototypical urban school sinking into quicksand. Low attendance, a high dropout rate, and an atmosphere of aimlessness. The police were there every day, I was told, because some of the students at Prospect Heights would otherwise prey on those from Clara Barton or on their fellow students.

Why was Clara Barton different? The students in the two schools come from similar backgrounds. And the environs of the schools include brisk entrepreneurs of crack and other heavy distractions from study.

One clear reason for the difference is that the students at Clara Barton know why they are in school. They have a fair idea of how school connects with what they want to do after they finish high school. And they are not anonymous. With a good sense of themselves because they know where they are going, they make it easier for the teachers to know and remember who they are.

Across the street, at Prospect Heights High School — as at many other schools across the country — the students who have not dropped out are serving time. Their names may be known to many of their teachers, but *they* aren't known. These students feel, accurately, that they are seen as being interchangeable with the other underachieving or nonachieving residents of this detention center.

Those who drop out are not missed, because their presence was barely felt when they were intermittently in class. Over the years, in reporting on schools, I have asked administrators in all the districts I have visited whether they keep track of dropouts, but I have yet to find a district that persistently does so. They do not want to be reminded of their failures.

Remembered, at least, are those who "act out"— if they do enough damage to persons or property. The others, who eventually disappear, are ghosts — frightened ghosts. Years ago, at what was then Benjamin Franklin High School in New York, I taught a class composed mostly of ghosts. It was a small class because the truancy rate at the high school was enormous. So was the ultimate dropout rate. Of those who entered the ninth grade, only 7 percent were graduated four years later.

In one of the class sessions, I read and discussed with them a fairly wide range of poetry — from Emily Dickinson to William Carlos Williams. This was in direct contradiction of the advice I had received from their regular teacher. "They are not interested in reading," she had told me, "or in thinking, for that matter. Just amuse them, and if you can't do that, tell them to write something, and read your newspaper."

I had discovered, however, that my students were interested in a lot of things. During one class, as we went through the history of the labor movement, the Puerto

Rican boys at the back of the room who professed to speak no English moved to the front when we began drawing up a list of demands for collective bargaining between the students and the principal.

After the class in which I had read and we had discussed some poetry, an extremely shy young woman came up and asked if I could tell her a little more about this Emily Dickinson. She did not say it then, but later she told me that it was weird — she felt some of the things that Emily Dickinson had felt so long ago. And very tentatively, she handed me some of her poems. She had never shown any of them to anyone in any school she had attended. She had not thought that anyone would believe she could write poems.

The Benjamin Franklin High School no longer exists under that name. Some years ago, it was metamorphosed into the Manhattan Center for Science and Mathematics. The teachers, the principal, and the community superintendent have made it a special school like the Bronx High School of Science. The students who come know why they are there, and no ghosts are allowed. That is, students are not permitted to become anonymous.

The attendance rate is very high, practically everyone is graduated, and nearly all go on to college. These students come from the same kinds of homes and "mean streets"— streets that are getting meaner by the year — as those who went to Benjamin Franklin High School. The latter were stereotyped, and gradually they became those stereotypes. But the students at the Manhattan Center for Science and Mathematics define themselves.

Stereotyping is hardly limited to poor blacks and Hispanics. I learned that again in the spring of 1988, when I met with all-white classes in a number of middle schools and high schools in rural and suburban Pennsylvania. I was there to tell them about the Bill of Rights and the Fourteenth Amendment. Like adults, most students are quite ignorant of their own rights and liberties — let alone anyone else's.

In one town, school personnel told me not to expect much in one of the high schools I would be visiting during the afternoon. Many of those students lived in trailer camps and some even in homes with dirt floors. They were not very verbal, I was warned, and, well, they just were not up to something like the Constitution. On the other hand, the school I would be in this particular morning had students whose fathers were executives of one sort or another. These students went to museums in Philadelphia with their parents. I should really enjoy these sessions.

It worked the other way around. For the most part, the students who went to the museums were certainly articulate but they were glib, more interested in showing how voluble they were than in what we were actually discussing. In the other school, where the teachers had warned me to expect almost no questions, we had the most spirited exchange during my visits to those Pennsylvania classrooms.

Their teachers wondered what had got into those students.

There are journalists who would know. Since the late 1960s, American public schools — with notable exceptions — have condemned more and more students to marginal lives. At the same time, however, newspaper reporting about schools in some cities has become much more knowledgeable and trenchant. In my experience, one can learn more about what works and what does not work from such newspapers as the *New York Daily News* and the *Chicago Tribune* than from many academic journals of education.

In May 1988, for instance, the *Chicago Tribune* published a series called "Chicago Schools: 'Worst in America.'" (The previous year, on November 7, the *New York Times* reported that Secretary of Education William Bennett had said that "forty-six percent of Chicago teachers send their children to private schools. The people who know the product best send their children elsewhere."

Tribune reporter Bonita Brodt made the following observations. They are not new. Dr. Kenneth Clark, among others, has been saying these things for years. But they are not believed by many teachers, by many principals, by many school boards, and by many legislators.

Brodt took due and vivid note of the wearying obstacles to teaching in urban schools, particularly with regard to class size. (In some Chicago schoolrooms, there are as many as thirty-nine children.) But she also emphasized:

> While it is true that children from low-income families can pose a challenge to teachers, particularly when they live in an isolated world where lessons taught might not be reinforced in the home, in a truer sense, many of these children are not that much different from children in any other school.

> They respond to teachers they feel care and respect them. . . . They challenge authority from time to time. . . . "She [the teacher] thinks we're stupid. She gives us all the answers. She don't know how to make us act, so we tear up the place." . . .

> The system deals with the most difficult children by evaluating them and using red ink to stamp their permanent record cards with the words "Child Study." The children are labeled "B–D" for behavior-disorder and placed in special classrooms.

> This is much different from the way the system deals with teachers who have trouble in school. It tolerates them and even compensates for the weaknesses.

Projects That Promise and Sometimes Deliver

During the 1960s, Paul Goodman, whose book about schooling, *Growing Up Absurd*, had considerable currency, invited me to accompany him to a New York City Council meeting on "Whither The Schools?" In the course of his testimony, Goodman told the legislators, "Just about every innovation in teaching and learning has been tried in the New York City school system — *once*." If it worked, it was not extended to other schools. If it did not work, not much effort was made to find out why.

Since then, some ideas have had positive effects and even changed some students' lives. But these innovations are not often exported. It's as if each town or city has to invent the wheel in its own time — if ever.

Consider Boston's Project Promise, begun by the city's superintendent of schools, Laval Wilson. I went to public school in Boston during the 1930s and 1940s; and while there were ineffective teachers and failing schools then, there was nothing like the desolation in many of Boston's classrooms now. The dropout rate is almost 50 percent, and the daily attendance rate is about the same.

Project Promise focuses on students likely to remove themselves from the school system, and, of all things, it gives them a third more school hours a week — including three hours of classes on Saturdays. In the Roxbury section of Boston, where I grew up, Mary Grassa O'Neill, principal of the Timilty Middle School, told Richard Louv of the Copley News Service (October 11, 1987): "By state law, we couldn't make students come in on Saturday, but 90 percent of our students show up on Saturday. We sold parents this idea by telling them it was the chance of a lifetime — this is what expensive private schools do, but you're going to get it free!"

While the parents may have been sold on the idea, the students would not have kept giving up free time unless the project made them feel differently about themselves. They were being told they were not hopelessly dumb. They were being told that the school *did* care whether they dropped out or not. They were being told that they were expected to be able to do the work — with this push. Such support is part of what makes the difference between anonymous children and those who feel they belong in school.

Boston's Project Promise also works with many children because it does something as elemental as providing everyone in a class with his or her own book. Jeff Cohen, a faculty member at the Timilty School for eighteen years, says: "A few years ago we didn't have enough math texts for every student. They had to hand their books in at the end of class. After Timilty was targeted for Project Promise, we started getting books. I remember the surprise on my students' faces when I told them that they could actually take the textbooks home."

Many of the schools in Boston, however, look as if they were built in Sam Adams's time and have been used heavily ever since, as do many urban schools elsewhere in the country.

No office or factory would be allowed to be in the condition of many American schools. Productivity would be impaired, and worker morale would be greatly lowered. But the enterprise of educating children is permitted to take place in buildings where chunks of ceilings are missing, bathrooms do not work, and rodents audit classes.

Students in those schools hardly get the sense that education is valued or that *they* are valued. And the same message, of course, is delivered to the parents.

In nearly all the books and other reminiscences of the "participatory democracy"— often not democratic at all — of the 1960s, there is practically no mention of a phenomenon of the period that gave hope to a goodly number of parents and children. Moved by the spirit and accomplishments of the civil-rights "revolution," many parents extended their demands for a reasonably decent way of life to the schools that kept failing their children.

One parent at a New York City Board of Education meeting I was covering rose in anger and desperation. I later found out he had been a school dropout in the South, came north, worked at a string of menial jobs, and wound up being attached to a machine in a factory—a job that paid him $90 a week. He had one child, and each year she fell further and further behind in school.

The father stared at the variously attentive members of the school board. "You people," he said, "operate a goddamn monopoly, like the telephone company. I got no choice where I send my child to school. I can only send her where it's free. And she's not learning. Damn it, that's *your* responsibility, it's the principal's responsibility, it's the teacher's responsibility, that she's not learning."

There was no answer from the board.

"When you fail, when everybody fails my child," the father's voice had become hoarse with grief and frustration, "what happens? Nothing. Nobody gets fired. Nothing happens to nobody except my child."

He never got a reply from the board of education.

Parents began to hold their own meetings about education, and they began to organize, at first, for integrated schools. But they soon found out that *Brown v. Board of Education* would work in most big cities only if suburban school districts were also included in the mix, and nobody in power—including the Supreme Court—wanted to go that far. So minority children became a majority in most schools, and, in some, there were no whites at all. Racial isolation is now part of the learning process for a considerable number of black students.

Parents went on to demand more black and Hispanic teachers, decentralization, community control of schools, one book per child, supplies that arrive before the middle of the year, and accountability. If a principal or a teacher were failing, parents thought they ought to be sent elsewhere, preferably out of the profession.

Some of these demands were politically unrealistic and, for that matter, undesirable. Community control could—and in some cases did—end up in rampant majoritarianism, with no place and no due process for heretics. But some of the demands made sense and could begin to bring sense to a system that mystified and ultimately paralyzed far too many of its clients.

Much of this parental hope that the schools can be transformed has evaporated. The system is so formidable a foe that it recalls those ancient fables of extraordinarily wily monsters. Harvey Scribner, a former chancellor of the New York City school system, described his job as dealing with a giant octopus. "You think you've got a handle on it," he would say, "but then all of a sudden, that tentacle breaks off, and twenty more take its place."

There are still parents' groups, however, trying to get hold of the octopus. And that kind of action is continually important—although some educators who abstractly lament the lack of parental involvement are not that pleased when parent activists actually appear in their offices.

Parents should, of course, help with their child's homework or at least make sure it gets done, but they convey a different kind of support to a child when they care enough to come to the school to try to change the odds against the student.

For instance, in a number of cities and some states, parents have organized to end corporal punishment in the schools. Only two allegedly advanced nations continue to allow the legal beating of school children as an "educational tool." One is South Africa; the other, the United States. Yet in practically all the books and monographs on the deficiencies of schooling in America, corporal punishment is hardly ever mentioned. Children who are physically abused in this way by teachers and principals — some to the extent of hospitalization — are blacks, Hispanics, and poor whites. It is a lesson in special education that stays with them for the rest of their lives.

And at least one group of parents — in alliance with teachers' unions — is engaged in a lawsuit against the octopus that should be widely emulated. In three Ohio school districts, class-action suits have been filed charging that the board of education has allowed class sizes to rise above state standards.

Meanwhile, certain neighborhoods are becoming active again. In the February 8, 1988, *New York Daily News*, Juan Gonzales writes of Community School District 6 in Washington Heights, where 80 percent of the public-school children are Hispanic, most of them Dominican. "It is," Gonzales notes, "the sixth poorest school district in terms of family income, has the lowest reading scores and is the most overcrowded. Its children have the city's second highest hospital emergency room use rate, because so many have no medical insurance or private physicians."

It is hardly news that a child who is inadequately fed or has a health problem is going to have trouble learning in school. In Washington Heights, parents and professionals in the community formed the North Manhattan Health Action Group, which discovered, as Gonzales reports:

"On average, Department of Health nurses assigned once a week to the district's overcrowded schools have about six minutes per child to do physical examinations, review records, meet with parents and teachers, make referrals and follow up.

"Of more than 1,500 pupils with vision problems, 74 percent never got follow up care."

The parents have gone on to pressure members of the New York City Council and the state legislature to act on the realization that more funds for health care are an essential corollary to the budget for education.

Principals — the head teachers, as they used to be called — should be chosen according to how well they know the needs of the children in their schools. Health needs, for example. And that test ought to include, of course, the extent to which they are willing to help meet those needs. To such principals, the students will not be anonymous.

More than twenty years ago, I came to know a principal in Harlem who taught me what a principal can be. It was a time when white principals were in mounting disfavor in Harlem and other black neighborhoods. But many Harlem parents told me that Elliott Shapiro, who was in charge of an elementary school, was an exception.

"In Harlem," a member of the Harlem Parents Committee said, "we either get principals who consider their work as just a job, a certain number of hours a week to be filled, or occasionally we get a liberal. The liberal feels he must help the heathen, but since he does indeed see the children as heathen, his attitude precludes his being of any help. Elliott sees them as children, and he has a strong sense of the importance — and individuality — of each one of them."

And Elliott Shapiro knew more about those children's lives than their scores in school. One afternoon, as we walked about the neighborhood — where he was a familiar presence — Shapiro was telling me about the housing conditions of some of the students:

"Across the street a house built for eight families has forty-five. Next door there are two houses with serious heating problems. Two winters ago, I spent hours trying to track down the owner, and finally I told the man who said he was only the agent that if heat weren't provided, there'd be a picket line of teachers and me. There was heat for the rest of the winter.

"Another time for another building, we found someone in the mayor's office who was vulnerable to picketing and he arranged for the city to take that building over. Nonetheless, the furnace remained broken, and it took us fifteen days of constant pressure to get it fixed. This was in the dead of winter with people sick in the building."

Although he was white, Elliott Shapiro was considered a member of that community, and that too was part of the learning process for the children in his school.

Schools That Open Their Windows to the Neighborhood

Deborah Meier, first a teacher and now head of Central Park East Schools in central Harlem, is an educator of such distinction that she is a MacArthur Grant Award winner. Speaking of the surge of apparent interest in education in the past four or five years, she says:

"I think we are in fashion. The question is, can we make use of what probably is a brief moment? It is enormously important that we think carefully about what it is that is most important to say during this period and try to push for a few of what we think are the most significant issues."

Her list includes smaller schools. ("The Norwegians passed a law that no school should be larger than 450. I would like to see that law passed here.")

She agrees with Paul Goodman, as I do, that no school should be so large that the principal does not know every child in it. And in a school of humane size, the child would know — and could therefore get help from — all the teachers, not just his or her own.

In this "brief moment," when public attention is more or less focused on education, another highly significant issue is the quality and scope of school leadership that ought to be the standard for all schools. This level of leadership should not only make every child justly confident of his or her ability to learn but also open the doors and windows of the school so that both children and adults can feel that education is indivisible — is a mutual process.

Many of the older school buildings look like the fortresses they were and still are. Once someone had graduated from such a redoubt, he or she seldom, if ever, returned — except years later, perhaps, as a parent. A parent and an outsider. They would come on parents' night or when their progeny was in trouble. But they do not feel welcome there. It is a school, and they are grown up.

This is a needless separation. For years, Herman Badillo, a former congressman from the Bronx, has been advocating schools that would be open nights, Saturdays, and summers, so that parents could take courses in the evening or on the weekend. Courses in English for parents newly arrived from other countries would be offered, as well as many others.

A partial example, already in existence, was described by Deirdre Carmody in the October 26, 1987, *New York Times.* New York State's Commissioner of Education Thomas Sobol had been much impressed by "his visit to an elementary school in Brooklyn, which stays open until early evening. He said he was impressed by seeing working parents who normally would be unable to pick up their children come to the school and be told, for instance, that their child needed glasses.

"'Not only was that school serving breakfast and lunch, but, bless me, supper too, at 5:30 in the afternoon.'"

Partially as a result of that experience, Sobol has decided on a pilot program that will turn ten elementary schools in poor neighborhoods in New York State into year-round centers of education open from early in the morning until evening seven days a week. There will be tutoring and weekend activities for parents as well as children. The idea lends itself to a considerable number of variations. In any case, for children in that kind of school the key advantage is that it will be much harder to feel anonymous—not fitting in and being afraid.

For many children, especially those in urban schools, fear is an integral part of each day—fear of being hopelessly dumb forever, or fear, in some cases, of being in enemy territory. To many children, everywhere is enemy territory. For even more, the fear is that there is no one to talk to, no one to help them make sense of their lives.

One of the most extraordinarily effective teachers I have ever seen was John Simon, who worked on Manhattan's West Side with children who had so baffled and so infuriated their principals that they were sent to Simon and his Dome Project in the basement of All Angels Church. Over much of a year, I watched him turn what one police official had called "feral youth" into readers, writers, and, in some cases, college students.

He told me one day about the basis of his "method." There is nothing revolutionary about it, nor does it require a charismatic teacher. It does require time for a teacher to be able to concentrate on those children who need someone to *hear* them. And by no means am I speaking only of children already characterized as "feral."

"First of all," John Simon told me, "you have to listen. When I start working with a child I don't know too well, I spend a lot of time listening to him before I try to suggest a course of study. I have never fallen in with that dumb notion that you have to start 'teaching' from the very first day of class—as if teaching is something that happens in a vacuum without having to take account of where each student is, in his head, on that first day of class.

"Where he is and where he's been. So I listen until I have a sense of his particular problems, and then we work together to find out how to resolve them. That way he's already learning. He's analyzing his own problems."

And the teacher then knows how and where to begin. "That kind of preliminary listening," Simon adds, "can reveal all kinds of signals. Take reading. In our class, long before we put a book in a student's hand, we talk with him. We listen to determine the kid's speech patterns, his dialect, and his idiolect. We listen for signs of aural confusion, for hints as to how good or how poor the student's ear is. We listen to find out if he knows many or few words, if he can express himself easily or gets frustrated trying to tell a simple story. That way we stay close to the actual source of the student's difficulty."

That way, the student knows there is a reason for him or her to be there.

During a quarter century of observing in schools, I have learned that the style of a teacher or principal is far less important than whether he or she sees each child distinctly. I have seen quasi-Summerhillian teachers infatuated with theory but ignorant of what children are actually trying to say to them. I remember a mathematics teacher in Harlem who conducted his class like a Marine drill sergeant but who also knew the particular insecurities and strengths of every child in the room — and they were well aware that he knew. They were poor and black, he was white, and he was convinced that all of them could do the work. And they did.

Educational Malpractice

For all the monographs and studies and reforms, schools still create many more failures than even moderate successes. In 1975, James A. Harris, then president of the National Education Association, testified before the Senate Subcommittee on Juvenile Delinquency that 23 percent of all the school children in the country were failing to graduate. And of those who did graduate, many were functional illiterates. These statistics included many white students.

"If 23 percent of anything else failed," Harris added, "if 23 percent of the automobiles did not run, 23 percent of the buildings fell down, 23 percent of stuffed ham spoiled—we'd look at the producer."

The national dropout rate is now at least 25 percent. This estimate is conservative, I would say, if other systems cook their figures the way New York City does, where well over 50 percent of black students and even more Hispanic students drop out.

What has not changed is the lack of outrage against the producers of this much spoiled human material. In the spring of 1988, the Carnegie Foundation for the Advancement of Teaching issued a report on the unrelentingly harsh bleakness of many urban schools. In one Chicago school, only 10 percent of the tenth graders were competent readers. The dropout rate in one Los Angeles school was 70 percent. In a Cleveland high school, the report noted, "lavatories for students have no light bulbs, the stalls have no doors and there is no toilet paper in the dispensers."

Ernest Boyer, president of the foundation and writer of most of the report, told the *New York Times* on March 16, 1988: "Teachers and principals feel powerless against the huge frustrating school bureaucracy, and students feel anonymous. No one notices if they drop out because no one noticed when they dropped in."

Like the president of the National Education Association in 1975, the writer of the 1988 Carnegie report was amazed that these conditions are so taken for granted:

"No other crisis—a flood, a health epidemic, a garbage strike or even snow removal—would be as calmly accepted without full-scale emergency intervention."

Yet making schools work is no mystery. There are still teachers who know how to listen. Ways have been found by administrators and teachers to make some classes smaller and even to create schools within the school. Students who were convinced that they were irretrievably dumb have triumphantly found out they were wrong.

So why are many millions of anonymous children still slogging through or dropping out of the schools? Because most principals and most teachers can safely allow this enormous waste of mind and spirit to continue.

The principal of the school at St. Brides Correctional Center in Chesapeake, Virginia, said in 1986: "We have some [inmates] who have high school diplomas but still are not able to read at the sixth-grade level, which is a sad commentary on their being pushed through school, right on through, until they got their diplomas."

There are many high school graduates who do not read above the sixth-grade level. In the 1960s and 1970s, a few of them tried to sue the school systems that had given them worthless diplomas. They claimed to have been the victims of educational malpractice.

I covered some of those cases, and I particularly remember a young man from Long Island, New York, who, on graduation from high school, could not read an employment application. He could not even read a restaurant menu. His mother told me she had been complaining to school authorities for years, and she had always been told that the boy was "coming right along."

When the lawsuit was filed, the school district did not claim anything was inherently wrong with the boy that made it impossible to teach him to read. They had just done the best they could, they said. But why was he passed along to the next grade year after year without being able to read? They had done the best they could, they said.

The New York State Court of Appeals—the state's highest judicial body—dismissed the case. There were two reasons, which had been echoed by other courts around the country confronted by claims of educational malpractice.

First, if the courts were to second-guess the professional judgments of public-school educators and administrators, the floodgates would open. Hordes of public-school graduates, unhappy with the damage done to them in their classes, would haul school districts and school personnel into court. Second, according to the courts, education is a complex and often delicate process beyond the ken of jurists.

School professionals often say that education is more an art than a science. I once told an appellate judge, however, that when a youngster has been moved up and through each grade until graduation and still cannot read, there is nothing delicate or artistically complex involved in that shoddy process. And "the system" is not to blame. Specific individuals are.

The judge, looking somewhat like Lewis Carroll's walrus on the briny beach as he ate the little oysters he had invited to join him, told me, "I deeply sympathize. I really do." But he went on to dismiss just such a case.

Marcia Robinson Lowry, director of the American Civil Liberties Union's Children's Rights Project, has been the losing lawyer in some of these lawsuits. But she is unbowed. The courts, she keeps pointing out, deal with delicate and complex decision making that is at the core of medical- and legal-malpractice suits. "It is no more difficult," she says, "to try to show that a teacher or a school administrator has not complied with professional standards than it is to make that case against a doctor or an attorney."

Furthermore, students who have been deprived of the very foundation of an education — being able to read — have constitutional grounds for suing. When the state undertakes to provide an education in its public schools, the state is then required to do just that. It is not required to provide the best possible education, but under the due process clause of the Fourteenth Amendment, it must give each child a reasonably adequate education. That is, due process of law cannot be just a promise.

Under the Fourteenth Amendment, moreover, no state can "deprive any person of life, liberty, or property, without due process of law." In agreeing to confer the benefit of education on its youngest residents, the state thereby creates a constitutionally protected property right. But when a high school graduate can't read, that property right has become valueless.

If a few courts throughout the country would finally recognize that educational malpractice can be as real and as severely damaging as medical malpractice, the resulting money verdicts would likely bring about more pervasive attention to each child in the schools than all the hortatory books and reports on the chronic crisis.

A teacher told me that he had allowed a senior who read on a sixth-grade level to graduate. "She would have been so humiliated if I hadn't let her go," he explained. Instead, she will be humiliated for the rest of her life, but there is nothing negative on the teacher's record or on that of his principal.

Overcoming School Failure:
A Vision for the Future

DOROTHY KERZNER LIPSKY
ALAN GARTNER

It is commonplace to note that today's schools are not only the product of an earlier era but are also outmoded in calendar, schedule, design, and structure for both children and adults. In recent years, the most notable response to such concerns has been state officials' action to raise requirements and to increase assessment activities. While appropriate, such reforms are too limited and too late. Rather, the schools need urgently to prevent failure and to develop better ways to meet the needs of students, teachers, parents, and the community.

It is clear that the schools of yesterday are not suitable for today. The demands made on the schools, the context in which they operate, and the circumstances of those who attend them, each and together require not minor changes but a new paradigm, that is, new organization and activities derived from new conceptualizations of learning and schooling. Tom Joe has presented the rationale for a comprehensive service-system approach to meet the full range of youth's needs.[1] The value of that approach is granted, but the approach here envisions a unitary system.

The bases of this system take into account changes that have occurred in the society at large. These include changes in the United States's place in the world economy, the United States labor force, and the composition and structure of American families.

The United States's place in the world economy has changed dramatically. For example:

• From the dominant creditor nation, the United States is now by far the world's leading debtor.

• In 1946, the United States produced 80 percent of all passenger cars in the world; it now produces barely a quarter of them.[2]

The United States labor force has also changed significantly. For example:

• In 1948, the United States labor force had an equal number of goods-producing and services-producing workers, and today the latter group is more than twice the former.

• Between 1970 and 1986, the percentage of mothers of children under eighteen years of age who were in the work force increased from 39 percent to 58 percent; for those with children under the age of five, the increase was from 29 percent to 50 percent.[3]

• A fifth of the nation's work force, 23 million persons, read at no better than an eighth-grade level, while "studies show that 70 percent of the reading material in a cross section of jobs nationally is written for a comprehension level of at least ninth grade."[4]

And the composition and structure of American families have changed. For example:

• In the past quarter of a century, six of ten American families consisted of a working father, a stay-at-home mother, and two or more children; this is now true of barely one in twenty families.[5]

• The median income of families with children dropped (in constant dollars) between 1975 and 1985 for all families, and especially for mother-only families. And the percentage of children under age eighteen living in poverty grew between 1970 and 1985, from 14 percent to 20 percent; this growth was true for all racial and ethnic groups.[6]

• From 1970 to 1985, the birthrate for unmarried minority teenagers decreased from 91 births per 1,000 to 79. The birthrate for white unmarried teenagers nearly doubled during the same period, to 21 births per 1,000.[7]

• Young people in their twenties are living with their parents longer, marrying later, and earning less money in proportion to older workers than was the case ten to twenty years ago.[8]

These economic and demographic changes require a response by the schools. In the past it was possible to see school failure as acceptable — there would be good or marginal work for those without an education — and it affected only a small and exceptional portion of the population. But the work and citizenship demands of the present no longer make such failure acceptable. Not only are greater demands facing workers, but also the percentage of youth in the labor force is shrinking and those remaining in it need to be more productive. The chief executive officer of Xerox Corporation, David T. Kearns, has pointed out that successful companies pay most attention to the customers who do not continue, the "dropout." Yet schools, he noted, suffer no consequence when students drop out; in fact, they are likely to hold the student at fault.[9] And the demographics point to a new norm. For example, in the fall of 1988, more than half of the enrollment in California public schools was for the first time "minority." California is now the fourth state where this is true, and it is a harbinger of changing demographics; in 1985, nationally, 29 percent of students under seventeen years of age were nonwhite or of Spanish-origin. By the year 2000, it is expected that they will constitute 34 percent of this age group.

The American people are willing to pay for improved schools. According to the annual poll of attitudes toward public schools sponsored by Phi Delta Kappa and conducted by the American Institute of Public Opinion, 64 percent of those surveyed said they would pay higher taxes to improve schools, an increase of 6 percent from 1983; the figure for parents of public-school children was 73 percent. And among all those surveyed, 88 percent said developing the best education system in the world is very important to the country's future, while only 65 percent said that about improving industrial production and 47 percent for developing a strong military.[10]

New Conceptualizations

It is not that schools have simply excluded students now called "at risk." Historically, a series of mandates has limited outright exclusion of children from schooling: the compulsory-attendance laws at the turn of the century, the child-labor laws of the 1920s and 1930s, *Brown* and subsequent school-desegregation cases, the Education of All Handicapped Children Act (P.L. 94-142) in 1975, and the *Lau* decision concerning the Limited English Proficient. Together, these actions provide a framework of mandates to include all students. In reality, however, the education of youth has become one of two systems—an ever-narrowing mainstream for some and various "alternatives" for a growing number of at-risk youth. Commenting on the first stage of the current school-reform efforts, Harold C. Hodgkinson pointed out that "virtually no state passed 'reform' legislation that contained specific plans to provide remediation to those who did not meet the higher standards on the first try—thus, almost all states were willing to have a higher drop-out rate from secondary schools in their state, even though the economic (leaving out the social) costs of this position will be very high indeed."[11] Hodgkinson noted that the more recent reform efforts have begun to address the needs of those who do not meet the standard, yet they fail to heed Benjamin Bloom's finding that "among the truly excellent performers in a wide range of fields from sports to music, natural talent is less of a factor than hard work and persistence."[12] This conforms with findings from studies of Japanese education in which parents think one works for success, in contrast to the American belief that it is ability or luck.[13] Hodgkinson's conclusion is that if the United States's goal "is to have all students meeting the higher standards," then Americans have not behaved as if they shared this ideal.[14]

And even when students stay in school, complete the regular programs, and graduate, their education is often inferior. For example, a study of high schools in New York City, Chicago, Philadelphia, and Boston documented the tracking that separates students. It reported that barely a third of the graduates read above the national average. A quarter of the graduates read below the ninth-grade level. Indeed, only a fifth of the entering class of 1984 both graduated and read above the national average. In a study for a business group in Minnesota, a state with "good" school systems and high percentages of high-school graduates, Howard Berman reported that among the graduates there is a persistent problem of illiteracy and a failure to learn to reason or to think creatively.[15]

The methods of exclusion are numerous, drawn from a long history involving what Joseph L. Tropea has nicely labeled "backstage efforts" to maintain order.[16] In urban school systems, despite compulsory attendance laws, it is not uncommon for as many as a third of the high-school students enrolled to be absent on any given day. And among growing numbers of the homeless and immigrant families, children are often not even enrolled. Albert Shanker, urging candor as to school failure, has written: "If you're real lenient, you might say we're educating 40 percent of our students. If you're real strict, maybe 10-20 percent. But no one could soberly claim that we're educating more than 50 percent."[17]

For those enrolled, there are designs that extrude some and separate and segregate others. The reform focus on so-called raised standards without a commitment to provide necessary additional services and assistance results in an increase in failures and those labeled "school dropouts." And those not forced out by failure — ascribed to the student but more often the school's — may be "pushed out" by the school culture that is hostile to many students.

But the most pernicious of these designs is the establishment of special services — separate curricula, programs, and classes. While done in the name of responding to special needs of students, they are rarely effective except in their segregating function. In New York City, for example, with an overall school population of nearly a million pupils, more than 100,000 students are in special-education programs, over 310,000 in federal and state remedial programs, and some 73,000 in the mislabeled "bilingual education." In sum, nearly half a million students are in separate programs. And in the extremes of such segregation, the city schools, in response to attacks on gay and lesbian students, set up a separate program for them several years ago rather than directly confronting homophobia.

The ostensible purpose of these programs is student benefit, and there is generally talk about returning students, newly strengthened, to the regular program. In truth, this rarely happens. Indeed, recent studies have shown that these programs are designed in ways incongruent with the regular education program — in curriculum, teaching strategies, and scheduling. Thus it is no surprise that for many students referral to these programs is a one-way ticket. Indeed, in special education, return to the mainstream is rarely expected. While the federal Office of Special Education Programs collects a massive amount of data on special education, it does not seek decertification data, that is, information about special-education students who return to the mainstream. In a letter to us, the director of the office wrote: "Thank you for your letter in which you ask about data concerning children who had been certified as handicapped and have returned to regular education. While these are certainly very interesting data you request, these data are not required in State Plans nor has the Office of Special Education Programs collected them in any other survey."[18]

The decision not to collect "interesting data" can conceivably be made for various reasons. For instance, policymakers may think that the data are unimportant, or they may fear the results or believe that the collection process is not worth the potential benefit. Indeed, collecting decertification data might be difficult, and it is likely to show an embarrassingly low level of return to general education. The major reason such data are not collected, however, probably has more to do with beliefs and attitudes — some implicit, some explicit — generally held about the purposes of special education and about special-education students. Indeed, negative beliefs about and attitudes toward students is at the heart of much of what needs to be changed in schools.

For those placed in special-education programs, there is the added benefit for schools that the pupils' test scores are not included in the "report cards" now used to monitor school-system performance. This device mirrors the practice in the 1910s, when concern about students called "laggards" led the schools to establish ungraded special classes whose pupils were not considered in the calculation of school efficiency. Similar disputes occur today in defining "dropouts" and "graduates."

Neither better data nor new definitions of those "at risk," however, will satisfactorily address the problems facing schools. Fundamental changes are needed in school-system goals, the conceptualization of education, and school practices. School systems must first acknowledge the belief that all students can learn and accept the responsibility to ensure that they do. Writing more than sixty years ago, Walter Lippman said, "If a child fails in school and then fails in life, the schools cannot sit back and say: 'You see how accurately I predicted this.' Unless we are to admit that education is essentially impotent, we have to throw back the child's failure at the school, and describe it as a failure not by the child but by the schools."[19]

The Nature of Intelligence

A new conceptualization is required, both as to the nature of intelligence and the characteristics of learning. Rather than viewed along a single dimension, as measured in today's so-called intelligence and achievement tests, there is the concept of multiple forms of intelligence — different ways of knowing and performing. So, too, schools need to break away from present conceptions of learning — many based largely on research about boys alone — and recognize, for example, differences in women's ways of knowing. Instruction that is premised on a single way of comprehension precludes a relativistic understanding that all knowledge is constructed, just as school organization that emphasizes competitiveness penalizes those whose "ethic of caring" stresses respect for others' views over absolutes of right and wrong.[20] Recently, studies about women's way of knowing have pointed out that such discoveries "may concern not just women but others on the margin as well."[21]

So, too, the schools need to expand their ways of knowing beyond narrow reliance on the physical and social sciences to include the arts and humanities. Lous Heshusius has pointed to "the untenability of the separation between fact and value, observer and observed, objectivity and subjectivity [which] are now seen as standing in the way of a fuller understanding of reality."[22] A related point was made by Seymour Sarason, who stated that the assumptions of the dominant scientific model are too reductionist and try to explain too much.[23] This "reductionist thought is . . . mirrored in behavioral objectives that reduce complex human processes to only the most obvious and observable behaviors."[24] Including the insights of artists and humanists would "restore the importance of recognizing and justifying appropriate values as a way of knowing."[25] And teachers would gain a fuller and more encompassing understanding of the range of humanity and human relationships.

The Individual as Learner

Along with a new understanding of intelligence must come new conceptions of learning, which is much more than the outcome of teaching—it is an activity of students. Whatever the roles of other resources—teachers, texts, and other curricular materials—the student is not an empty vessel to be filled but an active producer of his or her own learning.

Sound educational practice must draw from the research that indicates that students have different needs, learn in different ways, and progress at different rates. For some students it is a matter of learning quickly or slowly; for others it is needing first to see the whole and then the parts. Some learn best through listening, and they are advantaged in classrooms dominated, in John Goodlad's term, by "teacher talk"; yet others learn better by seeing, or discussing, or manipulating. The benefits of instruction attuned to student learning styles were the subject of a recent study at ten secondary schools that use a learning-styles instructional approach. These schools have three characteristics in common: (1) the vehicle for teaching and learning is the individual student, with classroom patterns changing with specific tasks or youngsters' preferences; (2) all learning is compatible with the students' assessed learning-style preferences; and (3) students assume major responsibility for learning.

While standard methods—lectures, reading assignments, and quizzes—work for some, different approaches like cooperative learning and computer instruction do so for other students. As Edward Fiske has observed: "Underlying this research is the assumption that, given enough time and the right kind of instruction, almost any student can learn what is expected. The trick is to use the best approach for each student."[26] A further advantage of such an approach is that it does not result in designs that have the consequence (if not the intent) of failing or segregating some in order to benefit others.

Programs of cooperative learning, developed by the Center for Research in Elementary and Middle Schools at the Johns Hopkins University and the Cooperative Learning Center at the University of Minnesota, have demonstrated the capacity to enable students of varying skills to work and learn together and to do so in a way that builds teamwork, now so valued in increasing worker productivity. One of the key features of such designs—students working together—was incorporated in a program to improve the performance of black students in calculus. "Through the regular practice of testing their ideas on others, students will develop the skills of self-criticism essential not only for their development of mathematical sophistication, but for all intellectual growth."[27] Another feature of cooperative learning is the recognition that one can learn by teaching; in other words, in tutoring the tutor may benefit most. This is especially true for students with special-learning needs, whether they are in general education or in programs for the handicapped.

The understanding that students possess multiple intelligences, the recognition that they are the active producers of their own learning, and the use of peer learning models are not simply interesting matters of learning theory or pedagogic practice. They have importance and consequences for the organization of schools and schooling. As Slavin has pointed out, they foster cooperative relationships among students, promote a new level of professionalism and collaboration among teachers, encourage community as well as school-based learning, and could lead to a less hierarchical and bureaucratic school structure.[28] An expression of this is seen in the Key School in Indianapolis. There, a group of teachers, building on Howard Gardner's multiple-intelligences concept, are working collaboratively "to nourish all of the intelligences and to coordinate the diverse forms of information being gathered about all the students."[29]

The Location of the Problem

Current education practice and even much of the reform effort to date operate on a deficit model: it identifies something wrong or missing in the student (or the student's family) when there is a learning or behavior "problem." Such an approach not only "blames the victim" but also identifies causes (such as family structure or poverty) beyond the scope of school effect.

The issue must be framed differently so that the problem is seen as a result of a mismatch between learner needs and the instructional or management system. The new conceptualization sees the child not as a failure but as a learner whose potential is being thwarted by the educational mismatch. Rather than a deficit-based model, it is strength-based, respectful of the student, using what the student knows and can do as the avenue to what needs to be learned.

An area for further expression of respect for students and their parents concerns choice of educational programs, schools, and even districts. There are serious equity issues here — the risk of "creaming" and the potential for differential availability of information on which choices are to be made. Yet the potential benefits warrant careful study of programs now beginning in Chicago and statewide in Minnesota and justify further development of other models. New school-site governance procedures also offer the potential to enhance parental, teacher, and student involvement and responsibility.

For students labeled "handicapped," there is a growing recognition that — at most — they differ in degree, not in kind from other students. This being the case, efforts are increasingly under way to educate them with other students. In some instances, this involves educating various groups of students — those now labeled "mild and moderately handicapped" along with students in remedial programs.

More fundamentally, new conceptualizations of fully integrated models have been put forth. And in districts like Johnson City, New York, and Olympia, Washington, and individual schools in Syracuse, New York, and Riverview, Pennsylvania, the full range of students with disabilities are integrated into a refashioned mainstream. While the particular designs vary, they have two practices in common. The first is the teachers' acceptance of responsibility for a diverse group of students, and the second is the development of classroom organization and instructional strategies that see opportunities, not impediments, in student diversity.

Various general-education reforms espouse inclusiveness of students labeled "handicapped" and recognize the changes necessary in classroom practices, teacher roles, and school organization. These include the reforms proposed by John Goodlad and Theodore Sizer, among others. The more than fifty schools in the Coalition of Essential Schools are implementing some of these ideas. And in a proposal for "bottom up" reform, Albert Shanker has "advocated for more schools which emphasize group learning—teams of students and teachers working together, developing individualized learning plans and dealing with content in ways students can participate more directly."[30]

Parental Roles

Just as the deficit model blames the student, it also blames the parents. Their race, their education, their poverty, or, in special education, their inappropriate response to the child's impairment become the cause of the problem. And when lack of parental involvement is recognized as a problem, most often the school's response is parent education; that is, parents are seen as lacking knowledge that school people have.

A different conceptualization sees parents as partners who not only have legitimate interests in their children's well-being but also possess valuable knowledge. Thus, if training is called for, it is just as appropriate for parents to train school people as it is for school people to train parents. The partnership model recognizes that each group comes to the relationship with different roles, different strengths. Parents' strengths include a permanent commitment to the student, long-term knowledge of the student, knowledge of his or her nonschool behavior, and access to the student outside the school day, as well as their own knowledge, experience, and work. Teachers' strengths include special knowledge of subject matter, child development, and pedagogy; a perspective on and distance from the student; and access to the student during the school day. In working together to build a partnership, teachers and parents need to recognize their shared interests in the student, to acknowledge their different but equal contributions, and to commit themselves to making the partnership work. Doing this gains the benefit described by Herbert J. Walberg, that "cooperative partnerships between home and school can dramatically raise educational productivity."[31]

A Non–Zero–Sum Game

The response to individual differences need not involve the exclusion of some, the extrusion of others, and the "dumbing down" of the curriculum for yet others, in order to produce a few more winners. On the contrary, schools can be organized so that all succeed. Indeed, that is the choice facing the movement for school reform. Will it continue down the current path of marginal change for a few, or will it engage in the work necessary to ensure the dream of public education— both opportunity and achievement for all?

In the current formulation, the choice to be made between equity and excellence is a false choice. The United States cannot afford to neglect either excellence or equity. That it has done so is attested to by an abundance of evidence, most recently in the report of the Commission on Minority Participation in Education and American Life, cochaired by former Presidents Jimmy Carter and Gerald R. Ford:

> America is moving backwards — not forward — in its efforts to achieve the full participation of minority citizens in the life and prosperity of the nation.

> If we allow these disparities to continue, the United States inevitably will suffer a compromised quality of life and a lowered standard of living. . . . In brief, we will find ourselves unable to fulfill the promise of the American dream.[32]

The question, then, is how to organize an educational system to achieve both excellence and equity for all students. A recent report by the Office of Technology Assessment offers a stark expression of the alternatives:

> The system could change in a way that makes learning more productive and fun while allowing teachers more time to spend with individuals as coaches or tutors. It could put more power in the hands of the learner, tailor instruction to each person's level of understanding and learning speed and technique, and make it easier for an individual to learn when instruction is most needed.

> Or, the system could create rigid centralization of course design, mechanical and impersonal instruction, national regulations, and a contraction of choice for both students and instructors.[33]

The issues, therefore, are not merely matters of pedagogy or even educational policy. Rather, the future direction of school reform becomes a question of what type of society is to be built and which values are to be honored.

NOTES

1. Tom Joe, "New Futures for America's Children," in this vol., pp. 214–23.

2. Peter Collier and David Horowitz, *The Fords: An American Epic* (New York: Summit Books, 1987), 419.

3. Select Committee on Children, Youth, and Families, U.S. House of Representatives, *U.S. Children and Their Families: Current Conditions and Recent Trends* (Washington, D.C., 1987), table 7.

4. L.A. Daniels, "Illiteracy Seen as a Threat to U.S. Economic Edge, *New York Times*, 7 Sept. 1988.

5. Harold C. Hodgkinson, *All One System: Demographics of Education, Kindergarten Through Graduate School* (Washington, D.C.: Institute for Educational Leadership, 1985), 3.

6. *U.S. Children*, tables 1, 3.

7. U.S. Department of Education, *Youth Indicators, 1988* (Washington, D.C., 1988), table 5.

8. Ibid., table 9.

9. David T. Kearns and Denis P. Doyle, *Winning the Brain Race: A Bold Plan to Make Our Schools Competitive* (San Francisco: ICS Press, 1988), 3-4.

10. Stanley Teske, "Drug Abuse Leads Nation's Concerns About Schools, Gallup Poll Finds," *Education Daily*, 26 Aug. 1988.

11. Hodgkinson, 11-12.

12. Ibid., 12.

13. U.S. Department of Education, *Japanese Education Today* (Washington, D.C., 1987).

14. Hodgkinson.

15. Howard Berman, "The Minnesota Plan: The Design of a New Education System," *American Education* 21, no. 1, 16-19.

16. Joseph L. Tropea, "Urban Schools' Backstage Order and Children At Risk: An Historical Perspective" (Paper prepared for the Rockefeller Archive Center Conference on Children At Risk, Mt. Kisco, N.Y., 1988).

17. Albert Shanker, "School Failure Needs Airing," *New York Times*, 11 Sept. 1988.

18. Patricia Guard, personal letter to Alan Gartner, 7 Nov. 1986.

19. Quoted in N.J. Block and G. Dworkin, *The I.Q. Controversy* (New York: Random House, 1976), 17.

20. K. Goldberg, "Among Girls 'Ethic of Caring' May Stifle Classroom Competitiveness, Study Shows," *Education Week* 7 (1988), 1, 24.

21. Nancy Lyons, "Learning from New Research About Women," *Education Week* 7 (1988), 32.

22. Lous Heshusius, "The Arts, Science, and the Study of Exceptionality," *Exceptional Children* 55 (1988), 61.

23. Seymour B. Sarason, *Psychology Misdirected* (New York: The Free Press, 1981).

24. Heshusius, 62.

25. Ibid.

26. Edward Fiske, "When Students Fail, the Fault May Lie with the Teacher's Methods," *New York Times*, 8 June 1988.

27. Albert Shanker, "Strength in Numbers," *New York Times*, 14 Aug. 1988.

28. R. E. Slavin, "Cooperative Learning and the Cooperative School," *Educational Leadership* 45 (1987), 7-13.

29. Jennifer Goldman and Howard Gardner, "Multiple Paths to Educational Effectiveness," in *Beyond Separate Education: Quality Education for All*, ed. Dorothy K. Lipsky and Alan Gartner (Baltimore: Brookes Publishing, 1989).

30. Quoted in A. Shecky, "The Reality of Education Reform," *Youth Policy* 10 (1988), 22.

31. Herbert J. Walberg, "Families as Partners in Educational Productivity," *Phi Delta Kappan* (February 1984), 17.

32. American Council on Education, *One-Third of a Nation*, a report of the Commission on Minority Participation in Education and American Life (Washington D.C., 1988), 1.

33. U.S. Office of Technology Assessment, *Technology and the American Economic Transformation Choices for the Future* (Washington, D.C., 1988), 48.

Schools and Moral Development

JAMES J. DIGIACOMO, S.J.

Most parents and other adults have paradoxical expectations of public schools. They hope that, besides teaching children to read and write and develop the other skills that will enable them to do the world's work, these institutions will also impart ideals, promote integrity, and contribute positively to character development. On the other hand, they object to any proselytizing or indoctrination. Schools are supposed to assist moral development but not "impose" values on children and young people.

They do not think that these expectations are contradictory, because they assume a societal consensus about a set of standards that are nonreligious and agreed upon by all decent people: for example, lying, stealing, violence, and abuse are bad; honesty, fairness, self-discipline, and industriousness are good. To some extent they are correct. The consensus does exist, and many children are helped in school to interiorize these values. The adults who work as teachers, administrators, and counselors want their students to turn out as decent, hard-working, responsible persons, and they strive with varying degrees of dedication and skill to contribute to wholesome personal development. But it is all too obvious that their success is limited. The incidence of violence, dishonesty, substance abuse, irresponsible sexual activity, and other forms of destructive behavior in and out of school convince many that the schools not only fail to contribute to children's well-being but may even exert a negative influence.

To judge the fairness of these criticisms, one must ask: How realistic are adult expectations? If the schools are indeed failing to fulfill reasonable expectations, why is this so, and what can be done to improve performance?

One of the biggest mistakes one can make is to equate education with schooling. To be sure, education goes on in schools. But children are constantly learning, absorbing messages in the home, on the street, and from the popular entertainment media — recorded music, radio, movies, and television. Many of these messages are freighted with value judgments about what is important, what is valuable, what is worth their attention and energy. And though the home and school may be presumed to be allies most of the time, even their combined educative influence finds a powerful counterpoise in the media. The latter are in many ways more influential than the home or school and in some respects hostile to their shared values. Any serious attempt at making schools more effective in imparting values and forming character must take these countervailing influences seriously and assess their effect on strategies of formal education.

Before analyzing the messages and measuring the influence of popular entertainment, it is necessary to consider the overall cultural context in which the media and schools operate. James Fowler rightly identified the dominant myth of consumer culture: "You should experience everything you desire, own everything you want, and relate intimately with whomever you wish."[1] Many young people accept this view of life. Anyone who tells them that some experiences are wrong or that they have no unrestricted right to sexual intimacy is seen as interfering with their inalienable right to pursue happiness. This implicit philosophy undergirds many people's ideals, judgments, choices, and action. It is expressed and reinforced through the stories and the songs of young and old. The most powerful source of this myth is, of course, commercial advertising, but it is not the only one. The plots of television and movie dramas almost invariably proceed from an affirmation of this philosophy and rarely deviate from the value judgments inherent in it.

Adults who criticize schools or who simply want to improve them should examine their own feelings about the dominant myth of American culture. Parents whose lives exhibit an uncritical acceptance of these priorities should not expect schools to give their children a set of values or moral standards that are in opposition to their own. Since the contradictions are not immediately apparent to all, however, a few classroom stories are in order.

A group of eleventh graders were reading about people who had stood up against injustice and oppression and suffered for their convictions. An opposing point of view was heard in a Billy Joel song, "Angry Young Man." No longer concerned with right and wrong, the singer believes in no causes, expresses no rage in the face of injustice. All he wants to do is survive. One student's written comment was: "I sometimes feel that Billy Joel is like me. I think the world is full of people looking out for Number One, and I presume that I will become like them. Although there are people of conscience who are concerned about others, they are a minority. And I feel that I must get all I can, because down the line no one would bend over backward in the real 'corporate world.'"

Another class of eleventh graders were discussing how to curb unwanted teenage pregnancies, specifically the strategy of dispensing contraceptives in schools. They had just read a counterproposal in which the writer said that it would be better to tell teenagers that sex "is an enriching and serious business between mature people who are emotionally, socially, and even economically able to accept the consequences. . . . Educate them in such things as family values, a healthy and integrated acceptance of sexuality, stability in marital relationships, a sense of obligation toward other persons, and willingness to accept the consequences of one's actions."[2]

One student replied: "I feel that this is impossible. The society in which we live is centered around two ideals: sex and money. Sex is used to make money, and money is used to get sex. These values are so instilled in our mind that the plan would not be able to succeed. If our world had more respect for sex, this plan would be great. I find it unfortunate that the world is as it is, but we should try to correct the problem, not run from it with an idea of great moral values."

Finally, a university dean, after talking about morality and television with a group of boys and girls in a Brooklyn public school, observed:

> Seemingly, today's television heroes — and heroines — whose immoral behavior is often sumptuously rewarded have become role models for many young Americans. As one young woman noted, Alexis on "Dynasty" "is bad. Like she's evil. She's vicious and bold and glamorous. And she's everything that any woman would want to be." When I inquired if that included her calculating behavior, the student replied, "yes, that too. She gets whatever she wants." One of her classmates, speaking of the character J.R. Ewing of "Dallas," added, "I sort of admire the way he can just corrupt everybody and not even let it affect him."[3]

Fighting Back

In the face of these deleterious influences, adults appeal for a renewed emphasis on moral formation. But in this pluralistic society, they do not agree on the kind of morality to be imparted. Pluralism poses its own problems for socialization. To avoid offending anyone, educators have devised one response: value-neutral education. Such teaching tries to inform youngsters about options, encourages interaction and discussion of these options, but studiously refrains from endorsing any one of them for fear of imposing solutions in controversial areas. Secretary of Education William J. Bennett made this observation on sex education:

> This is a very odd kind of teaching — very odd because it does not teach. It does not teach because, while speaking to a very important aspect of human life, it displays a conscious aversion to making moral distinctions. Indeed, it insists on holding them in abeyance. The words of morality, of a rational, mature morality, seem to have been banished from this sort of sex education.
>
> To do what is being done in these classes is tantamount to throwing up our hands and saying to our young people: "We give up. We give up teaching right and wrong to you. Here, take these facts, take this information, and take your feelings, your options, and try to make the best decisions you can. But you're on your own. We can say no more."[4]

Young people need more help than this. They need guidance, role models, and encouragement from committed and caring adults. But to what are adults committed? How deep are their convictions about what constitutes morally responsible behavior? How firm is the consensus about the so-called basic civic virtues? Allan Bloom has said that any professor can be sure of one thing: almost every student entering the university will say he believes that truth, especially moral truth, is relative.[5] Moreover, the university experience is not likely to challenge this assumption, since moral relativism is a fairly entrenched position in the world of higher education. Nor is this moral philosophy limited to academics. Sociologists repeatedly confirm its pervasiveness in the citizenry at large. William McCready of the National Opinion Research Center at the University of Chicago concluded: "Americans don't respond to moral imperatives. They increasingly behave any way they want to. They've been told to trust their consciences, and that's what they're doing."[6] When this marks an advance from uncritical reliance on external authority to a search for conviction based on evidence and argument, people are on the road to moral maturity. But the authors of *Habits of the Heart* indicated that something else is at work when they explored the underpinnings of this attitude in the popular mind:

> For many, there is no objectifiable criterion for choosing one value or course of action over another. One's own idiosyncratic preferences are their own justification. The right act is simply the one that yields the agent the most exciting challenge or the most good feeling about himself.
>
> In the absence of any objectifiable criteria of right and wrong, good or evil, the self and its feelings become our only moral guide. But if the individual self must be its own source of moral guidance, then each individual must always know what he wants and desires or intuit what he feels. He must act so as to produce the greatest satisfaction of his wants or to express the fullest range of his impulses.
>
> Utility replaces duty; self-expression unseats authority. "Being good" becomes "feeling good."[7]

This perspective shows up in some striking ways in teaching materials used in many schools. The sex education resources referred to by Bennett give arguments for not engaging in sexual intercourse and try to make students "comfortable" with that decision. His comment is arresting: "You sometimes get the feeling that, for these guides, being 'comfortable' with one's decision, with exercising one's 'option,' is the sum and substance of the responsible life. Decisions aren't right or wrong, decisions simply make you comfortable or not. But American parents expect more than that from their schools. Most Americans want to urge, not what might be the 'comfortable' thing, but the right thing. Why are we so afraid to say what that is?"[8]

Although not all Americans consider morality as residing only in the eye of the beholder, enough of them do to have a significant effect on how not only adults but also young people think about right and wrong. For many people "morality" has come to mean the intrusion of external and coercive authoritarianism. Young people show in a variety of ways that they have absorbed this mentality. They are extremely reluctant to call any behavior "wrong"; the worst label they can apply to the most antisocial actions is "stupid." In their minds, criminals are not evil but "sick." The most heinous atrocities are not wrong but "gross." More than language games are being played here. Ethical judgments become little more than an exercise in aesthetics. But a society that cannot in principle commit itself to basic moral truths has nothing left but a shallow utilitarianism clothed in the shibboleths of "freedom" and "privacy."

When young people engage in destructive behavior in the name of freedom, adults express indignation and call for tighter discipline and control. But their children, aware of the unspoken rules of adult society, see this as a hypocritical enforcement of standards that their elders themselves do not believe in. Adolescents especially resent this seemingly arbitrary imposition. One eleventh grader wrote a reply to a magazine article in which the author argued that the mere distribution of contraceptives in schools was unlikely to decrease the number of teenage pregnancies but might increase it. Completely ignoring the evidence and arguments advanced by the author, the boy responded: "Your stand on contraceptives is really a personal opinion. If parents would allow the contraceptives, teenagers might agree to [sic] their parents because of the willingness of parents to allow freedom of choice. A good family discussion on sex, its true value, contraceptives, and love would give teenagers freedom to make their own decisions without feeling pressured by parents. This is only my opinion, much like, I believe, your article was. You seem to be forcing your opinion on people and that puts a negative tone on things." This peculiar form of self-righteousness reminds one of Bloom's observation: "The inevitable corollary of . . . sexual interest is rebellion against the parental authority that represses it. Selfishness thus becomes indignation and then transforms itself into morality."[9]

A Double Standard

No matter how hard adults try to place reasonable limits on children's freedom and to inculcate standards of responsible behavior, their efforts are likely to fail as long as they are perceived by the young as maintaining a double standard. If privacy is equated with nonaccountability and accepted as the ideal of the moral life, then adolescents will view all moral imperatives as equivalent to the arbitrary limits placed on children. And any attempt by schools to reinforce moral standards will not only be rejected but also resented as an effort to postpone the rewards of maturity and perpetuate childhood.

Young people notice, for example, how adults carry on the debate about that most divisive of issues, abortion. Those who believe in abortion-on-demand do not call themselves "proabortion" but "prochoice." They insist that they are arguing not for abortion but for people's right to choose whether to abort. The unfortunate effect of this kind of argument is to preclude any meaningful dialogue on the question of whether abortion is the unjust taking of human life. The unspoken but inescapable premise of such an argument is that whatever choice one makes is right, so long as it is made freely. Of course, the same people who make this argument forbid their fellow citizens to make free choices to rob, rape, and sell drugs, but no matter. Children hear this nondebate and rightly conclude that adults disagree not about the moral quality of choices but about the right to choose. It does not matter what one does so long as it is done freely. And, of course, one should feel comfortable with it. Anyone who criticizes a choice is at best guilty of bad manners and, at worst, of violating another's privacy.

These observations are bound to enrage many readers and perhaps dissuade them from reading further. But even those who find these ideas uncongenial must admit that in the present climate of opinion it is unrealistic to expect schools to make a meaningful contribution to moral formation. Schools do not operate in a vacuum. The proliferation and refinement of the media make even the least literate of youngsters sensitive to what is going on in the larger society. They sense that the older generation wants to saddle them with a burden of ideals and taboos that even they do not accept. As children see it, the mainsprings of adult behavior are not justice, honesty, and self-discipline but aggression, greed, and self-indulgence. This is an overstatement, of course, but it is normal adolescent moralizing, born of disillusionment and fueled by the popular media portrayal of adult motivation. At any rate, the moral crisis among young people seems to be partially a function of the moral confusion and fragmentation in adult society, and the mote in one group's eye can hardly be removed without attending to the beam in the other's.

This should not be interpreted as a counsel of despair. Within the limits imposed by cultural myths, schools can do much to combat the present malaise and assist in children's moral development. At the outset, it must be understood that socialization is a game that must henceforth be played by new rules. In the past, it has meant inducing children to accept the values of adult society. But in a pluralistic, fragmented society lacking consensus in many areas of moral concern, public education must employ more complex strategies. There is a built-in tension in American society between a commitment to individualism and a desire for community. This stress spawns paradoxes like the desire to socialize children without agreeing on the way of life that is considered desirable for them.

The question is: How can schools promote a desirable pluralism without encouraging rootlessness and contributing to fragmentation? How can they encourage tolerance and openness and still avoid lapsing into anomie? This problem lies at the heart of the issue of moral education. Most Americans are deeply committed to freedom of conscience and the preservation of individual liberty. They fear the influence of Moral Majority types and other zealots who would manipulate information, intimidate dissenters, and discourage critical thinking in their single-minded determination to impose a set of values and a way of life. These fears are well grounded. But it is important to understand the roots of the anger in such people. They think that the schools have betrayed their children by creating an amoral, value-free vacuum to be filled by those less responsible vehicles of informal education, television, and other media. For all their shortcomings, they understand what many of their adversaries fail to grasp: that freeing children means more than leaving them alone. In their anxiety to fill the vacuum, zealots may undermine the foundation of a free society. But if they are extremists, it is because they are polarized by a society that, they feel, has closed its eyes to their legitimate fears and concerns.

A Third Way

There is a large group of people who receive little publicity but who have the power to break the paralyzing deadlock described above. They perceive the bankruptcy of value-neutral schooling but recoil from the excesses of reactionary indoctrinators. Their existence is barely acknowledged by media analysts who do not know how to fit them into convenient stereotypical categories. They want to exercise responsible authority in the lives of their children and to guide them without stifling initiative or discouraging healthy responsibility and self-determination. They believe that even the thorniest and most divisive ethical issues are susceptible to reason and dialogue and that children can be taught the skills of moral analysis and decision making. One would be tempted to call them a silent majority if that sobriquet had not been preempted. At any rate, these people are looking for a way out of the present impasse. What can they reasonably expect of their schools by way of moral education?

One thing educators can do is to help children understand the roots of the differences among people. Youngsters are already aware of the differences, but they are a source of confusion until they are addressed in an organized, intentional way. Louis Raths, Merrill Harmin, and Sidney Simon described this confusion and its consequences:

> Being exposed to so many different alternatives, perhaps the child was left with *no* ideas, but instead absorbed just the confusion. It is possible that the biggest contribution these media made was to baffle the child's nascent understanding of what is right and what is wrong, what is true and what is false, what is good and what is bad, what is just and what is unjust, what is beautiful and what is ugly.

> Out of this welter of traveling and communication, there came not only confusion and uncertainty but also the idea that perhaps anything was all right, nothing really mattered, that while many people were different, there was nothing particularly significant in the differences. One way of life was as good as another. Nobody really was an example of what was the right way to be.[10]

With due attention to the age and ability of students, teachers can help them to discern the unstated premises from which people work, the taken-for-granted worldviews and value systems that underlie choices and life-styles. Young people are capable of this kind of analysis with help from their teachers. They can begin to see that their lives are not necessarily predetermined by forces over which they have no control but can be shaped by conscious, free decisions. They can see how people take different paths, depending on what is more important to them: comfort or achievement, things or people, self-indulgence or service, pleasure or sacrifice, competition or cooperation, egoism or altruism, amorality or integrity. They can begin to grasp the consequences of these choices, how their decisions may affect themselves and society.

This kind of education helps students to answer not only questions like, How can I succeed? but also questions like, What is success? What kind of person do I want to be? What are the sources of life's deepest satisfactions? Here are the well-springs of personal morality, the sources from which ethical stances derive and moral choices flow. If this sounds too philosophical, that may be due to the drift toward instrumentalism and vocationalism that characterize much education. A 1987 survey of American college freshmen by the American Council on Education and the Higher Education Research Institute found that only 39 percent put great emphasis on developing a meaningful philosophy of life, the lowest proportion in twenty years. This kind of superficiality leaves a vacuum to be filled by the insistent, manipulative messages of consumerism. A record 76 percent of the freshmen said that being financially well-off was a key goal, a number nearly double that of seventeen years before. The survey director concluded: "Despite Newsweek's announcement that greed is dead, our data show that it is alive and well. Students still tend to see their life being dependent on affluence and are not inclined to be reflective. Obviously we are seeing something very profound in the society."[11]

What prevents schools from being places of reflection and discussion about values? It is resisted by the well-founded fear of teachers (and, even more, of administrators) that taking positions on moral issues is almost sure to offend those in the community who hold different opinions. According to Raths, Harmin, and Simon: "If someone was for something, someone else was against it; and to avoid controversy, schools began to stand for nothing. Teachers turned toward 'teaching the facts.' In communities of strangers . . . people with many different backgrounds, it became easier to have schools which themselves represented an absence of consensus. Moral, aesthetic values were quietly abandoned as integral parts of the curriculum."[12]

As a result, educators have become skilled at laying out options, delineating choices, and, with studied neutrality, encouraging children to clarify in their own minds what seems important or right to them. Students are prodded not to look for the truth but for what they feel comfortable with. There are no "right" or "wrong" choices, only those that each individual finds agreeable. This can be legitimately termed enlightenment of a sort, but not guidance.

To do better than this, schools would have to attempt something very courageous: they would stand for something. Individual teachers would delineate options and explore the roots of pluralism and controversy with their students. They would encourage critical thinking, stimulate curiosity and questioning, and welcome reasonable disagreement. While respecting the individuality and freedom of students, they would challenge them. Discussion of moral issues would be analytical, rational, and respectful. Opinions and people alike would be subject to criticism. But—and most threatening of all—teachers themselves would feel free to agree with some of their students and disagree with others, and to assert their own convictions.

This last proposal will be rejected out of hand, because it threatens the harmony of the school community. Educators have become painfully sensitive to anything that may cause controversy. As it is, harmony has indeed been purchased but at a heavy price. American schools have become bland environments characterized not by the healthy, invigorating clash of opinion and the excitement of discovery but by a deadening dissemination and regurgitation of "facts." They are the last place anyone would go to find out what life is all about. No wonder children are bored. They are taught by people who feel constrained to muffle their deepest convictions about what is right and true and just in the interest of a surface placidity. So, to find out what is really important and how to get it, they turn to the "educators" who have the biggest budgets and the fewest restraints — the hucksters of popular culture. All the evidence indicates that such "teachers" are quite effective and that the children are learning very well indeed, so well that countless parents fear they are losing their children to a way of life that contradicts every important value for which they stand. And then they wonder why their schools do not help to turn the tide.

Taking Risks

The people who run and teach in schools will be understandably nervous about trying the new (old?) approach to education proposed here. Some of them assume that parents *want* schools to be neutral, even mute, in matters of morality and values. Others suspect that forthrightness in such matters will inevitably cause some complaints from adults who object to what is being taught. Ideologues will cry "indoctrination" at the first sign that someone is trying to teach something more than the "facts." In such a climate, people will fear for their jobs, decide that prudence is the better part of valor, and go back to business as usual. But does it have to be this way? Schools can reflect the pluralism of the public not by ignoring the divisions among competing elements but by promoting dialogue, even debate, among them. If America is indeed a free marketplace of ideas, then educators should be permitted not only to display their wares but to promote them.

But suppose students do not share their teachers' opinions. What happens then? Obviously, these views must not be imposed, nor should students be pressured by either overt or subtle sanctions to conform. In any society, no matter how homogeneous, freedom should be respected and encouraged; in a pluralistic one like ours, this should be even more evident. Both parents and students would rightly object to anything smacking of indoctrination. Teachers should aim not at agreement on specific issues but at a shared willingness to pursue standards derived not from an external source but from the young person's own thinking and struggle.

One of the great virtues of our society is respect for diversity. This should not and need not be sacrificed as educators strive to contribute to moral enlightenment and growth. The challenge is to maintain a devotion to searching for the truth without losing regard for those whose search leads to conclusions and commitments in conflict with one's own. Voltaire said it best: "I disapprove of what you say, but I will defend to the death your right to say it." The present state of affairs is unsatisfactory not because the differences among people are accepted but because the roots of these differences are not addressed and hence are regarded as insignificant. The opposite error, no less undesirable, would be to try to obliterate those differences at the price of freedom.

Good teachers know how to steer a middle course between such extremes. Every day, in a variety of subjects, they prod their pupils along the road to learning even as they make allowances for limitations of talent and maturity. Teachers of literature are accustomed to promoting sound interpretation and criticism without stifling independence of thought. They know how to make students feel accepted even when their opinions are not. If these teaching skills could be put to work in the field of moral education, much good could be accomplished.

There are, of course, risks involved in turning schools into centers of ferment rather than leaving them as information sites and skill factories. It is dangerous to let people express, in front of the children, their thoughts and opinions. Feathers will be ruffled, sacred cows will be gored, parent-teacher sessions may go on longer, and school-board meetings could even suffer a diminution of civility. But these signs may not portend destruction but stirrings of life.

The alternative would be the status quo. In their headlong rush to the shelter of neutrality, schools have unwittingly become havens of the unexamined life. In their anxiety to offend no one, they have become eunuchs incapable of impregnating their students with anything remotely resembling a passion for truth. But they are not harmless, either. While the hypocritical tastemakers of mass culture hide behind First Amendment fortifications and conduct their hard-sell assault on the minds and hearts of the young, those who are supposed to be allies of parents are mute. All this reminds one of Edmund Burke's famous aphorism: "The only thing necessary for the triumph of evil is for good men to do nothing." It is not a question of choosing between danger and safety, but of deciding which dangers to confront.

Some will interpret this as an assault on liberalism. But there is a difference between liberal education and the education of liberals. Liberal education steers a middle path between the extremes of value-free schooling and indoctrination and tries to help students choose their lives. It recognizes that the young will never find their way through the maze of ignorance and self-deception without coming into vital, even abrasive contact with caring adults who demonstrate their own commitment to honesty, truth, and justice. It is not even important that these adults believe or say the same things; indeed, it is probably not desirable. It is important that they clearly stand for something more than self-aggrandizement and infect their students not necessarily with their own beliefs but with their devotion to the search for enlightenment and righteousness.

There are certainly schools where good things happen, where teachers do more than transmit information and skills: they challenge and inspire young people. Moral education takes many forms, from the English class where literature is a springboard for serious reflection to the history class that grapples with social issues, to the adults who simply demand honesty and settle for nothing less from anyone, beginning with themselves. But these are bright spots on a drab landscape and will remain so as long as schools reflect a society muddled in its thinking, unsure of what it believes, and protective only of a lonely individualism. A community fragmented in its values and commitments should not be scandalized when its schools do little more than mirror its own divisions and uncertainties.

Educators do not have to be uncertain trumpets, and many of them are more than that, but it takes an unusual store of moral conviction and courage to rise above the general level of mediocrity. In the present moral climate, where teachers march to many different drummers, a clear and firm note of moral leadership is bound to be a bit of a surprise.

NOTES

1. James Fowler, *Stages of Faith* (New York: Harper & Row, 1981), 20.
2. Joseph Bernardin, "Abortion and Teenage Pregnancy," *New York Times*, 22 Jan. 1978.
3. Herbert London, "What TV Drama Is Teaching Our Children," *New York Times*, 23 Aug. 1987.
4. "Sex and the Education of Our Children," *America*, 14 Feb. 1987, 121–22.
5. Allan Bloom, *The Closing of the American Mind* (New York: Simon & Schuster, 1987), 73–74.
6. Kenneth Briggs, "Religious Feeling Seen Strong in U.S., " *New York Times*, 9 Dec. 1984.
7. Robert Bellah et al., *Habits of the Heart* (New York: Harper & Row, 1985), 75–76.
8. Quoted in ibid., 122.
9. Bloom, 74.
10. Louis Raths, Merrill Harmin, and Sidney Simon, *Values and Teaching* (Columbus, Ohio: Charles E. Merrill Publishing Co., 1966), 17–18.
11. Deirdre Carmody, "To Freshmen, A Big Goal is Wealth," *New York Times*, 14 Jan. 1988.
12. Raths, Harmin, and Simon. 20.

Schools That Serve Children

FRANK J. MACCHIAROLA

The contributors to this volume make it eminently clear that the conditions of America's children have provoked a crisis of enormous proportions for the children, their families, and the nation. These problems call into question the suitability of some of the most important institutions that serve children, particularly schools.

This essay will analyze and comment on some of the changes that have affected children, many of which are described in greater detail elsewhere in this volume, and then delineate the characteristics of the schools that can most effectively serve children. Finally, it will integrate some of the most important recommendations that experts have made regarding school improvement and evaluate their suitability in the context of what works best for children. Most of what has been advanced in behalf of children comes with an ulterior purpose and another constituency to be served. Unlike the causes of adults, the causes of children must be undertaken by surrogates. Long experience has taught me that the interests of these surrogates are rarely the simple interests of the children.

Several characteristics of the condition of America's children are most striking, not only because they are severe but also because they are recent. Within less than a generation, children have lost a great deal of the support that society had long given them. As a result, they have suffered in a number of significant ways. They have not been the center of family life, and they have grown up with less and less adult support. Since the advent of the single-parent household and mothers in the labor force, children are increasingly not participating in family and community life in traditional ways, and no alternative structures have been developed to meet their vital needs. They are more and more at a loss as to what behavior is appropriate. They share fewer values of a society that has fewer values to share. Whether one focuses on the children's physical well-being or on the moral aspect of their condition, it is apparent that serious needs are not being adequately addressed.[1]

The effect of the lack of care and attention is so significant that it calls for major changes in the way that the family, church, school, and society deal with our children. For as a society and as families, we have not provided the kind of structure that youngsters need if they are to prosper and grow. Often, we are overwhelmed by other things in our lives and rationalize that other structures and institutions are providing our children with the kind of lessons they need to be taught. Parents need to increase their involvement with the institutions that serve their children. The school and family connection — whether one means that the schools are to deliver community services or simply that parents are to visit schools more often to check on the progress of their children — must be a central focus of the fundamental reform that must occur. The school has to reach out to the parents so that there can be a real understanding and appreciation of the youngster's school work. Children need their parents' concern and involvement. And public institutions, particularly schools, need to encourage and support this connection. Finally, institutions like child care, paternal leave, and flexible work arrangements must be better developed so that parents can more adequately manage responsibilities to their children.

This volume makes it abundantly clear that a great deal more has to be done. Children are often without the benefit of adult counsel and guidance. And this reality holds true across lines of race and class. Moreover, it is clear that children need the kind of discipline that emanates from the home with the full force of family support. The child who is pushing at the limits of discipline must meet a strong counterforce that represents what the youngster actually needs. Often, when children express the desire to be free from the restraints of parents, they are actually crying out for it.

In order to deal with the condition of America's children in school settings, it is necessary to strengthen their preparation for school. The development of a sense of community — starting with the home and what it does to encourage and support children — is essential in order to effect fundamental change in schooling. The habits of children in the home, the attention to the clothes that children wear, the hours that they are permitted to spend out of the home, and the participation of the youngster in family activities — all must be attended to by the family. And while parents often have so many other responsibilities that it is difficult to do all these things, they must be aware of the price to be paid for their inattention. When many of these parents consider the cost of sacrificing the needs of their children, they may be unwilling to do so.

The assumption of new roles by mothers who are now in the workplace, and the change of the basic family structure with the increasing number of single-adult households, without the development of institutional arrangements to support families, have placed an extraordinary burden on the children. When children have an opportunity to talk about what this change means for them, many see it as a form of deprivation and say that they have borne the burden of the changed situation, particularly the increasing anonymity and the deterioration of many of the necessary conditions for community within the home. More and more children come from poor families and face the additional problem of being discriminated against by the larger society.

One challenge to the children of America that must be added to those described above is a changing society. The United States — particularly its cities — is undergoing some significant demographic changes. The wave of immigration has brought increasing numbers of Asians, blacks, and others from the Third World and has drastically changed the characteristics of the population. As a result, children are called both to understand and to thrive in circumstances where inclusion is called for. These changes should not be simply tolerated but celebrated. This is not easy for children to do, particularly when they are not encouraged at home to accept these changes with a positive and optimistic spirit. All too often, parents and other adult Americans have made it clear to youngsters that intolerance — or downright hostility toward many of these new Americans — is acceptable behavior. There is little doubt that children in the school setting, for example, when left to their own devices, and when free to form their own judgments based on their own values and understanding, do a better job than adults in similar situations. The students' positive attitudes, encouraged by the teachers, must form a basic part of the value system in the school.

This essay deals with three basic areas of schooling: (1) what the school means to the community; (2) how the school does the work of schooling; and (3) what the children do in the school setting. Today, the school is a much more important institution in American society than at any previous time in its history. This is true from at least two perspectives. First, a youngster cannot expect to succeed in American society without a high-school education. No skilled jobs can be found without a diploma. The concept of the "dropout" reflects the society's growing recognition of the importance of a high-school education for all children.[2]

Second, the school must do the work of many institutions that have lost their effective role in the society. In addition to the family, institutions that have deteriorated include churches, neighborhood and community groups, and other social and religious institutions that once existed in great strength in the United States. The schools can no longer concentrate on education in its most formal sense and thereby satisfy its responsibility to children. School professionals must transmit their values to America's children without complaining that the burden has been taken off the shoulders of others and has fallen primarily on their own.

Because of the importance of the school, some significant changes must occur in the kinds of things that schools must do. After all, the school was developed as a place where students would be educated, and it was not unusual for students who did not need a diploma to drop out. And so at the turn of the century high schools graduated only about 10 percent of those who had started. Today a school should graduate all of its students.

In addition, effective schools are places where students receive a great deal more service. Not only must schools have breakfast and lunch programs, but the school day must be extended well into the evening, and extracurricular activities must be expanded. The school must be available in the evening for activities involving parents and community residents as well as students. The school must shape students' values in ways that go beyond the formal aspects of schooling. This development has naturally been uneven. Many professionals and governing boards for local schools complain that the school cannot be all things to all persons. But the fact remains that the school is required to meet more of the students' needs, and the literature continues to cite these types of changes as the ones that have been made by the successful school.[3]

This development is all the more important in high school, where students have to struggle to find themselves and to define their roles in the school setting and in life itself. For in high school, students are simultaneously children and young adults, and they have to be encouraged to join with others in common activities. Participation in school activities comes naturally to some students, but others approach school with a very limited understanding of themselves and of what they are capable of becoming. They want to be included, to feel part of the school and what it represents, but find it difficult to understand just what is expected of them. The rules for inclusion in the mainstream of the school are often vague, and high-school students are usually bashful or awkward — despite bravado — when they approach their peers and teachers. It is therefore imperative that the schools be organized to deal with *all* children and make them feel that they have a positive and welcome role to play in the school. But reform must be initiated cautiously. Some reforms that seem to enhance requirements in the name of quality and seem to eliminate classes and programs that are not useful may actually drive youngsters from school. Rather than emphasizing that public education is inclusive, these standards often make it appear to some students that the school program is not meant for them. They get the impression that school is going to be too hard for them and they would do everyone a favor if they left. The movement toward higher standards — a movement that is basically correct in my view — must therefore be accompanied by an attitude that tells youngsters that they are expected to succeed, that the school will help them to succeed, and that these higher standards are intended to include rather than exclude them from school and a diploma. For too long, children have been getting the message that education is the concern for only some of them. They have been told — again and again — that they are not expected to succeed.[4]

It is not accidental that the dropout statistics in most large cities in the United States have shown little improvement in response to an enormous effort already five years in the making. There have been appreciable gains in student performance among the students who usually do well, but success still eludes those having the greatest academic problems. The reason is clear. The youngsters, particularly those who are suspicious of the efforts of adults, have not understood that we truly expect them to be successful. What they hear about increasing standards still signifies exclusion for many of them. The school must therefore be a community. All children must sense that they can succeed and that all the people in the school community are unambiguously committed to their success. Such a strong and ringing affirmation of their place within schools is necessary not only because schools are still suspect places. It is also necessary because the society at large, as well as many families, have not made children feel wanted and welcome.

Too many of them feel that they are a burden or an inconvenience to the larger society.

School, then, is a place to make things happen, a place for success to be encouraged — and perhaps virtually guaranteed. It is a place for developing values and for promoting a sense of citizenship, not just for teaching formal subjects. And the school is accessible at all hours of the day and well into the evening, where children can meet and play with their friends.

The next question concerns the meaning and the technique of schooling. The first and most significant factor in the success of schools is the necessity of a principal who assumes responsibility for the well-being of the school. The principal is an instructional leader, and more than that: he or she ensures that there is a school community that is willing to fulfill the school's responsibilities to each member of that community. The principal takes the blame for failure and is willing to assign credit for success. The literature on the subject of effective schools is in unanimous agreement that the school needs strong leadership.[5] It also agrees that there are no requirements as to this leader's age, gender, particular educational background, or experience. Some evidence suggests that knowledge of and experience with reading programs is tied to school success. And there are strong findings that link the principal's success to administrative style. The accessible and open person who is not threatened by the strength of the teachers and demonstrates a willingness to change is the preferred school principal. Selection procedures are critically important, and assessments of the principal and his or her program are absolute requirements for an effective school. According to the literature, shortcomings have concerned the method of preparing, appointing, evaluating, and replacing principals. The literature criticizes the teachers colleges and state departments of education for the criteria they regard as significant. School boards are criticized for their selection procedures. Often, many people observe, the job of school principal is obtained through success on the football field or in the political clubhouse. In addition, experts say, it is rare for principals to be evaluated and removed for reasons having to do with school performance.

The job of principal cannot be done effectively forever. Methods have to be in place for reassigning principals from time to time. The school board that governs the local schools must be willing to face the task of removing and replacing the principal when it is appropriate. And it must do so in ways that reflect its understanding of school success.

In addition to the principal's leadership, there must be a sense in the school that the students can learn and that they can do the kind of work necessary for success. Children need to believe in themselves; when the school takes as its working proposition that all youngsters can succeed, a basic step toward success has already been taken. The signs of high expectation are encouraging and hopeful ones, and through them the school becomes a place for good things to happen. The positive signs are important not only from the standpoint of the children, but they also stimulate teacher success. As the literature clearly shows, the teacher who believes that the students in the class are gifted will be more successful with those "gifted" youngsters.[6] Such students do better in school than those who are in fact gifted but whose teacher has not been told that. It is clear, then, that encouragement makes the difference. And from the standpoint of the school community itself, the ingredient of respect added to high teacher expectations makes the school a happier, more caring, and more effective place to be.

The effective school is also distinguished by its tone. Students no longer sit frozen in fear during instruction periods or during their recreation period. But in too many instances the school has been out of control, with students and intruders wandering in various parts of the building. For too long, many schools have delegated responsibility for the basic demeanor of the school to security guards. The tone of the school must be set by the school community; hence it must be regulated and governed by decisions and actions of that community. And it is the teacher who can do the most effective job disciplining the students.

The literature indicates that the value of order is essential in every successful school.[7] The students must know what is expected of them from doing homework to attending classes to obeying the established rules. In the effective high school the students are involved in developing and administering the rules. Such an involvement ensures that the student has begun to act in ways that will permit the development of a sense of citizenship and a sense of community. And discipline is not enforced simply to permit learning to occur. While that would be reason enough, it is also part of the lesson of life that the school provides. Thus, the school reinforces routines of self-discipline that will help youngsters in their lives at home, with family, and with friends. Children have to be taught the benefits of order and structure, particularly in a world that pays less attention to those important lessons.

The effective school has also given a high priority to the acquisition of basic skills. It knows that there is a basic logic to the way that students learn and that the pleasure gained from reading is directly related to the ability to read. Such a realization means that the school will attend to certain basics before turning with confidence to advanced skill levels. Yes, great books can be read by those who are struggling to read, and aspects of discovery that are important to maintain enthusiasm among youngsters can be part of the curriculum. But until students have acquired basic skills, the schools will not be successful in truly instructing these children. Obviously, this is more critical for youngsters from disadvantaged families that do not reinforce basic-skills education. In such situations, the school must forcefully attack the problem of youngsters who have not mastered basic skills. The school must concentrate its efforts on reading, mathematics, and writing.

In being successful with the most disadvantaged children, the school fulfills its most important obligation to democratic principles. Such a public school minimizes the distinctions between class by providing the students who are most disadvantaged with the most essential of their needs. And so, with basic competence acquired in school, the student living in poverty is given an important tool that can be used for self-improvement and real achievement.

A school that is focused on student success also realizes that youngsters who advance through the grades through social promotion will be frustrated by the work they are asked to do later. In addition, these youngsters are embarrassed by having to do remedial work. A strong focus on basic skills, a promotion system based on student achievement, and a careful, considerate approach to the issues of remediation are necessary parts of an effective school.

The effective school takes the work of the students seriously and assesses their progress. Regular testing is a positive aspect of the effective school, and the student's program for improvement is based on the assessments that have been made. The effective school appreciates and uses data in the design of its programs. There is an important need to be careful in both the design and implementation of tests. Critics justly complain that tests are not related to the program of instruction. Criticism has also been justifiably made about the overuse of tests and the overreliance on testing in many situations. Students have indeed been overtested, and the test results have not been correctly used. The effective school ties its testing program to its instructional program. It continually improves its testing program and explains its benefits to the parents. It also ties test results to the necessary role of the parent in the supervision of homework.

The effective school concept is a powerful one, because it discredits the theories used to excuse poor student performance. Social-science data have been so effectively employed in this area that teaching professionals have to attribute their failure to the many identified disabilities of the students. Poverty levels, discrimination, "broken" families, and low self-esteem have all been used by many professionals to excuse themselves from meeting the basic responsibility of educating all their students.[8] In the context of the philosophy of doom and gloom that was so prevalent in the United States in the 1960s and 1970s, many Americans felt that the situation in public education was hopeless and that certain students were destined for failure. That opinion has greatly changed as a result of the effective schools movement and the determination of many professionals to make the system perform adequately. The effective school literature and the movement that grew up around it has put in place many educators who accept the challenge of educating all of the children under their care. And it is a fundamental principle that must undergird successful school reform.[9] For a project or a program must be directed principally in the classroom, with the most critical part of the dynamic taking place between teacher and student. Real reform must take into account this relationship and the environment in which it occurs.

A principal contention of this essay is that the development of the school community is the most critical factor in the success of schooling. While this is certainly so in terms of my experience with public education, it is reinforced by the work that James Coleman has done to explain the success of Catholic parochial schools, most significantly those that serve many poor and non-Catholic children in the inner cities. The results of his work demonstrate that the critical issue is not support from the outside in the form of more resources and more dollars.[10] This is not to minimize the importance — indeed necessity — of an adequate budget. The simple matter, however, is that the development of community within the school is far more potent than support from without. As these schools continue to be successful, even as they include virtually all applicants in the school community, they provide a model that can well be used to improve public schooling. The model is built around the formation of community. And in that community, parents are critical actors.

Still, the school reform movement has also taken strength recently from many social institutions that had been for the most part indifferent to the issue of schooling. The 1983 report of Secretary of Education Terrell H. Bell, *A Nation at Risk*, was presented to an American public that had not had the opportunity to examine the issue of social performance for many years.[11] The public's interest in schools had waned, and the business community had had an extremely limited set of involvements with public education. Since that report, the reaction has been overwhelming. A number of states have acted to increase the support from private sources for the public-school system and to develop many programs and activities designed to increase business involvement and partnerships with schools. Public education has got the attention of business organizations like the Committee for Economic Development and the Business Roundtable.[12] Issues of concern have ranged from the quality of leadership and governance of schools and school systems to what students learn in school and how that learning can make them better citizens and employees. A great variety of programs has been introduced in many parts of the country; individual businesses have established numerous programs that have made the school community recognize that a sense of caring and concern is part of what many businesses have seen as their corporate social responsibility. Thus, schools have an opportunity to take advantage of the sense of good will toward public education that characterizes the work and effort of many Americans who are concerned with the success of future generations.

The final part of this essay is devoted to suggesting what must be emphasized if schools are going to be successful in serving America's young people. As I have indicated throughout, most important is the development of a community within the school. The school has to understand that it serves as more than a location, that the students and faculty are there to interact with one another and to grow. The concept of community, that students and faculty owe one another mutual respect and that neither can succeed without the other, must be part of the ethic of the school. In the spirit of that community, the institution is transformed. In that community, teachers are not afraid to represent themselves and their values to the students, who are not afraid to have their values shaped and influenced by adults. They are not afraid to have their beliefs and practices put to the test by teachers who continually challenge them to do better. In the same way, teachers remain open to students who help the teachers reshape their own values. Dialogue results from the interaction of each upon the other.

In the context of real reform the school must also take a greater responsibility for linking students with future careers. In the past, except for special programs in the areas of vocational education, the American high school saw itself as a precollege institution. Thus the successful student was college bound; the corollary was that the student not bound for college was unsuccessful. Teachers who were concerned about success, and who saw success in the terms just described, largely ignored the phenomenon of the student who was not going to college. As a result the school had a hierarchy of values built into its academic offerings and its social settings as well. This can no longer be the case. The school — while encouraging students to perform at their maximum — must also convey the understanding that student success can occur even if college does not immediately follow a student's high-school education. Teachers must carefully walk the line between accepting youngsters' decisions about their future and encouraging them to do the best they can. In the 1980s, many students have interrupted their studies and returned to school when they were ready to take advantage of the opportunities offered by a postsecondary education. This is now a reasonable option, and students must know that it is available and that it does not mean that a student is not acting inappropriately by choosing to defer, or even not attend, college.

One of the most important tasks of the school is to introduce students to the meaning of responsible work. All too often students, even by the time of their graduation from high school, are unable to perform tasks that are necessary for success on the job. These include the simplest activities, such as reporting an absence from work by a telephone call. Values like punctuality and regular attendance are found neither in the curriculum nor in the conventions and rules that regulate student behavior. Newly hired high-school graduates are often surprised to learn what their employers and fellow employees expect of them. The program of instruction can introduce these life experiences by formally presenting these values to the student as part of the curriculum, but such values can also be acquired as a by-product of the right kind of instruction and the results that are expected of the students. The school must make it clear that it encourages the kind of work from students that will also teach them to be successful in their employment. Schools that are sensitive to this responsibility will put students to work in ways that are rare in schooling today. The students will engage in peer tutoring, whereby they instruct one another, reinforcing the meaning of their own work. Peer tutoring programs are a part of the basic program of the effective school. Students are also encouraged to collaborate on joint projects. When the school appreciates both the need to work and the relationship of work in school to work in life, the school encourages team projects in term papers and other activities in which students are jointly engaged as a part of their academic endeavor. When student work becomes more appreciated, students do not hesitate to work collaboratively or to submit their work to constructive criticism by their fellow students. When this takes place, the students' willingness to learn from others will prepare them for some important lessons of life.[13]

The effective school must also value the work and productivity of its staff. School administrators often ignore the need to be productive and accountable in the delivery of their service to the youngsters. They are used to spending the funds that the school board has allocated to them, but they do not sense the responsibility to spend them effectively and efficiently. As a result, especially when evaluated by those in the business community, the schools pay too much attention to the spending of their budgets and too little attention to ensuring that these funds are well spent.

The values of school administrators are on the input side of the equation. School officials demonstrate these values to argue that they have been underfunded or that certain results cannot be forthcoming because of the budget cuts that they have been asked to absorb for the particular school year. This approach focuses on needs, but it tends to downplay the ways in which the school staff themselves are able to meet those needs. School officials will often tell their staffs that they are excused from achieving a successful result. Instead of challenging the staff to make do with what is available, the focus on inputs does not give them a strategy to use in order to achieve greater successes and increased productivity. School leaders must hold staffs accountable for developing alternative strategies that will result in success even in the face of less taxpayer support. In this regard, the experience of parochial schools, which get by with a fraction of the support that is received by the public schools, is again most instructive. Their staffs are told that the support they will be given from tuition and other assistance is limited, that they are expected to produce, and that voluntarism will play an important part in the activities of the school. As a result, they do produce, and their per-dollar performance far outstrips that of the public school. They are successful in many of the same neighborhoods and with many of the same children. This type of productivity is beneficial in and of itself as well, for it fosters self-reliance and instills the will to survive and the determination to prosper.

Schools must also be places where teachers feel that they are expected to excel. It is increasingly clear that all too often teachers have been asked to perform tasks that are inconsistent with their experience and their worth. All too often they are seen as the lowest level of the production line that is responsible for the education of the children. This perspective has to do with the fact that teachers often get the feeling that they are left to fend for themselves in the classroom. Their only companions for the day may be the children, and they are lost to the rest of the world for the entire school day. As a result, teachers have rarely viewed themselves as being treated as creative. When they do have a strong and determined sense of themselves and their responsibilities, as they often do, they have it in the face of many of the structural problems that they endure. Until the spurt in teacher salaries over the past five or six years, they also felt it in the way in which society was compensating them for their service.

This concept of the undervalued teacher has been in vogue in education. According to that theory, the teacher should be given a greater role to play in the instructional program of the school. There are various forms of the empowerment strategy, and the teachers' unions have been instrumental in promoting them. They are attractive to the teachers because their powers and prerogatives have been taken away from them. They have had more and more teaching time taken away by paperwork, and they have had a great deal of discretion about what they teach taken away by changes in the curriculum. It is important for aspects of this teacher-empowerment movement to be successful, particularly those that make the teacher more responsible for the management of classroom instruction. The relationship between teaching and learning is often confused. When we concentrate on learning, for example, we pay less attention to the particular teacher's methodology. Instead, we measure whether the students have learned what they were supposed to learn.

In a setting where the focus is on teaching, supervisors examine the teacher's technique and style. They focus on the lesson and attempt to determine whether it meets the objective of the curriculum. In the process of supervision, all eyes are on the teacher, and the job is well done when the lesson has been well taught. This approach to teaching is a time-honored one, and most teachers and supervisors are familiar with it. But it is based on a leap of faith. The relationship between a lesson well taught and a lesson well learned is not quite as direct as one might at first think.

In a setting where the focus is on learning, the success of the lesson is much harder to discern. For success depends on how well the students have learned the subject. The test of the student's performance is a measure of the teacher's success, and the relationship is direct. The school that has developed a sense of itself in terms of community will find the concept an easy one to understand. When the students in the community are doing well, the teachers are doing well. The teachers therefore have a direct investment in the success of their students. Success in the classroom on the part of the teacher, then, is the key to student success. It is, from my perspective, the most critical point that is being overlooked in the effort to improve the performance of America's children.

The school reform movement has not yet addressed school success in the stark terms put forward here. It has not invested in the mutual success of the students and the staff. We are still rather tentative in the way in which we define success in the school setting, and society is afraid to acknowledge its dependence on a system of shared beliefs and common understandings.

The theme of this essay has been the need for the school to be a community where students feel that they are challenged, supported, and encouraged to be successful. Students are more in need of this kind of institution than they have ever been. And schools are capable of becoming the kinds of institutions that can guarantee success for almost all students. School-effectiveness literature has shown that this is the case, and for almost a decade the most forceful proponents of children's rights have been challenging our will to provide successful schools. But schools can be successful only if they adhere to the criteria described in this essay. There must be a sense of success built into any program. There must be an administration in place that seeks success and can guarantee it. And there must be a supportive atmosphere, one in which the students are truly expected and helped to succeed.

Notes

1. Some of the major data have been reported in U.S. Department of Education, Office of Educational Research and Improvement, *Youth Indicators* (Washington, D.C., 1988).

2. The United States government's recognition of this situation is found in a unique and joint publicaton of three federal departments: U.S. Department of Labor, U.S. Department of Education, and U.S. Department of Commerce, *Building a Quality Workforce* (Washington, D.C., 1988).

3. This has been cited in many publications. See, e.g., Special Issue on School Effectiveness, *Social Policy* 15 (Fall 1984).

4. An attempt by the U.S. Department of Education to deal with this need is found in U.S. Department of Education, *What Works: Researching About Teaching and Learning* (Washington, D.C., 1986) and *Schools That Work: Educating Disadvantaged Children* (Washington, D.C., 1987).

5. See *Schools That Work*.

6. Thomas F. Good, "Teacher Expectations and Student Perceptions: A Decade of Research," *Educational Leadership* 38 (February 1981).

7. See *Schools That Work*.

8. In a 1987 survey of public high-school principals conducted for the Center for Educational Statistics of the U.S. Department of Education, major obstacles to school improvement were cited as those outside the school—students and families—rather than those within the school over which they have some control. See U.S. Department of Education, Office of Educational Research and Improvement, *Center for Education Statistics Bulletin* (May 1988) (CS88–422).

9. This is clearly recommended in a new publication of the Council of Chief State School Officers, *School Success for Student at Risk: Analysis and Recommendations of the Council of Chief State School Officers* (Orlando, Fla.: Harcourt Brace Jovanovich, 1988).

10. James S. Coleman and Thomas Hoffer, *Public and Private High Schools: The Impact of Communities* (New York: Basic Books, 1987).

11. National Commission on Excellence in Education (the Bell Commission), *A Nation at Risk: The Imperative for School Reform* (Washington, D.C.: U.S. Department of Education, 1983).

12. For an excellent example of this type of report, see Committee for Economic Development, *Children in Need: Investment Strategies for the Educationally Disadvantaged* (New York, 1987).

13. The publications from The William T. Grant Foundation Commission on Work, Family and Citizenship, *Youth and America's Future*, are most instructive in this area.

Children versus the State: The Status of Students' Constitutional Rights

ROSEMARY C. SALOMONE

Legal rights, entitlements, and personal liberties have escalated since the 1960s. Spurred on by the early gains of the civil rights movement in the pursuit of equal dignity for racial minorities, group after group has used the legal system and the political process to achieve similar recognition. The poor, the handicapped, women, linguistic minorities, and the elderly have all pressed their claims before Congress, state legislatures, and the courts and have engaged the organs of government in an interplay of policy making with broad social consequences. Throughout this uneasy process, the U.S. Supreme Court has played a pivotal role in defining the contours of rights granted by the Constitution. As a result of what has been termed "judicial activism," groups that traditionally lacked a political voice have made significant strides by stating their claims in the language of constitutional rights. One such group whose legal status itself owes much to the constitutionalization of rights is children.

Modern thinking on children's rights and on the relationship among the child, the family, and the state has its roots in the writings of classical historians and philosophers, including Aristotle, Thomas Hobbes, Jean Jacques Rousseau, and John Stuart Mill. Framed in the context of parental obligations, their arguments primarily focused on a universal right of children to receive maintenance, protection, and education from their parents. More recently, social thinkers and activists have extended this obligation to the state. Government, it was argued, must protect children from youthful misjudgement, from the ills of society, and even from their parents. Nineteenth-century reformers pressed for child-labor and compulsory-education laws to protect children from the exploitive dangers of industrialization. States created separate juvenile courts in the early twentieth century in an attempt to address issues of child abuse, neglect, and juvenile delinquency.

These reforms were based on the notion that children were different from adults and therefore needed to be treated differently in order to protect themselves and society at large. Nevertheless, the concept that children have rights validated in the law is not only a recent phenomenon but a revolutionary one.[1] In fact, the idea that children have independent rights and a special legal status did not gain ground until the 1960s. At that time, children's rights activists piggybacked on the civil rights movement and attempted to include children within the category of persons who could advance legally recognized claims and assert public entitlements. These latter-day reformers redefined the relationship of the state with the child. No longer was the state acting in parens patriae, shielding the child from harm. The state had both a negative responsibility not to intrude unnecessarily into the child's life and an affirmative obligation to provide services and benefits.[2]

This bifurcated rights-entitlement approach to children in the polity led to certain inconsistencies in national policy making. On the one hand, children were to be treated the same as adults as a matter of constitutional right; that is, children were to enjoy the same scope of civil liberties as adults — freedom of speech, freedom from unreasonable searches by government officials, the right to equal protection of the laws, and the right to procedural due process. On the other hand, it could not be denied that children had different needs stemming from their inability to care for themselves. They were therefore entitled to certain government services and benefits — child care, food, and prenatal care.

While the individualistic rights-based approach prevailed as a matter of constitutional law in the judicial arena, the protective entitlement-based concept dominated legislative policy making. Through the 1960s and early 1970s this situation was not unlike that of other "protected" groups — racial and linguistic minorities and particularly the handicapped — for whom the equal opportunity movement translated into the right to be treated with equal respect and the right to special treatment in receiving government services.

This philosophical incoherence in the law of children's rights, however, was short-lived. Since the early 1970s a growing conservative perspective on the Supreme Court has gradually changed the course of constitutionalism and rejoined the rights-entitlement dichotomy into a unified protectionist concept. Court decisions, based on underlying notions of federalism and separation of powers, and framed in the language of state and local autonomy, community values, and limitations on the judicial role itself, have increasingly focused on the differences between children and adults and have significantly narrowed the scope of the child's constitutionally protected freedoms. Justices who affirm equality and liberty principles are now a fading minority on the Court, while the supporters of governmental and parental authority are gaining a strikingly powerful voice.

This essay addresses this evolving perspective as demonstrated in leading cases decided by the Court over the past twenty years. While the Court has demonstrated an increasingly limited view of children's constitutional rights in a broad spectrum of cases, the discussion focuses on children's rights in the public school setting.[3] It is in the educational sphere that children experience the most frequent contacts with government officials whose conduct must conform to the constitutional standards established by the Supreme Court. Specifically, the essay focuses on children's rights to freedom of expression, due process, and privacy, as these represent constitutional spheres in which the Court has made increasingly strong statements affirming official authority to limit the constitutional rights of students.

The essay attempts to demonstrate how the political viewpoint of the Court's growing majority—founded in federalism, separation of powers, constitutional theory, and traditional social mores—has shifted the balance of interests and thereby effectively diminished the constitutional status of children, specifically public secondary-school children. The analysis highlights flaws in the Court's reasoning and underlying assumptions and concludes with a discussion of the policy consequences, including potential abuses of government power that flow from the Court's inclination to straitjacket children's constitutional rights into the protectionist ideology of nineteenth-century social reformers.

Educational Rights and Liberties

From its very origins in the common school more than a century ago, American education has served a dual role. Public schooling promotes self-growth of the individual and also meets the needs of an industrialized democratic society. At times this dichotomy in function has proved difficult to reconcile, particularly for the Supreme Court, whose function it is to protect individual interests from majoritarian overreaching while maintaining the social order for the common good. In the context of children's rights, this traditional duality of individual versus the state takes on a third dimension in the child-family-state relationship.

In recent decades the Court has been called on with increasing frequency to define the rights of students, parents, and school authorities, but judicial attention to this problem dates back to the 1920s. At that time, the Court began to articulate a "progressive" model of education emphasizing "a participatory educational process with maximum student interaction and independent thought." That model held sway until the early 1970s when the Court gradually began its transition to a more pronounced emphasis on schooling as the inculcator of fundamental societal values under what has been termed a "cultural transmission ideology."[4] That transition has held serious implications for the status of children's rights in the school setting.

Two early cases laid the foundation for parental rights to control the education of children free from unreasonable state intrusion. In *Meyer v. Nebraska*,[5] the Court struck down a state law making it a misdemeanor to teach a subject in a language other than English to children who had not completed the eighth grade. While the case specifically addressed the right of teachers to pursue their profession, the Court relied also on the interests of parents to control the education of their children and on the interests of the child. In *Meyer*, the Court explicity rejected a Platonic model of education whereby "no parent is to know his own child, nor any child his parent."[6] Such an effort by the state to control the inputs and outputs of education in order to promote the state's interest in homogeneity would intrude on the rights of teachers, parents, and children. Two years later, in *Pierce* v. *Society of Sisters*,[7] the Court more definitively addressed parental rights when it unanimously invalidated a state law requiring parents to send their children to a public school. According to the Court, the liberty of parents to direct the education of their children includes the right to enroll them in a private school. The Court could find "no general power of the state to standardize its children."[8]

Five decades later, in the context of a claim to free exercise of religion under the First Amendment, the Court returned to *Meyer* and *Pierce* to uphold parental rights to direct their children's education. In that case, *Wisconsin* v. *Yoder*,[9] Amish parents claimed that enforcement of the state's compulsory education law beyond the eighth grade gravely endangered the free exercise of their religious beliefs. The Court was careful to limit its opinion to the peculiar facts of Amish life — a 200-year history of deep religious convictions that are shared by an organized group and that are intimately related to daily living. However, the Court, in broad *dictum*, reaffirmed the "primary role of parents in the upbringing of their children" as one that "is now established beyond debate as an enduring American tradition."[10]

Meyer, Pierce, and *Yoder* are clearly "parents' rights" cases. To say that they demonstrate a clearly articulated ideology of schooling taking shape on the Court would be stretching the analysis beyond reason. Nevertheless, they do give evidence of the Court's willingness to circumscribe the state's indoctrinative power over children. In that sense, they hint at a student's "right to freedom of conscience or belief," albeit one derivative of and dependent on parental authority. While all three cases have little value as legal precedent per se (*Meyer* and *Pierce* were decided on the now-repudiated doctrine of Fourteenth Amendment substantive due process, and *Yoder* turned on the peculiar facts surrounding Amish life and religious beliefs), they have remained the legal touchstones for parent-child rights asserted against governmental overreaching in the educational sphere. In the past two decades, these rights have been articulated in the language of other provisions in the Constitution, particularly the First Amendment free-speech clause, the Fourteenth Amendment guarantee of procedural due process, and Fourth Amendment protections against unreasonable search and seizure. The Fourteenth Amendment expressly limits *state* action. The Court has also extended the First and Fourth Amendments beyond federal action to that of local- and state-government officials by incorporating those provisions within the "liberty" interest of the Fourteenth Amendment.

Freedom of Expression

The First Amendment to the Constitution states that "Congress shall make no law . . . abridging the freedom of speech." The Court relied on that amendment two decades after *Meyer* and *Pierce* in *West Virginia Board of Education* v. *Barnette*[11] when, for the first time, the Justices established definitively that public-school students have constitutional rights. Here the Court struck down a state statute requiring all public-school students to salute the American flag. Relying on First Amendment freedom of expression, the Court laid the groundwork for a student's right to freedom of conscience or belief in an often-quoted statement: "If there is any fixed star in our constellation, it is that no official, high or petty, can prescribe what shall be orthodox in politics, nationalism, religion, or other matters of opinion or force citizens to confess by word or act their faith therein."[12]

The Supreme Court did not return to the issue of the students' interest in freedom of belief until the late 1960s in *Tinker v. Des Moines Independent Community School District*,[13] a case that represents the high-water mark of the students' rights movement and the Court's implicit embrace of a progressive ideology for public education. In *Tinker*, the Court struck down a school's prohibition against the wearing of black armbands to protest the Vietnam War. Relying on First Amendment freedoms and citing *Meyer*, *Pierce*, and *Barnette* for support, the Court clearly affirmed that "students [do not] shed their constitutional rights to freedom of speech or expression at the schoolhouse gate."[14] Even more broadly, the Court stated that "students in school as well as out of school are 'persons' under our Constitution. They are possessed of fundamental rights which the state must respect. . . ."[15] School officials may limit free expression only where it "materially and substantially" interferes with school discipline or infringes on the rights of other students.[16] In *Tinker*, the Court appeared to disregard both the inculcative aspect of public education and the maturity level of the students, who ranged from thirteen to sixteen years of age. In fact, the Court would never again make such a bold, sweeping statement of children's rights in any context. Within three years of the *Tinker* decision, four new members would take their place on the Supreme Court, ushering in a more constrained view of children's rights. (Warren E. Burger replaced Earl Warren as Chief Justice, while Justice Powell replaced Justice Black, Justice Blackmun replaced Justice Fortas, who had written the *Tinker* opinion, and Justice Rehnquist replaced Justice Harlan.)

The Court waited more than a decade before it again addressed specifically the issue of values inculcation and suppression of ideas within the public schools. In *Board of Education v. Pico*,[17] high-school students challenged the school board's decision to remove certain "objectionable" books from the school library. Unlike its predecessors *Barnette* and *Tinker*, the *Pico* case forced the Court to weigh the right of students to receive information (a right derived from free-speech rights) against the right of school officials to protect children from vulgar and indecent speech and to determine the values to be inculcated through the public-school curriculum. But the *Pico* decision is a studied lesson in court confusion and ambivalence. None of the seven separate opinions of the Justices garnered majority support, while the majority was swayed by only one vote. This outcome clearly pointed to a Court that was struggling to define the scope of student rights and school authority. The plurality opinion, written by Justice Brennan, begged the broad question. It narrowed its application to the school-library setting, establishing the library as a special place where students enjoy a broad "right to receive information and ideas" and where the school board can only choose from among books that apply educationally relevant criteria and are not founded in partisan politics. However, the opinion upheld the school board's discretion in prescribing the curriculum. According to the plurality, in curriculum matters, school officials could rely on their duty to inculcate community values. With all seven opinions stressing a values-inculcation model of schooling, *Pico* clearly signaled a decline in the constitutional status of students' rights and a return to the protectionist concept of state authority evidenced in the early days of this century. The Court's clearest statement of that perspective with regard to free-speech rights came in the closing days of the Burger Court in *Bethel School District No. 403 v. Fraser.*[18]

Theoretically, the First Amendment free-speech clause broadly encompasses not only freedom of expression but also freedom of thought and belief.[19] But these rights are not absolute. Practically, they must often be reconciled with conflicting societal values and objectives.[20] The *Pico* case touched on these competing interests, particularly society's interest in promoting community values within the local public schools. *Fraser* presented the Court with an additional interest to weigh in the constitutional balance — that of the other students who were a captive audience to what school officials and the Court considered to be an "offensively lewd and indecent speech" given at a high-school assembly. In *Fraser*, a seventeen-year-old senior delivered a speech nominating a fellow student for elective office. The speech, given before a voluntary assembly of students ranging in age from fourteen years upwards, began with the words, "I know a man who is firm — he's firm in his pants." The speech continued, peppered with sexual innuendo. The day after the speech, Fraser was suspended three days for having violated the school's disruptive-conduct rule and was removed from a list of graduation speakers.

In addressing the free-speech claim, in an opinion that clearly spells out the Court's emerging ideology of schooling and students' rights, seven members of the Court upheld the authority of school officials to discipline a student for engaging in such conduct. In fact, the Court drew a distinction between the constitutional rights of adults and children in a school setting, recognizing that school officials may limit certain forms of speech that they deem "inappropriate" and contrary to community values. According to the majority, "the inculcation of these values is truly the 'work of the school.' " School officials act *in loco parentis* in order to protect children "from exposure to sexually explicit, indecent, or lewd speech."[21] The Court distinguished *Fraser* from *Tinker*, where the penalties imposed were related to a "political viewpoint," political speech deserving the highest constitutional protections. Justice Brennan, concurring in the judgment, upheld the authority of school officials to restrict "disruptive language" in accord with the *Tinker* standard. But he took exception with the majority's suggestion that the school officials in *Fraser* were legitimately acting to protect younger students. To his mind, Fraser's speech was "no more 'obscene,' 'lewd,' or 'sexually explicit' than the bulk of programs appearing on prime time television or in the local cinema."[22] Justice Marshall, in dissent, viewed the majority opinion as an erosion, not an application, of the *Tinker* standard, since the school board had failed to present sufficient evidence of "material disruption" to the educational process.

Underlying the *Pico* and *Fraser* cases is a fundamental tension between the autonomy of the student as a self-determining individual with the full panoply of constitutional rights and the authority of public-school officials acting as arbiters and protectors of community values or preferences. This tension surfaced again in *Hazelwood School District* v. *Kuhlmeier*,[23] where the Court advanced one step further on its developmental path toward a protective notion of children in society and an ideology of schooling that is firmly grounded in community power and values inculcation. In *Hazelwood*, former high-school students who had been members of the school's newspaper alleged that their rights had been violated when the principal deleted two pages from a given issue because of two objectional articles: one describing student experiences with pregnancy and the other discussing the impact of parental divorce on several students who attended the school.

Writing for a six-member majority, Justice White upheld the action of the school principal. While the opinion opens with a reaffirmation of student rights to freedom of speech as articulated in *Tinker*, it quickly distinguishes *Tinker* as a case of personal political expression from the current issue of school sponsorship. It then moves on to an elaborate discussion of community preferences, power, and values as articulated by public-school officials. The entire discussion focuses on the newspaper as part of the curriculum. School authorities may exercise greater discretion and control over student expression when it takes place in school-sponsored activities, whether within or outside the traditional classroom setting. The Court suggested, in astonishingly broad *dictum*, that educators may censor student expression in this vaguely defined curricular context, in order to secure each of three objectives: "that participants learn whatever lessons the activity is designed to teach, that readers and listeners are not exposed to materials that may be inappropriate for their level of maturity, and that the views of the individual speaker are not erroneously attributed to the school."[24]

The majority maintained that *Hazelwood* is an extension of *Fraser*, which appears to have replaced *Tinker* as the guidepost on students' First Amendment rights to freedom of expression. The opinion is replete with references to *Fraser*: "a school need not tolerate speech that is inconsistent with its 'basic educational mission'";[25] "a school may refuse to sponsor student speech . . . or conduct otherwise inconsistent with the shared values of a civilized social order."[26] These broad statements of government authority over individual expression evoked a caustic dissent written by Justice Brennan, and joined by Justices Marshall and Blackmun. While the dissent opened by recognizing schooling as values inculcation under the authority of school officials, it also warned of the potential danger of officials' abusing that power to censor speech that "might subvert . . . their own perception of community values."[27] The dissent reaffirmed the *Tinker* standard of "material and substantial disruption" and cautioned that the school's mandate to "inculcate, moral and political values is not a general warrant to act as a 'thought police' . . . to cast a perverse and impermissible 'pall of orthodoxy' over the classroom,"[28] or to "assume an Orwellian 'guardianship' of the public mind."[29] For at least three Justices on the present Court, education continues to serve a dual function — not merely to promote community goals but to foster individual thought as well.

While *Tinker* was a natural point on the developmental road from *Meyer* and *Pierce* and through *Barnette*, cases decided since *Tinker* appear to have carried the Court on a tortuous journey to an unanticipated destination. *Tinker*, like its predecessors, viewed free speech not only as an end in itself but also saw an instrumental function to be served by allowing students to express themselves freely. The state could impose restrictions only under the most compelling of circumstances that threatened the social order. According to this instrumental rationale, free speech trains students for participation in democratic self-government and advances the search for truth and knowledge. As the Court stated in *Tinker*, "the Nation's future depends upon leaders trained through wide exposure to that robust exchange of ideas which discovers truth 'out of a multitude of tongues, [rather] than through any kind of authoritative selection.' "[30]

In *Pico*, however, the Court exercised far more caution in addressing the substantive claims. In fact, while Justice Brennan's plurality opinion established a student's "right to know" that is derived from free-speech rights, it also sidestepped the scope of that right by framing the constitutional standard against which school-board action is to be judged in procedural terms. *Pico's* motivational test requires school boards to examine their own objectives when removing library books in order to determine whether their decision is based on educationally relevant criteria or "narrow, partisan, or political" motives to suppress a particular idea or value.[31] This notion of "structural due process" has some practical merit. It forces government decision makers to establish decisional structures that engage a broad spectrum of viewpoints and thereby avoids imposing an official orthodoxy while preserving institutional autonomy. In this way, the Court is removed from determining or assessing the substance of the school board's decisions. By deflecting the controversy away from ideology toward the less volatile direction of procedure, the Court did not need to address the controversial value choices that generally lie at the heart of these cases. Nevertheless, from the student's rights perspective, the problem lies in the ambiguity of "educational relevance" as a standard and the potential it carries for abuse of discretion by school officials who can use it as a mask for political suppression.

The narrow interpretation of *Pico* seems to be only a minor digression on the Court's constitutional course. School officials must establish procedures and guidelines for removing books from a school library; they must consistently follow those procedures; the procedures themselves must include the views of all interested persons within the school community. Viewed in the context of *Fraser* and *Hazelwood*, however, *Pico* represents the Court's initial step in a new doctrinal direction that turns away from the "school as marketplace of ideas" concept of *Tinker*, away from the notion of education as a participatory process of self-discovery, and toward a more definitive values-inculcation model of schooling. The plurality's *dictum* and *Pico*, excluding curriculum decisions from the scope of its holding, is a harbinger of *Hazelwood's* curriculum rationale. And the Court's emphasis on process demonstrates a deferential approach to official decision making that clearly surfaces in both *Fraser* and *Hazelwood*.

These latter cases are radical departures from *Tinker*. In fact, they are much more akin to Justice Black's dissenting opinion in that case wherein he disclaimed "any purpose . . . to hold that the Federal Constitution compels the teachers, parents and elected school officials to surrender control of the American public school system to public school students."[32] In both *Fraser* and *Hazelwood*, the Court purported to uphold *Tinker* by distinguishing the political nature of the speech at issue in that case from *Fraser's* "indecent" or "lewd" speech and *Hazelwood's* issue of school sponsorship. By distinguishing the cases on their facts, the Court avoided the necessity of addressing *Tinker's* "material and substantial disruption" standard. While the *Fraser* majority discussed the harmful impact of the speech on the audience, no evidence surfaced in the district court that Fraser's words significantly disrupted the school program or infringed on the rights of other students. Without expressly overruling *Tinker*, the Court eviscerated it in *Fraser*, and by citing *Fraser* extensively in *Hazelwood*, the Court reaffirmed its course.

Both *Fraser* and *Hazelwood* place broad discretion in the hands of school officials to determine what forms of expression are acceptable or appropriate in the school setting. By failing to establish any standards or guidelines in either case, the Court has relegated students' expressive rights to the will or whim of school officials who may or may not represent community values. Further, these cases leave no room for dissenting views or for the robust exchange of ideas, and they seriously underestimate the level of sophistication demonstrated by the vast majority of today's high school students. Not only is education essentially a process of values inculcation, but the trend in Supreme Court thinking would allow a majority within a community, acting through its local school officials, to impose an orthodoxy of beliefs and viewpoints and suppress dissenting voices. This is a far cry from the progressive notion of schooling as a participatory process.

Procedural Due Process

The second area in which the Court has articulated an increasingly narrow view cf students' rights concerns the procedures followed in school disciplinary cases. The Fourteenth Amendment says: "No state shall . . . deprive any person of life, liberty, or property, without due process of law." The procedural safeguards guaranteed by the due process clause are rooted in the notion that "personal freedom can be preserved only when there is some institutional check on arbitrary government action."[33] More than a century ago, the Supreme Court noted that due process counts among "those fundamental principles of liberty and justice which lie at the base of all our civil and political insitutions."[34] Underlying the concept of due process is a concern for fairness in governmental decision making and the view that "fair" process will lead to the "right" result. The American political and legal culture focuses on a particular form of proceduralism — the due process hearing.

The application of due process rights for students received scholarly attention long before it became a matter of judicial concern. In 1957, Warren Seavey of the Harvard Law School published an article in which he criticized the courts for having failed to afford suspended students the minimal procedural protections "given to a pick-pocket. . . ."[35] Three years later, the Fifth Circuit Court of Appeals in *Dixon* v. *Alabama State Board of Education*[36] held that students on the college level are entitled to a due process hearing before being expelled or suspended for disciplinary reasons. In the years following *Dixon*, every circuit court followed the Fifth Circuit's lead. They disagreed, however, on the elements of an adequate hearing, the length of suspension that would trigger due process guarantees, and which nonsuspension penalties would require a hearing.[37]

Beginning in the late 1960s, the Supreme Court began to lay the groundwork for a theory of due process rights for children. The context was not education but the juvenile justice system. In *In re Gault*,[38] the Court held that the *parens patriae* model of the juvenile court system did not justify denying juveniles the right to notice of the government's charges against them, the right to counsel, the right to remain silent, and the right to confront and cross-examine adverse witnesses. In other words, most of the procedural guarantees afforded adult defendants in criminal trials were to also apply to juveniles. In *Gault*, the Court unequivocally stated that children, as individuals, have constitutional rights of their own. Children were no longer to be mere "subjects of paternalism." The Court rejected the assumption that institutions ostensibly designed to act in the best interests of children always did so but looked at the realities of the juvenile justice system and concluded that children risking incarceration should enjoy certain due process rights that were coextensive with those of adults. Three years later in *In re Winship*,[39] the Court held that the standard of proof "beyond a reasonable doubt" was applicable to both adult criminal trials and juvenile proceedings.

In 1975, the Supreme Court addressed the issue of procedural rights in the school setting in *Goss* v. *Lopez*.[40] Quoting *Tinker* for the proposition that students do not "shed their constitutional rights at the schoolhouse door,"[41] the Court held that students suspended from school for ten days or less were entitled to notice of the charges against them and at least an informal hearing or opportunity to be heard. Such short-term suspensions implicated both a "property" interest, that is, an entitlement to education drawing from the state's compulsory education law, and a "liberty" interest in the student's good name and reputation. On the question of how much process is due, the Court required very little: oral or written notice of the charges and the opportunity to present the student's side of the story. The Court expressly stopped short of allowing the student to secure counsel, to confront or cross-examine witnesses, or to call witnesses on the student's behalf. But *Goss* was decided by a bare majority on the Court.

The dissenting opinion, written by Justice Powell and joined by Chief Justice Burger, Justice Blackmun, and Justice Rehnquist, concluded that a suspension of ten days or less did not assume constitutional dimensions. The dissent drew a distinction between the rights of children and those of adults and recognized the broad discretion of school officials in prescribing and controlling conduct in the schools. For the dissenting Justices, the role of the school in teaching the "lesson of discipline" is no less important than teaching children to read and write.[42]

In *Goss*, Justice Powell warned that we would not "foresee the ultimate frontiers of the new 'thicket' the Court now enters."[43] Nevertheless, the four dissenters together with Justice Stewart appeared to have cleared that thicket just two years later in *Ingraham v. Wright.*[44] Here the Court, in an opinion written by Justice Powell, held that paddling students as a means of maintaining school discipline violated neither the Eighth Amendment's prohibition against cruel and unusual punishment nor the Fourteenth Amendment due process clause. Addressing the due process claim, the majority concluded that while paddling did implicate a student's liberty interest, state common law remedies for excessive corporal punishment satisfied the requirements of due process. According to the majority, the civil and criminal sanctions for abuse that are available under state law, when "considered in light of the openness of the school environment," would effectively deter teachers and school authorities from meting out excessive corporal punishment.[45]

The dissent, written by Justice White, pointed out the flaws in the majority's reliance on tort remedies as an adequate protection against erroneous and excessive paddling. First, under state law, the teacher would be protected from suit as long as he acted in "good faith"; and, second, even if state law would permit the student to sue for "good-faith error," the student would already have suffered irreparable physical pain.[46] All the dissenting Justices called for a *Goss* "'informal give-and-take between student and disciplinarian' as a 'meaningful hedge' against the erroneous infliction of irreparable injury."[47] The dissent further took exception to the majority's holding that the Eighth Amendment's prohibition against "cruel and unusual punishment" protects only criminals. While the dissenting Justices were careful not to suggest that "spanking in the public schools is in every instance prohibited by the Eighth Amendment," they criticized the majority's extreme view that the amendement never proscribes "corporal punishment in public schools, no matter how barbaric, inhumane, or severe."[48]

The underlying rationale and the practical implications of *Ingraham* are indeed troubling to the advocate of children's rights. The majority opinion denotes a decided retreat from the Court's expansion of those rights as seen in the decisions of the previous decade. *Ingraham* clearly marks a new direction. While Justice Powell's majority opinion quotes from *Tinker* to reaffirm "the comprehensive authority of the states and of school officials . . . to prescribe and control conduct in the schools,"[49] the tone of the opinion and the result are far afield from *Tinker.* Pervading *Ingraham* is an undercurrent of authoritarianism that is clearly absent from *Tinker*. The majority's cost-benefit analysis of the procedural due process claim weighs heavily on the side of preserving institutional autonomy. For Justice Powell and his colleagues, the benefits to be enjoyed by the individual and society in avoiding a "minimal" risk of error are outweighted by the administrative burdens and potential impairment of the teacher's ability to maintain discipline when the prepunishment hearing results in the rejection of the teacher's recommendation.

This rationale is flawed in several respects. First, it does not consider the individual and institutional benefits to be gained from the appearance of fairness in school disciplinary procedures. One could make a cogent argument that schools are microcosms of society and serve as the training ground for democratic principles. The school is the setting where students first develop not only respect for government authority but also faith in the democratic process. Even more startling is the assumption, implicit in *Ingraham,* that even though teachers may be absolutely wrong on a disciplinary matter, they should nevertheless be permitted to inflict corporal punishment in order to preserve their authority over their class.[50] Finally, the majority opinion is a direct repudiation of the underlying rationale of *Goss.* The *Goss* majority recognized the need for a presuspension hearing in order to unravel the facts that often turn on conflicting evidence in disciplinary cases. Yet similar conflicting facts or extenuating circumstances can also accompany the infliction of corporal punishment for violation of school rules. In fact, one of the plaintiffs in *Ingraham* testified at trial that he had been paddled for not having sneakers to wear in physical-education class. In reality, his sneakers had been stolen and his family could not afford to purchase another pair for him. A prepunishment hearing would have revealed the circumstances surrounding the violation of a school rule that hardly merited physical punishment at all.

A synthesis of *Goss* and *Ingraham* would mean that students are entitled to a minimal hearing before being removed from school for a mere ten days or less but are denied similar procedural protections when school officials can potentially inflict bodily harm, at the least violating their personal dignity through the imposition of physical punishment. These cases clearly do not square with each other.

Right to Privacy

The third area in which the Supreme Court has eroded the scope of students' liberties is the right to be free from unreasonable searches and seizures in the school setting. This right is based in the Fourth Amendment to the Constitution, which protects "the right of the people to be secure in their persons, houses, papers, and effects, against unreasonable searches and seizures." The amendment further requires that a search warrant be issued only upon "probable cause." The Court has extended the "probable cause" standard to cases where expediency may permit a search even without a warrant. Underlying Fourth Amendment protections is a fundamental recognition that individuals have certain expectations of privacy and personal security that government cannot invade. Underlying the probable-cause standard is an understanding that government needs effective methods for addressing breaches of the public order.

As any school teacher or administrator knows, breaches of school rules and policies and even the law are common, particularly at the secondary level. In recent years, the media have bombarded us with images of the dark side of school life — students carrying weapons, taking or dealing in drugs, and school officials overwhelmed with the burdens of maintaining order. The issue of student searches raises broad questions concerning official authority and the nature of schooling, similar to those raised in other disciplinary contexts. Do school officials act *in loco parentis* as was traditionally thought; that is, do they act in place of the parent in the interests of the child even when meting out punishment, or are they exercising public authority for the public good while holding the interests of the child only secondary? Are public-school officials bound by the strictures of the Constitution (here the Fourth Amendment), or does the unique nature of the school setting and the need to maintain a safe and effective learning environment exempt them from the amendment's dictates? More specifically, what expectations may students reasonably have that school officials will not search their automobiles, lockers, purses, and persons for evidence of impermissible or illegal activity?

The Court grappled with these questions in its 1985 decision in *New Jersey v. T.L.O.*[51] The facts of this case are common in today's public schools. A teacher found T.L.O., a high school student, smoking cigarettes in a school rest room. When questioned by the vice prinipal, she denied that she had been smoking. The vice principal demanded to see her purse and, upon examination, found a package of cigarette rolling papers commonly associated with marijuana. He proceeded to search through the purse and found marijuana, a pipe, plastic bags, a substantial amount of money in one-dollar bills, a list of students who apparently owed T.L.O. money, and two letters implicating her in marijuana dealing. The vice principal reported the incident to the police and turned the seized items over to them. Subsequently, the state brought delinquency charges against her, and T.L.O. moved to suppress the evidence on the grounds that it had been illegally seized and that the search violated the Fourth Amendment.

Judging from the opinions generated by the case and the bare majority joining in Justice White's opinion, at the heart of *T.L.O.* were controversial issues over which the Court was deeply divided. The one point on which all the Justices agreed was that public-school students come within the protections of the Fourth Amendment. In fact, the majority opinion is somewhat misleading in tone, opening with a broad reaffirmation of students' constitutional rights and a student-oriented vision of schooling. Citing *Barnette, Tinker,* and *Goss* as its guides, the majority rejected the doctrine of *in loco parentis* as inaccurately applied to the contemporary student-school relationship. According to the majority, "school officials act as representatives of the State, not merely as surrogates for the parents, and they cannot claim the parents' immunity from the strictures of the Fourth Amendment."[52]

Yet, despite the almost convincing rhetoric upholding the privacy interests of public-school students, the majority in *T.L.O.* distorted the traditional standard of probable cause to the point where, in effect, students scarcely enjoy Fourth Amendment rights in the school setting. Balancing the privacy interests of school children against the need of school officials to maintain order, the majority lowered the level of suspicion of illicit activity necessary to justify a search. In other words, the unique nature of the school setting justified the majority's abandoning the standard of probable cause for a more relaxed one of "reasonable suspicion." According to the majority, this reasonableness standard involves two inquiries: whether the search was justified from the beginning and whether the search was reasonably related to the circumstances that had justified it. A search would be justified "at its inception" if school officials have reasonable grounds to suspect that the student has or is violating either the law or a school rule. Measured against this standard, the search of T.L.O was found to be reasonable.

The conceptual flaws and the inevitable consequences of the majority's reasoning were best examined by Justice Stevens in his separate opinion in which he criticized the majority's relaxation of the probable-cause standard and its test for determining "reasonableness." Justice Stevens rightly conceded that school officials' warrantless searches of students are reasonable when undertaken to stem "violent, unlawful, or seriously disruptive conduct."[53] However, the majority's approval would justify a search if school officials suspect that it will reveal evidence that the student has or is violating either a law or a school rule, no matter how trivial. As Justice Stevens aptly put it, "a search for curlers and sunglasses in order to enforce the school dress code is apparently just as important as a search for evidence of heroin addiction or violent gang activity."[54] Both would be considered "reasonable" at their inception, and both could lead to the uncovering of other evidence that would be handed over to law enforcement officials to be used in subsequent criminal proceedings. Justice Stevens suggested an alternate standard, one more directly furthering the school's interest in maintaining order, whereby school officials would be permitted to search a student when they have reason to believe that the search will uncover evidence that the student is violating the law or engaging in conduct that is seriously disruptive of school order or the educational process. Such a standard, which ties the extent of the intrusion to the severity of the suspected offense and the degree of school disruption, flows more directly from both the common law and the case law.

T.L.O. raises another concern that goes more to the functions of schooling and the importance of teaching democratic principles. It cannot be denied that "the schoolroom is the first opportunity most citizens have to experience the power of government."[55] It is the place where children learn democracy, not just in theory but in action. Yet the majority seemed to miss this significant point in both *T.L.O.* and *Ingraham.* These cases show that the school environment is something separate and apart from the principles it engenders and, even more startling, that government officials can at times wield their power without adequate limits imposed by society or law. If these are hard truths emanating from the nation's highest court, they clearly undermine conventional notions of schooling and, ironically, the Court's own rhetoric on the importance of education in preparing students for good citizenship.

Balancing the Interests

The foregoing discussion tracks the Supreme Court's attempt to define the scope of the public-school student's constitutional rights within a changing ideology of schooling. The case law demonstrates that the Court has recently moved from a progressive vision of schooling as a participatory process to a view of education as a mechanism for inculcating societal and community values. A parallel development has been the Court's changing view of children from self-determining individuals to persons in need of state protection. This shift in perspective has resulted in an erosion of the constitutional status of students and a marked increase in the discretion afforded school authorities in treating student behavior that deviates in any way from what they consider to be the norm. The Court has strained to fit its changing ideology into the doctrinal framework of the past. Recent cases are replete with references to *Barnette*, *Tinker*, and *Goss* as the foundations of student rights. Nevertheless, cases such as *Ingraham*, *Pico*, *T.L.O.*, *Fraser*, and *Hazelwood* indicate an evolving viewpoint on the Court that weighs heavily on the side of institutional autonomy at the expense of individuals rights.

Even the most ardent advocate of children's rights must admit that public schools over the past two decades have been besieged with disciplinary problems from within and have become the object of public scorn and dissatisfaction from without. According to a recent U.S. Department of Education Survey, 44 percent of public-school teachers reported more disruptive behavior in their schools in 1986-87 than they had five years earlier, and 29 percent reported that student behavior "greatly interfered" with student learning.

No one can doubt the need for school officials to maintain a safe and effective learning environment. No one can challenge their authority and responsibility to make curriculum choices. No one can deny the uniqueness of the school setting and the inherent tension that such a uniqueness brings. Parents turn their children over to the state and thereby delegate certain authority to school officials, but these officials do not serve as surrogates for the parents. Obviously, they do not always act in the best interest of each child but must look to the larger good of all the students in making administrative and educational decisions. In that sense, school teachers, administrators, and school-board members are clearly agents of government whose discretion must be circumscribed within the limits of constitutionalism. American schooling operates within a strong political culture of local control, governed by popularly elected boards theoretically representing the will of the community. But deeply embedded in the social and political fabric and transcending constitutional law is a notion that government must not suppress freedom of thought and belief and must deal fairly.

These dualities have shaped the development of student rights into a balancing act, where the Court shifts the weight from one side to the other, based on what appear to be result-oriented legal and practical rationales. In the disciplinary cases addressing due process and privacy interests, the Court appears to have utilized a cost-benefit analysis, weighing the school's need to maintain its own institutional integrity, efficiency, and effectiveness against the interest of students that school officials will treat them fairly and openly. In bowing toward the school's interests, the Court contradicts its own ideological framework. If the primary function of public schools is truly to inculcate societal values, they should teach students about the need for responsible government to engender popular confidence and loyalty. Yet the Court's decisions, particularly in *Ingraham* and *T.L.O.*, where students were not afforded even the rudiments of fair and honest treatment, seem to teach a contrary lesson. These would have been easy cases for the Court to decide otherwise within a values-inculcation model of schooling. And yet a majority of the Justices chose not to do so, leaving a constitutional doctrine that places almost unbridled discretion in the hands of school officials, renders principles of fairness and privacy as a matter of constitutional right almost a nullity in the school setting, and leaves the students' interests to the vagaries of state constitutions and statutory law, which apparently have not provided adequate protections from disciplinary abuse. According to the National Committee for Citizens in Education, over the past five years the group's hotline caseworkers have counseled 2,800 parents who claimed that their children suffered the consequences of negative discipline practices. Most of these complaints concerned corporal punishment, which is still legal in thirty-nine states and out-of-school suspensions for trivial offenses or truancy.

The First Amendment cases present a more complex set of issues. No doubt the Court's broad pronouncement in *Tinker* is difficult to reconcile with its waffling toward a rough procedural accommodation in *Pico* and its far more limiting language in *Fraser* and *Hazelwood*. While the facts of *Tinker* are clearly distinguishable from those of the later cases, it is essentially the Court's shift in underlying ideology and the implications of that shift for school practice that most troubles critics of the majority opinions in those cases.

Be that as it may, the twenty years between *Tinker* (1968) and *Hazelwood* (1988) witnessed a crisis in values throughout the country and a conservative backlash to the perceived excesses of progressive education. No longer does a widely held consensus exist on the political and social values to be reflected in the school's implicit and explicit curriculum. Issues like sex education, abortion, feminism, and school prayer are tearing communities apart. Dissenting voices are heard from the political right as well as the left. This chaotic state has proved particularly troublesome for the Supreme Court Justices who are straining to develop and apply constitutional doctrine within a political ideology of local control and community power and an evolving ideology of schooling based on values inculcation. But do the school board and school officials necessarily reflect community values? And even if they do, can the majority in a community impose an orthodoxy of beliefs on the minority and thereby suppress dissenting voices? Can the "curriculum" be so broadly defined as to permit school officials almost boundless discretion and thereby foreclose students from all channels of critical thought and debate, including the school newspaper and student government?

Judging from the Court's most recent decisions in *Fraser* and *Hazelwood*, a majority of the Justices appear to answer yes to all three questions, at least when school officials are suppressing speech that they consider "lewd," "indecent," or "educationally inappropriate," given the age of the audience as judged against traditional or conservative standards. No doubt, these traditional values represent those of the majority of the Justices as well. One wonders how the Court would come out on a similar case brought by conservative dissenters challenging the suppression of speech or the imposition of a more liberal orthodoxy. The Court recently avoided addressing such an issue by denying review to a case brought by fundamentalist Christian parents who challenged a state-approved reading program used in the elementary school on the grounds that it included topics like feminism, evolution, and magic and thereby represented values inimicable to their religious beliefs.[56] By denying review the Court let stand the appeals court decision rejecting that challenge and upholding the authority of school officials to make curriculum decisions.

Given the level of sophistication of most modern-day secondary students, the Court's best attempt at resolving the First Amendment dilemma still lies in *Tinker's* "material and substantial disruption" standard. This preserves a safe and effective learning environment while preventing school officials from imposing an orthodoxy of beliefs or suppressing critical thought. The Court's next best effort was seen in *Pico*. There the plurality opinion utilized a procedural approach and applied a motivational test, at least to the school-library setting. School officials could remove books from the school library as long as the removal was based on "educational relevance" and not on a "narrowly partisan or political" motivation. But in *Pico* the Court also recognized broader official discretion when making curriculum determinations. Apparently, the majority of the Justices completely cast aside even this limited procedural standard when presented with countervailing interests of the wider student audience in *Fraser* and *Hazelwood*.

Putting together the Court's major pronouncements on schooling in the past two decades, at least those made in the context of the cases discussed in this essay, the Court has moved in the direction of handing over almost unbridled discretion to local school officials. What are the practical implications of this trend in Court thinking? First, without clearly defined standards against which to judge their conduct, school officials will be more likely to make arbitrary administrative and educational decisions with little regard, if any, for their impact on individual students. Second, extending the Court's ideology to its logical extreme, schools will no longer serve as arenas where ideas can be tested and challenged in the search for truth; the curriculum will inevitably become narrowed to reflect a set of neutral (i.e., noncontroversial) values, and students will be deprived of the stimulation and challenge necessary to develop creative minds. But most important, despite the Court's rhetoric reaffirming the student's constitutional rights, the majority's refusal to establish clear procedural guidelines for protecting those rights has not only divested them of any vitality but is creating a school climate in which students may develop a cynicism toward government authority. Perhaps this symbolic or perceptual impact of the trend in Court thinking is the most damaging of all from both individual and societal perspectives.

This is not to suggest that federal judges should involve themselves in the daily operation of public schools, second-guessing the substantive decisions of those trained to make educational and administrative choices. But the Supreme Court should establish parameters to ensure that the conduct of school officials complies with fundamental constitutional values. *Tinker* and *Goss* represent an attempt on the part of some of the Justices to strike that delicate balance. It would be wise for the Court, as an institution, to reconsider its current hands-off approach and reassess the merits of safeguards that guide the process of official decision making without determining the outcomes.

NOTES

1. Michael S. Wald, "Children's Rights: A Framework of Analysis," *University of California, Davis Law Review* 12 (1974): 256.

2. Martha Minow, "Rights for the Next Generation: A Feminist Approach to Children's Rights," *Harvard Women's Law Journal* 9 (1986): 9.

3. See, *e.g.*, *McKeiver* v. *Pennsylvania*, 403 U.S. 528 (1971) (children in juvenile court not entitled to the same right to trial by jury as afforded adults); *Parham* v. *J.R.*, 442 U.S. 584 (1979) (children not entitled to an adversarial hearing before commitment to a mental institution); *H.L.* v. *Matheson*, 450 U.S. 398 (1981) (state law may require unemancipated minor to notify parents before obtaining an abortion); *Schall* v. *Martin*, 467 U.S. 253 (1984) (state may authorize detention of juveniles who pose a serious risk of committing a crime).

4. William B. Senhauser, "Education and the Court: The Supreme Court's Educational Ideology," *Vanderbilt Law Review* 40 (1987): 941.

5. 262 U.S. 390 (1923).

6. Ibid., 401-2.

7. 268 U.S. 510 (1925).

8. Ibid., 535.

9. 406 U.S. 205 (1972).

10. Ibid., 232.

11. 319 U.S. 624 (1943).

12. Ibid., 642.

13. 393 U.S. 503.

14. *Tinker*, 406.

15. Ibid., 511.

16. Ibid., 513.

17. 457 U.S. 853 (1982).

18. 106 S. Ct. 3159 (1986).

19. Alexander Meikeljohn, *Political Freedom* (Port Washington, New York: Kennikat Press, 1948), 75.

20. Thomas I. Emerson, *Toward a General Theory of the First Amendment* (New York: Random House, 1966), 26.

21. *Fraser*, 3165, citing *Tinker*, 508.

22. Ibid., 3168 (Brennan, J., concurring).

23. 108 S. Ct. 562 (1988).

24. Ibid., 570.

25. Ibid., 567, citing *Fraser*, 3166.

26. Ibid., 570, citing *Fraser*, 3165.

27. Ibid., 574 (Brennan, J., dissenting).

28. Ibid., 577, citing *Keyishian* v. *Board of Regents*, 385 U.S. 589 (1967).

29. Ibid., 577, citing *Thomas* v. *Collins*, 323 U.S. 516 (1945) (Jackson, J., concurring).

30. *Tinker*, 512, quoting *Keyishian* v. *Board of Regents*, 385 U.S. 589, 603 (1967).

31. Stanley Ingber, "Socialization, Indoctrination, or the 'Pall of Orthodoxy': Value Training in the Public Schools," *University of Illinois Law Review* (1987): 83.

32. *Tinker*, 526 (Black, J., dissenting).

33. Lawrence Tribe, *American Constitutional Law* (Mineola, N.Y.: Foundation Press, 1988), 664.

34. *Hurtado* v. *California*, 110 U.S. 516, 535 (1984).

35. Warren A. Seavey, "Dismissal of Students: Due Process," *Harvard Law Review* 70 (1957): 1406-7.

36. 294 F.2d 150 (5th Cir.), *cert. denied*, 368 U.S. 930 (1961).

37. Mark G. Yudof, "Legalization of Dispute Resolution, Distrust of Authority, and Organizational Theory: Implementing Due Process for Students in the Public School," *Wisconsin Law Review* (1981): 901.

38. 387 U.S. 1 (1967).

39. 397 U.S. 358 (1970).

40. 419 U.S. 565 (1975).

41. Ibid., 574, quoting *Tinker*, 506.

42. Ibid., 593 (Powell, J., dissenting).

43. Ibid., 597.

44. 430 U.S. 651 (1977).

45. Ibid., 678.

46. Ibid., 693 (White, J., dissenting).

47. Ibid., 695, citing *Goss*, 583-84.

48. Ibid., 692.

49. Ibid., 683, citing *Tinker*, 507.

50. Irene Merker Rosenberg, "*Ingraham* v. *Wright*: The Supreme Court's Whipping Boy," *Columbia Law Review* 78 (1978): 99.

51. 469 U.S. 325 (1985).

52. Ibid., 336-37.

53. Ibid., 376 (Stevens, J., concurring and dissenting).

54. Ibid., 378.

55. Ibid., 386.

56. *Mozert* v. *Hawkins County Public Schools*, 827 F.2d 1058 (8th Cir. 1987), *cert. denied*, 108 S. Ct. 1029 (1988).

The Power of Community Service

DIANE P. HEDIN

This essay will focus on the impact of community service on students — on their education and their values. But caution must be exercised in framing the case for community service primarily in terms of its capacity to improve the character of adolescents. If the objective is real change in the way young people view their obligations to the community, it cannot be assumed that the young person is the prime beneficiary of service. Youth community service is powerful because it benefits the community as much as it does the student. It is powerful because it changes the role of student from being solely a consumer of educational services to a contributor to others. What is important about community service is that young people are being asked to give of themselves, to share their problem-solving skills, their empathy, their sensitivity, and their concern for other people.

That is not to ignore or depreciate the capacity of community service to enhance value development or citizenship education. But the argument for expanding service opportunities as remedial education for selfish and unconcerned teenagers is troublesome. The litany of the sorry state of adolescent values is all too familiar: Young people have never been more self-centered, more concerned with money, power, and status and less concerned about helping others. Youth have never been more violent, out of control, and beyond the influence of their parents and the community.

The usual evidence given to support this position comes from Astin's annual American Council on Education survey of incoming college freshmen, which indicates that the goal of "being well off financially" rose from 29 percent in 1970 to 76 percent in 1987. In contrast, "developing a meaningful philosophy of life" was important to only 39 percent in 1987, compared with 83 percent in 1967.[1] Another study often cited is that of the Gallup Poll on volunteering, which indicates that volunteering among eighteen–twenty-four-year-olds decreased from 54 percent in 1981 to 43 percent in 1985.[2] Nearly all calls for community service list the grim statistics on teenage pregnancy, drug abuse, and crime (all of which are actually on the decline).

This line of analysis argues that the changing values of young people themselves are primarily the source of the problem. But it is equally plausible that youth
mirror the dominant values of the larger society and that, more than at any other
time in the last twenty years, youth hold values quite similar to adults on achievement and success. In fact, in the late 1960s and early 1970s when young people
did not hold those values, many adults pressured young people to abandon anti-
materialistic and politically progressive beliefs. Blaming young people for not being
more altruistic and other-centered than their adult models is unfair; indeed, it
is a variation on the theme of blaming the victim.

It also seems particularly unfair for educators to blame adolescents for being
self-centered in view of the nature of the educational institutions, which are designed primarily to help some young people achieve at the expense of others. There
is competition for a limited number of academic and social prizes—being in the
top 10 percent of the class, acceptance at top universities, merit scholarships,
homecoming king or queen, and so on. Despite some welcome movement toward
cooperative learning and refocusing on values and youth service, those movements
are really at the periphery of the educational debate. Still at the center are calls
for more frequent testing, higher academic standards, more uniform curriculum,
and the like. When educational policymakers offer high-minded statements about
the importance of service, citizenship, and concern for others, one must ask whether
implementation of such policies can coexist with the current focus on a narrow
band of academic achievement.

Another disincentive for the young to be engaged in service has to do with the
value the whole society places on paid work during the teen years. Less than twenty
years ago, only about 40 percent of high-school students worked after school; now
nearly 80 percent of sixteen–eighteen-year-olds work at least fifteen hours per week.
Again, youth accurately reflect one of the larger values of American society: making
money is more important than spending one's discretionary time in service to
others. In most American corporations, even though voluntarism in the community is viewed as an important civic responsibility, few employees get time off
to volunteer. Being on the job and doing what an employee is paid for is viewed
as far more important than providing volunteer service, and it appears that secondary schools follow the same philosophy.

In addition, sentencing lawbreakers to do service offers a highly contradictory
message about the value that society attaches to meeting unmet social and environmental needs. The courts ought to quit using community service as a punishment for everything from drunk driving to vandalism to sexual assault. While
it may be a successful intervention for some acts of adult and juvenile delinquency,
this practice does great harm to the development of a service ethic for all members
of the community.

The current movement to establish community service as a new Carnegie unit
or extracurricular activity brings with it a set of problems that may keep service
programs from fulfilling their greatest potential—a pathway to knowledge and
academic growth. After all, for most schools and most educators, the central focus

of the enterprise is the accumulation of knowledge, academic learning, and the growth of the intellect. To pigeonhole service as an extracurricular activity used exclusively to improve the values of young people is almost surely to condemn it to a short life. Moreover, a rich body of theory and some research demonstrate that community service can have a positive impact on young people's intellectual development.

Community service is particularly effective in helping motivate the learner. Finding ways for students to become truly engaged in their education seems to be one of the major problems that schools face. A Minnesota Youth Poll conducted a few years ago asked high-school students what they thought was the leading problem in school, the same question the Gallup Poll has asked adults for twenty years. In contrast to the adult response (lack of discipline for seventeen of the twenty years and drug abuse for the other three), youth believe lack of motivation to learn is the greatest problem. They say: "Kids just really don't care." "Most are so bored they don't pay attention to anything." And "lack of enthusiasm is one of the biggest problems."[3]

Boredom is probably a function of what seems to many students an unfathomable gap between the curriculum and their everyday lives. Community service can help young people see the connection between academic content and real problems they themselves face. I have seen students sit with rapt attention while I read the regulations governing nursing homes. They were interested because they had volunteered to serve in a nursing home that had no recreational program and little stimulation of any kind. They wanted to know whether the home was violating the law and whether the director could be forced to allow the students to add a recreation component. Here seemingly "boring" information was valuable because it would be used to make a difference in the lives of the elderly residents. Community service provides the critical missing link for many students, an opportunity to apply academic learning to real human needs and to make the knowledge gained usable in one's thinking beyond the situation in which the learning occurred.

The other key way in which service can improve academic learning is that it improves retention. Few facts learned as children, as teenagers, or as adults are retained. But when one applies information, there seems to be less loss of particular facts. James S. Coleman has suggested that the "quick rate of loss of human memory seems to be better inhibited by the memory of an action taken and the environmental response than by the organizations of principles and ideas from which the facts may be inferred."[4] Or put more simply by Ralph Tyler, "knowledge is like fish, if you don't use it right away it won't keep."

Components of Effective Community Service Programs

What students get from a community-service program depends, of course, on its quality. The task here is to identify the components that are usually present if learning and growth occur. Of course, even if all seven features of effective programs are present, not all students will show significant increases in social responsibility or knowledge about the phenomena in which they are involved. What individual students gain varies greatly, because there is no general educational experience for the whole group; each student has an idiosyncratic community-service experience.

The usual variables that one might assume to be significant—amount of time spent volunteering and the setting in which the volunteer works—are not automatically the most important. For example, one-time experiences are usually dismissed as of little value, but one day spent working in a soup kitchen feeding and interacting with people too poor to buy food could affect a young person's consciousness in a way that picking up litter in a park for a day might not.

Similarly, the place of service does not necessarily produce good outcomes. Some students working in a shelter for battered women or a nursing home, in the midst of extraordinary human drama and suffering, are capable of reducing their volunteer service to a series of routinized tasks without really interacting with the residents and can leave their twelve-week assignment the same as when they came.

Besides the amount of time and the placement, what are the features of a volunteer assignment that are likely to lead to student growth as well as valuable service being provided for the community? At least seven components of a service experience are necessary but not sufficient conditions for growth to occur, and they will be described through an example of one exemplary service project.

1. *Genuine tasks that both the young people and the community think are worth while.* At the beginning of the school year, a teacher and students at Hopkins High School in Hopkins, Minnesota, started reading about an elderly woman named Mrs. Bain in the newspaper and hearing her story on the television news. Media coverage had elevated the significance of her plight in the eyes of the students.

Mrs. Bain, eighty-eight years of age, was evicted from her home after being charged with reckless driving and assaulting a police officer. She lived in a tiny, ramshackle house in the midst of a wealthy upper-middle-class suburb. After being arrested for driving fifteen miles an hour in a minimum-55 zone, she was placed in a psychiatric hospital for assessment, her dogs and cat put in the pound, and her possessions removed. The city was ready to bulldoze her house when an investigative reporter started writing about Mrs. Bain, and it was later found that she was not mentally ill. The city officials had a problem—what to do with Mrs. Bain. Dan Conrad, the teacher who runs a community-involvement program, called the city manager to find out if there was anything his students might do to help defuse the situation.

2. *Opportunities for others to depend on the actions of young people.* In community service, students ought to be engaged in activities with real consequences for others. In this case, what Mrs. Bain most needed was someone to help her maintain her independence, or she would end up in a nursing home. This meant she needed help from the students in getting groceries and cleaning up her house (the city officials still insisted that she maintain her home in such a manner that it was not a fire or safety hazard). Moreover, she refused to accept any form of

help from the city; she was still furious with the city officials. But she felt a kinship with some of the students, who also often felt like pawns of "the authorities," and she welcomed their visits and their assistance.

3. *Tasks that challenge and strengthen the students' thinking — cognitively and ethically.* For community service to engage the students, the tasks must not be trivial but call on the students to use their most complex thinking skills. The Mrs. Bain case confronted the students with an array of ethical questions. For example, they had to consider why she was willing to accept their help but not that of the bureaucracy. Why is it difficult for public social services to reach the people who need their help the most? How can social services be offered in a way that preserves a person's dignity? What is the appropriate amount of power and authority that the city government can use to respond to the neighbors who did not like the way Mrs. Bain lived, i.e., what are the rights of the majority versus the minority?

4. *Making decisions and having responsibility to affect the direction of the project.* The situations in which young people learn the most are ones in which they have the opportunity to determine what needs to be done at developmentally appropriate levels of responsibility. When the students went to Mrs. Bain's house, they did not have a detailed job description to guide their work. The plan had to be developed in consultation with Mrs. Bain, by observing current conditions at her home and finding out what the other students were doing to help her.

For optimal student growth and for making a worthwhile contribution, students should be asked to make decisions that match their current level of development, not far beyond or far below their problem-solving capacity. A student with little initiative who requires a high degree of structure and a "detailed job description" would not do well at Mrs. Bain's home. Often the students who are labeled "rebellious" or who do not follow directions well do better in such a setting because they have a higher degree of initiative.

5. *Working together with adults and youth on common tasks.* As an antidote to what was described above as the self-centered nature of schooling, projects that allow students and teachers or youth workers to plan and work cooperatively to achieve some goal are preferable. While the usual pattern in providing help to Mrs. Bain was that students worked in teams, one Christmas a project involved all thirty-six students in the class. It started with a comment from Mrs. Bain: "I've got a crazy idea; I want my big pine tree in the front yard decorated for Christmas." She described how she had planted the seedling fifty years before — a seedling she had carried from her childhood home in northern Minnesota. Far from thinking it was a crazy idea, the students and their teacher were intrigued with it.

There were a number of factors to consider. Since she had almost no money, using electric lights was not an option, and the students had to devise decorations on a scale large enough to be seen on a forty-five-foot Norway pine. The industrial-arts teacher offered to donate materials and woodwork-shop class time to cut huge Christmas tree ornaments in the shape of stars, balls, and bells. A paint store donated iridescently bright paint. Finally, the fire department let the students borrow its ladder truck, which could reach the full length of the tree.

After local television stations heard about the project, the story appeared on the news. For the first time, Mrs. Bain achieved attention not for violating safety regulations but for the beauty of her Christmas decorations and the breadth of her friendships.

6. *Systematic reflection on the service experience.* In effective community-service programs, action is not separated from reflection. One of the best supported findings of research about community service is that students learn most (knowledge about the people for whom they volunteer, attitudes about being responsible and being active citizens, and problem-solving skills) when they are in programs that have regular opportunities to process and talk about their direct experiences.

Volunteering to help Mrs. Bain was in the context of a social-studies course for seniors, who worked in the community four days a week (a total of eight hours) and had a classroom session for two hours a week. The theme of the course was human development, and theories of how people grow and develop through the life cycle were studied. Moreover, students studied theories and practice in the art of helping others. They kept a daily journal; they were asked to develop critical incidents to highlight problems in their field placement for which they needed ideas from their fellow students and teacher. For the students who worked with Mrs. Bain, the course work on developing effective skills in working with people (empathy, communication, listening, and counseling) and content about gerontology (the particular needs and concerns of the elderly and arguments for and against various housing arrangements) have direct and immediate application.

7. *A final product of the students' effort.* Discovering the full meaning and significance of the volunteer experience often requires the students to pull together their array of feelings, new knowledge, new attitudes, and new perspectives into a final product that allows them to preserve the experience and apply its implications in another context at another time. Students who worked with Mrs. Bain were required to write a final "expert paper" in which they related their experience as an "expert" working with the elderly. The students were also required to do library research on the topic and offer their own generalizations and insights about working with this population. In other community-service programs and projects, students have produced videos documenting their work, written a set of guidelines or tips to a new group of students on how to work with a particular problem or population, helped orient the incoming volunteers, and so forth.

Outcomes of Community Service

While it is unlikely that even the best programs have all of these components fully present, when more of them occur the chances of positive results are clearly improved. When this is the case, what will happen to the student's growth and learning? There are two sources of evidence. The first, and most common, is qualitative data—the observations of adults and young people who have been involved in community-service programs, their self-reports, journals, interview data, testimonials, and the like. Often these sources of data are dismissed as "soft," that is, not serious or real evidence. "Real" data, in the eyes of most educational evaluators and policy analysts are quantitative data—featuring standardized instruments, paper and pencil tests, control groups, random assignment, and so on. Both kinds of evidence are available about the impact of community service, and both have their place. Evidence from quantitative methodologies is more limited, though a body of research will be described below that shows a strong trend toward social, personal, and academic development being fostered by community service. On the other hand, evidence from qualitative, anecdotal, observation data is far more consistent in suggesting community service is a useful, enjoyable, and powerful learning experience; that set of evidence will also be explored in more detail later.

Quantitative Research on Academic and Social Personal Outcomes

The case was made above that community service is a way to improve academic learning. The evidence is strongest for peer tutoring and teaching. Using a technique called meta-analysis, several researchers have combined the findings of many tutoring studies and have found that increases in reading and mathematics achievement scores, both on the part of the tutor and tutee, were found consistently. The changes in reading and mathematics knowledge tend to be small, modest, and incremental, as is the case with most learning and growth; full-scale conversions happen, sad to say, infrequently. Indeed, tutoring was found to be a more effective tool for raising academic outcomes than a technologically oriented approach of computer-assisted instruction.[5] In scattered cases, students in community participation outperform their fellow students on standardized tests for factual knowledge of subjects like local government and politics, but as frequently no difference is found.

It is likely that positive academic outcomes are found more frequently for tutoring because it is the form of community service that is most "school-like," and the methods of assessment closely parallel the tutors' experience. In contrast, when standardized instruments of factual knowledge are used to assess what students gain in more expansive and complex experiences, such as internships and projects in which students play multiple roles in unfamiliar settings like social agencies and hospitals, the instrumentation is too narrow to tap the array of knowledge gained.

In broader forms of intellectual development, several studies have probed into the impact of service on processes of thinking—such as problem solving, open-mindedness, and critical thinking. Wilson found that students who participated in some kind of political and social action in the school or wider community became more open-minded.[6] Conrad and Hedin found that students' problem-solving ability as measured by reactions to a series of real-life problems increased more for the students in community-service programs than for those in comparison groups. Furthermore, students' ability to solve complex problems improved substantially when they had encountered problems similar to those presented in the test and the program had deliberately focused on problem solving. Students who had neither discussed their experiences with teachers and fellow students nor had encountered problems similar to those presented in the test showed no more change than students in conventional classrooms. Other studies have focused on the skills learned through direct experience. Consistently, these studies show that high-school students can become competent in counseling, teaching, classroom management, basic social-research skills, and case presentation.

Not only do well-run, well-conceptualized community-service programs affect students' knowledge and intellectual capacity, but they can also influence social-development outcomes (e.g., level of personal and social responsibility, civic involvement, commitment to basic democratic values) and psychological development (e.g., self-esteem, moral development, ego development).

Conrad and Hedin studied twenty-seven school-sponsored programs featuring direct participation, such as community service, community study, career internships, and outdoor adventure, and found that most students in participatory programs did improve in social and personal responsibility.[7] Stephen F. Hamilton found similiar results with a groups of 4-H members engaged in various forms of participation — child care, community improvement programs, and the like.[8] Fred M. Newmann and Robert A. Rutter found community-service programs increased students' sense of social responsibility and personal competence more than did those in control groups.[9] Stephen F. Hamilton, Conrad and Hedin, and Marilyn Luchs all found that youth in experience-based programs gained more positive attitudes toward and increased their associations with adults and the type of institutions and people with whom the students were involved. Studies that have probed political efficacy and attitude about subsequent civic participation have had mixed results. An equal number of studies find and do not find increases on these dimensions.

The effect of community participation on self-esteem has been the psychological variable most commonly investigated. Increases in self-esteem have been found for students in the role of tutors, service providers for the mentally disabled, and in more general helping roles. Newmann and Rutter reported that students involved in community-service projects increased on a dimension closely related to self-esteem, a sense of social competence on such tasks as communicating effectively to groups, starting conversations with strangers, persuading adults to take their views seriously, and the like.[10]

A number of studies have assessed the impact of service experiences, such as being a peer counselor, interviewer, and teacher, on moral and ego development. The typical, though not universal, outcome is that students gain in both moral and ego development. A general conclusion of theory and research about developmental education is that moral and ego development can be enhanced by educational programs that allow the exercise of empathy and role-taking and action in behalf of moral and social goals and offer "experiences of moral responsibility and independent moral choice."[11]

In summary, quantitative research on the impact of community service suggests that this approach can and often does have a positive effect on intellectual and social-psychological development of student participants. Researchers consistently report a heightened sense of social responsibility, more positive attitudes toward adults and others, greater understanding and more active exploration of careers, enhanced self-esteem, growth in moral and ego development, more complex patterns of thought, and greater mastery of skills and content directly related to the experiences of participants. Findings are mixed on whether community service increases political efficacy and later participation in civic affairs. Only rarely does participation result in higher scores on standardized tests of factual knowledge, with the clear exception of academic achievement scores for students in the role of teacher or tutor.

Findings from Qualitative Research

While there is a considerable body of evidence on the positive impact of community service, the studies mentioned above have been subject to the criticisms leveled at nearly all research in natural rather than experimental settings—lack of true control groups, lack of randomization, inadequate instrumentation, researcher bias, and the like. Yet anyone who has worked with or evaluated community-service programs cannot help being struck by the consistently high regard in which they are held by students, teachers, community supervisors, parents, and those being served. This gap between what quantitative and qualitative methodologies uncover about community service should suggest that the practice is so varied, idiosyncratic, and complex that richer and more varied sources of data than typically gathered are necessary.

A recent example of a community-service project in which the author was involved will illustrate this dilemma. The scene was a soup kitchen, and the project was a meal prepared and served by a group of sixth and seventh graders to the 300 people who came that Saturday noon for a free meal. The students and the parent volunteer who supervised them had solicited food at their school and supermarkets, prepared a hearty soup, homemade bread, and cupcakes, and served the meal.

The day was a series of dramatic, unpredictable, and powerful events. For example, my three-year-old son accompanied me to the soup kitchen. When we walked in the door, a young woman with a child said to me: "If you have a child, you know you can go to the front of the line." There was no escaping one conclusion—the differences in appearance between a middle-class person and a mother with a child who rely on soup kitchens are negligible. It reminds us of the fragility of our advantaged circumstances.

The next thing that happened, equally difficult for an educational evaluator to anticipate, was my child's reaction to the place and its implication for my view of myself. My little boy kept his hand over his nose and constantly complained about the smell. The combination of vegetables in the soup had produced an unpleasant odor. But what occurred to me was that my child had been so sheltered in a sanitized environment that he seemed incapable of adapting to a new, unfamiliar one—a devastating indictment of my child-rearing practices.

Next the director of the soup kitchen talked about why it was crowded. Another surprising thing—he did not agree with most antihunger advocates that soup kitchens are filled at the end of the month because food stamps run out. Instead, he offered the classical conservative argument that "these people" are not planful and careful in budgeting their money and that their food stamps and welfare check would be sufficient if they did not squander their money in foolish ways. How could an evaluator anticipate the appropriate pretest questions that would demonstrate that my assumptions about the kind of persons who run these facilities were wrong?

Many more unanticipated events occurred, but the most surprising happened during the debriefing after the meal. It started out in the usual way, with the students observing that a variety of persons used the soup kitchen; they commented on how many looked like "ordinary" people, how appreciative they were, how difficult it was to make conversation because people seemed embarrassed to be there, and so on. The bombshell came when a sixth-grade girl quietly suggested that the students could have done more and that the parent volunteer who supervised the project had done too much of the work. She observed that the parent had made all the homemade bread and cooked the soup by herself. The girl said, "You know, I kind of think that us kids should have taken more responsibility and I know next time we could do more."

It appeared that the experience was accomplishing everything one might hope for, that the student learned that feeding the hungry is so important and consequential that she reconsidered her earlier behavior and vowed to put forth more effort in the future. Rather than applauding her sentiment, the parent volunteer became very angry and accused the students of not appreciating her hard work. She told them they had not done their share; and if it had not been for her, the people would not have been fed. The students yelled back, telling her that they had offered help, such as going to her house to bake the bread, but she refused their assistance. The parent become progressively more angry and left the room.

The debriefing continued, and the event provided insight into why it is difficult to capture the richness and complexity of community service through traditional evaluation techniques. The parent's reaction paralleled the mistakes educational evaluators often make. First, she had thought that the only way to succeed was to achieve the predetermined outcome—that the students offer great gratitude for all the parent had done and ask forgiveness for not having contributed more. The students' point of view, that they had learned from this experience but that they were capable of far more responsibility, was not the "correct" response. The parent also made the second error often committed by educational evaluators—that all the learning must happen immediately, at least before the posttest. I saw several of the students a week later, and they were talking about a new project they were planning to undertake with a different adult leader. If fact, there had been some change, growth, and learning; but because it was not completed at the time of the debriefing at the soup kitchen, the parent assumed they had gained nothing. My day at the soup-kitchen project demonstrates that community-service experiences are often too complex, illusive, and unpredictable to capture their sensibility through traditional evaluation methods. Rather, the power of service is better understood by letting the service providers themselves describe its meaning and value through journals, interviews, essays, and the like. Below are some journal entries of high-school students in a community-service course. These excerpts will illustrate student growth and change in the same domains as for the quantitative data, first social-psychological outcomes and then intellectual development.

The first entry speaks to the importance of being in a new role (other than pupil) as a way for adolescents to discover and affirm their competence and shed their perception of themselves as passive and powerless. A senior in high school writes:

> As I walked through the hallway [of the elementary school on my first day of leading children in theater experiences] I realized what I had gotten myself into . . . a challenge. But as I step through the door I transform from student to person. . . . The first day went extremely well, but I'm glad I don't have to go through it again. Now I return to school and become student again.

Increased levels of social and personal responsibility can often be an outcome of community service. In the following journal entry, a student suggests that becoming more reliable and committed to his work was a result of his relationship with a child, not the demand of an authority for conformity to a rule:

> As I entered St. D's it was my joy to see Adam wearing a smock covered with paint washing his hand at the sink. "Hi," I said. "Did you go to school yesterday?" he replied shortly. "Yes," I said guiltily. "Why didn't you come?" he demanded. "I didn't have a ride to get back from here," I explained thinking as fast as I could. When I started to touch his shoulder he jerked away and said, "Don't." So I left him alone. . . . I felt like a criminal.

Community service can broaden students' range of the people, places, and problems with which they feel a connection. It allows adolescents to break out of the isolated world of their peers. A young man who volunteered in a nursing home wrote about his connection to the elderly, a group he had avoided and disdained:

> I have come a *long* way though. I remember my first few days at Oak Terrace. I was scared to touch people, or the doorknobs even. And I used to wash my hands after I left there every single day! Can you believe it? Now I go and get big hugs and kisses from everyone. Get this—I even eat there! That's a horror story for some people.

Service allows young people to explore different parts of themselves. In the first quotation the young woman became a person, not a student, through her new role as teacher. A young man who chose to work with infants recognized that he had a capacity to be nurturing and caring:

> I didn't think they would give the job to a guy. Society has always thought that men were too tough to handle children and that they didn't know how to handle them correctly, or wouldn't want to. Well, I was out to prove them wrong. The first day I was

told that I was the first male to join the staff of the day care in 17 years. And it wasn't that great at first. I had to change diapers, wipe noses, bottle feed them and most of all, put up with their bloody whining and crying. I started to think that maybe I bit off more than I could chew. . . . All I can say is that I really love those kids. Can you believe that? Enjoying being with babies? Well, they've really affected my life and I'll miss them.

This essay has made the case that community service could have an impact on stimulating a key dimension of academic development—"higher-level thinking." Service experiences can provide an arena for allowing adolescents to focus their critical thinking capacity on the major questions in their lives: Who am I? Where am I going? Is there any point to it all? The fundamental issues are those of relationship, significance, connection, suffering, meaning, hope, love, and attachment. The following journal entries and portions of essays illustrate such critical thinking. In the first quotation, working in an elementary classroom stimulated a sixteen-year-old girl's thinking about the tendency human beings have to hide emotions and feelings as they "grow up" and to cut themselves off from connections to other people:

> My kids have so much love, touching, caring affection toward me and one another. It is amazing how much better you feel about yourself after getting all of this loving affection. It makes me wonder where, and when, we lost all that love and affection? You never see it in high school. In what grade does all this stop? Why does it stop? Does it have to stop? Does our society put such pressure on us that if boys hold hands in elementary school they will be laughed at and get the image of fags? Do parents, teachers stop this relationship or is it the whole environment in which we live?

An encounter with a child in a day-care center provoked a young woman to raise profound questions about the nature of human relationships and what seems to be an inherent tendency of people to inflict pain and injustice on others:

> "I don't want you," he stated defiantly. I just shrugged my shoulders and told him I liked his shoes. I said they were "cool and looked good." So we discussed his shoes. Somehow the subject changed to Scooby-doo. "I used to watch that a lot," I exclaimed. Adam told me that Scooby fell down into a tree while being chased by some man who was mad. This is the important stuff. Talking to a tiny person about Scooby Doo. It beats all the death in El Salvador. It puts El Salvador worlds away. Of course, you don't want to tell this kid that he's going to grow up in a sick world with a demented society where people die for nothing. Kids don't understand. Adults don't either. Why mention the fact that as he gets older he will be confused, judged by others; no they aren't God but still it's their self-appointed task to judge you, or worse you may become an asshole. The worst thing about assholes is that they don't realize that they are assholes. It's sad. So you talk to this tiny person and the world can stop or pass you by and it just doesn't matter. Anyway, Adam the brat became my friend.

Learning from service, like any real learning, is highly personal, dependent on both the learning environment and the individual learner. Not every service experience is a success. Some placements are barren, and some students do not respond to even the richest environment. But the above comments are not anomalies, special cases, or rarities. Young people are curious; they are seeking, wondering about themselves and their world. The power of service is that it places young people in a context in which the learning is real, alive, and with clear consequences for others and themselves. It does not reach everybody, but it reaches a far higher percentage — and more deeply than any other method that I have tried. For that reason, community service ought to have a prominent place in schools for adolescents.

NOTES

1. "Freshmen Found Stressing Wealth," *New York Times*, 14 Jan. 1988.
2. Independent Sector, "Americans Volunteer 1985" (Washington, D.C., 1985), 7–9.
3. Diane P. Hedin and Paula Simon, *Minnesota Youth Poll: Youth's Views on School and School Discipline*, Minnesota Report 184, Agricultural Experiment Station, University of Minnesota, 1983, 21–22.
4. James S. Coleman, "Differences between Experiential and Classroom Learning," in *Experiential Learning: Rationale, Characteristics and Assessment*, ed. Morris T. Keeton (San Francisco: Jossey-Bass, 1977), 54.
5. Diane P. Hedin, "Students as Teachers: A Tool for Improving School Climate and Productivity," *Social Policy* 17 (Winter 1987): 42–47.
6. T. C. Wilson, "An Alternative Community Based Secondary School Education Program and Student Political Development" (Doctoral dissertation, University of Southern California, 1974), 97–99.
7. Daniel E. Conrad and Diane P. Hedin, "The Impact of Experiential Education on Adolescent Development," in *Youth Participation and Experiential Learning*, ed. Daniel E. Conrad and Diane P. Hedin (New York: Haworth Press, 1983), 65–67.
8. Stephen F. Hamilton and L. Mickey Fenzel, "The Impact of Volunteer Experience on Adolescent Social Development: Evidence of Program Effects," *Journal of Adolescent Research* 3 (1988): 71–73.
9. Fred M. Newmann and Robert A. Rutter, *The Effects of High School Community Service Programs on Students' Social Development* (Madison: Wisconsin Center for Education Research, University of Wisconsin, 1983), 34.
10. Ibid.
11. Lawrence Kohlberg, "Stages and Aging in Moral Development: Some Speculations," *Gerontologist* 13 (1973): 500.

New Futures for America's Children

TOM JOE
DOUGLAS W. NELSON

As other contributors to this volume have indicated, many of the country's children are failing to grow into successful, productive adults. Not only are large numbers of students leaving high school before graduation, but an equally alarming number of graduates are ill-prepared for higher education or for an increasingly competitive labor market. These trends, moreover, are likely to continue until American communities find more effective ways of defining responsibility, establishing accountability, and integrating efforts among and within the key community institutions that affect the preparations and prospects of young people.

The Annie E. Casey Foundation launched an initiative in 1988 to assist five cities better to prepare youth for productive adulthood. Known as "New Futures," the initiative represents an ambitious strategy designed to enable selected communities to forge reformed institutional environments in which more young people can grow into successful, contributing adults. Although the goals of New Futures parallel other efforts by foundations, corporations, and states, the Casey initiative proceeds from a distinct set of assumptions and principles that collectively warrant analysis and debate by those interested in the general reform of public policy toward youth.

In 1987, the Annie E. Casey Foundation began a search for five midsized American cities that appeared willing and capable of making a visible and sustained commitment to restructuring their local youth-serving institutions. After a lengthy screening process that included site visits to some twenty-four cities, ten cities were chosen to develop plans, five of which were ultimately funded by the foundation.

To assist the cities in developing their plans, the foundation produced a document entitled "A Strategic Planning Guide for the New Futures Initiative." Written by the Center for the Study of Social Policy, the guide conveyed the foundation's sense of the depth and scope of the problems facing youth today, and it set forth a basic conceptual framework for both analyzing and addressing the needs of at-risk youth. This guidance grew out of a review of the relevant literature and an assessment of recent "best practice" initiatives from around the country. The guide identified four specific goals of the initiative: (1) to improve the academic level of at-risk students; (2) to increase school attendance and graduation rates; (3) to increase youth employment after high school; and (4) to reduce the incidence of adolescent pregnancy and parenthood.

Following a six-month planning process in which the ten cities developed detailed, multiyear plans, the foundation, in April 1988, selected five cities — Dayton, Ohio; Lawrence, Massachusetts; Little Rock, Arkansas; Pittsburgh, Pennsylvania; and Savannah, Georgia — each to receive between $5 million and $12 million over the next five years. The foundation required the cities to match its resources on at least a dollar-for-dollar basis; thus the total five-year budget for the initiative is expected to reach over $100 million.

The purpose of this essay is not to report on the cities' progress in implementing their plans but to outline the conceptualizations of at-risk youth problems and the central strategies for community action that shaped the development of those proposals. While it is too early to judge whether these ideas will prove effective, they are presented here as an instructive illustration of one deliberate attempt to incorporate current thinking about "what works" into a comprehensive approach to positive change for children.

An Institutional Analysis of the Problem

The seriousness of the problems afflicting many young people is now largely beyond debate. Whether it is functional illiteracy, teen-age pregnancy, juvenile crime, dropping out of school, or inadequate preparation for employment, most Americans are prepared to identify one or more of these issues as serious threats to the future of the coming generation. Unfortunately, however, there is far less agreement about what, if anything, can be done about any of these issues. The dilemma, in the eyes of many, is that most serious youth problems appear to be rooted in circumstances that cannot be easily altered. Poverty, family background, individual aptitudes — the evidence indicates — are the correlates for much of the academic underachievement, the lack of motivation, and the high-risk behavior that underlie youth problems. If social institutions cannot do much about the causes, so the argument goes, they are unlikely to do much about the consequences.

In some quarters, this view has become an excuse for inaction. Schools are not responsible for the economic, social, cultural, family, or individual problems that put some young people at risk; accordingly, they should not be held accountable for overcoming or resolving them. The same argument holds true for local governments, employers, community organizations, and even human-service agencies. At best, these institutions can try to compensate, ameliorate, or remediate the individual manifestations of disadvantage, but they can do little to prevent its occurrence or frequency.

There are, of course, different perspectives, and the Casey Foundation's New Futures initiative illustrates only one point of departure. In a sense, New Futures begins with a firm rejection of the notion that academic failure, teenage pregnancy, and dropping out are the inevitable consequences of aptitude, character, or even the constraints of class ethnicity and family status. Instead, New Futures sees these youth problems as the failure of community institutions to do what they can do to equip youngsters with the expectations, opportunities, supports, and incentives they need to become aspiring, responsible, and successful adults. From this vantage point, poverty, ethnicity, and personal differences are not viewed as irrelevant. They are seen as challenges to youth-serving institutions, not intractable determinants of individual destiny.

Informing this whole perspective is the view that schools, government, business, service agencies, and other local institutions have real power to create environments that actually shape the values, self-esteem, expectations, and behavior of at-risk youth. In a sense, it presumes that the shapers of community institutions have a choice; institutions can either reinforce social and economic disadvantage by communicating (through their policies, practices, and structures) low expectations, negative labeling, cultural bias, and limited opportunity for those at risk, or they can address these risk factors by creating countervailing environments based on the premise that all young people are able and are "entitled" to succeed.

Such an analysis, it should be clear, implies a demanding agenda for institutional change, and the New Futures program conveyed just such an ambitious challenge to its participating communities. In its planning guidelines, the Casey Foundation asked local leaders to think of New Futures not as an opportunity to add new categorical programs targeted narrowly to dropouts or failing students but as a process for reexamining and reforming the ways that schools, social services, media, employers, and others reinforce talent, self-esteem, aspiration, and achievement in all young people.

Principles of Institutional Reform

In order to help communities respond to this broad challenge of reform, the foundation attempted to translate its general assessment of the failure of community institutions to help all youth succeed into more focused principles that could serve as practical guides for community change. Among the most significant of these reform principles were (1) the crucial impact of reward, recognition, and incentive structures on the shaping of self-image and choices among youth; (2) the critical importance of concentrating on preventive institutional changes rather than on remedial programmatic responses; and (3) the need for mechanisms that enable large institutions to fashion individualized responses to specific aptitudes, interests, and problems.

Recognition and Rewards

The first of these themes — the emphasis on recognition and rewards — has been used by the Casey Foundation as a concrete way of describing how existing institutions tend to fail with at-risk youth. The key contention here is that conventional grading systems, the use of visible ability tracking, the reliance on curricula and teaching methods that respond to a limited range of learning styles, traditional discipline and suspension policies, existing eligibility rules for health and social services, and customary selection bias in job training and hiring — all of these accepted characteristics of contemporary youth-serving institutions contribute to, if not actually cause, failure among at-risk youth. They do so because they not only serve as barriers to successful experiences for some at-risk youth but also as powerful sources of stigmatization, alienation, low self-esteem, and limited aspirations for many others. New Futures, in effect, asks communities to identify these institutional reinforcements of failure and replace them with a more pluralistic and positive set of incentives. More specifically, it recommends consideration of more flexible curricula to accommodate a wider range of aptitudes and learning styles, the introduction of positive rewards for effort and achievement by less competitive students, and the introduction of more integrated and universal (i.e., less labeled) approaches to meeting the special learning, developmental, and support needs of some youngsters.

To some degree, the plans of all New Futures cities have incorporated elements of this principle. In Dayton and Pittsburgh, for example, an extended school day has been proposed as a vehicle to broaden the range of learning activities beyond the narrow confines of the current academic curriculum. Little Rock is planning a systematic reduction in its use of "pull-out" programs in order to lessen the negative labeling and stigma currently attached to its remedial and compensatory teaching efforts. Similarly, Pittsburgh has decided to eliminate its "general education track"— a modified curriculum path that has been seen as a reinforcer of low aspirations and, for some, as a route to underachievement and dropping out. In Savannah, after-school "success clubs" are being designed as ways of recognizing and rewarding the effort and aspiration of students who had been the object of low expectations. Finally, all the cities' plans include some form of proposed employment guarantee or college-access assistance to provide a visible incentive for staying in school and graduating.

Prevention and Early Intervention

A second major theme rooted in the Casey Foundation's institutional-change approach is its emphasis on preventive thinking. The focus here has been framed in deliberate contrast to many recent at-risk youth initiatives that target high-school dropouts, pregnant teenagers, or those who are at clear and imminent risk of these problems. It is not that these youth are inappropriate targets for special assistance; obviously, they are. From the Casey perspective, however, an exclusive preoccupation with these "symptomatic" youth too often distracts attention from the institutional problems that contributed to their negative outcomes. Dropping out of school without job prospects is characteristically the last stop on a path that begins with problems in elementary or middle school. Poor grades or the perceived inability to accomplish something that is valued in one's preteen years leads to reduced interest and motivation, worsening attendance, and still lower grades. This deepening failure breeds alienation, lowered self-esteem, more risk-taking behavior, and disciplinary sanctions. Peer and institutional labeling further diminish aspirations, leading finally to dropping out either as a way of avoiding further failure or as an admission of defeat.

New Futures represents an attempt to address the institutional dimensions of this cycle, not just its individual and ultimate casualties. It asks communities to identify and initiate practices and policies that prevent academic disengagement, reduce the probability of consistent failure, and respond to risk factors before they become hardened into diminished confidence and foreclosed aspirations.

One upshot of this preventive orientation is a heavy emphasis on the middle-school years. In Dayton's proposal, for example, almost all the initial New Futures interventions and reforms are concentrated on two targeted middle schools whose students have been disproportionately vulnerable to later adolescent problems. To a somewhat lesser but still significant degree, comprehensive middle-school reform also shapes the initial Pittsburgh and Little Rock interventions.

The prevention theme has also been reflected in proposed city efforts to increase their institutional capacity for early identification of potential risk factors. Lawrence proposed to develop an individual, annual "futures plan" for each of its public-school pupils, beginning in the sixth grade. This plan, developed by parents, teachers, and students, proposes to identify possible needs and vulnerabilities before they become problems. A similar early identification component has been built into Savannah's concept of a Stay Team—a multidisciplinary middle-school–based process for assessing and addressing emerging special needs. The concern for early identification also surfaced in the cities' information-systems and case-management proposals—both of which are discussed later in this essay.

The prevention theme is even more obviously paramount in the foundation's approach and the cities' planning response to problems of teenage pregnancy and parenthood. All the city proposals call for some upgrading of family-life and sex education and for the extension of such curricular components to earlier grades. In addition, the Savannah, Little Rock, and Pittsburgh proposals include developing or expanding preventive-health information and services targeted to teenagers.

Mechanisms for Adapting Institutional Responses to Individual Needs

The New Futures postulate that all children can succeed does not in any way presume that all children are the same. On the contrary, the operative notion is that each child embodies unique aptitudes, interests, vulnerabilities, and needs. A central challenge—perhaps the critical challenge—in the New Futures approach thus becomes the task of making universal or broad-based institutions (i.e., schools, human-services agencies, the labor market) responsive, accessible, and attuned to a broad array of individual characteristics.

Historically, the effort to build this kind of bridge between institutional functions and individual needs has led to categorization. Within schools, this tendency has led to a heavy reliance on group tracking and programming—gifted education, special education, academic and "general" curricular paths, remedial and compensatory programs, and even, in recent years, specialized initiatives for prospective dropouts.

Within human services, the proliferation has been even more extensive and more specialized. In response to the diversity of human needs, government and private efforts in every community have created a spectrum of separately organized, separately governed, and separately funded support resources, such as general health, mental health, recreation, youth services, income maintenance, child welfare, housing assistance, job placement, and employment training. Moreover, each of these agencies tends to have its own target populations, its own eligibility rules, and its own patterns for referral, access, and assessment.

However understandable in intent, this process of categorization has carried with it almost as many problems as solutions. At best, it has led to the arbitrary fragmentation of a whole person's problems and at least has promoted some measure of artificial and usually harmful labeling. At its worst, it has left individuals with the pressing need to struggle with systems that are too incomprehensible, inaccessible, untimely, or insufficient to make an effective difference with their real problems. These limitations are abundantly clear when viewed from the vantage point of at-risk youth. Indeed, the failure of social, family, and health-service systems to provide coordinated, timely, and effective support to socially and economically disadvantaged children is one of the reasons that schools have been asked to take on so many responsibilities for the welfare of children.

New Futures attempts to address this overarching fragmentation problem in behalf of youth in a straightforward way. It does so by first encouraging the creation of coordinating structures at the community's highest political and policy levels, by promoting linkage and access and by integrating mechanisms to address more fully individual child needs. The first of these strategies is reflected in the New Futures requirement that participating communities organize and maintain a multisector, politically empowered "collaborative" initially to plan and then to oversee the city's at-risk youth-reform agenda. In addition to developing a consensual and communitywide priority on the problems of youth, the collaborative is also expected to be a multisector forum for developing more focused, mutually reinforcing, and integrated policy and institutional responses to those problems.

The particular form these collaborative structures have assumed varies somewhat among the New Futures cities. Savannah, through state-enabling legislation, created a state, county, city, and school-district Youth Authority with explicit legal authorization to pool, manage, and expend tax resources from all constituent levels of government. In Lawrence, a city ordinance created a Youth Commission attached to the mayor's office but including designated state, school-district, and citizen representatives. In the remaining cities, the collaboratives have been organized as special-purpose, not-for-profit corporations, chartered to administer directly (or through lead agencies) New Futures–related resources and activities.

Despite these formal differences, the membership on the collaboratives is strikingly similar across all the cities. It includes the highest level representation from the schools, cities, and counties (e.g., mayors, city managers, superintendents, county executives); all include representatives of major local employers or business organizations, local directors of key health, social-service and employment-training agencies, juvenile-court officials, and varying numbers of persons representing parent, church, provider, and community-organization interests. Two of the collaboratives include youth members, and all but one have members from state government.

In every city, the collaborative employs direct staff. These individuals are responsible for administering the group's on-going policy-making functions as well as providing day-to-day oversight of the implementation of New Futures interventions. The collaboratives generally retain fiscal control over the foundation and match funds allocated to planned interventions, although most have chosen to delegate fairly wide budget latitude to schools and other key implementing institutions in their community. The one consistent exception to this delegation, however, is case-management activities. In every city, the collaborative retains close fiscal and management control over the proposed case-management staff. In fact, in Little Rock and Savannah, the case managers are collaborative employees.

This is not surprising, given the Casey Foundation's conceptualization of "case management" as the vehicle for integrating multiple resources, supports, and services around individual youth needs. It is, in essence, the client-level analogue to the collaborative's policy-level coordinating function. Indeed, under New Futures, the two functions are envisioned as reciprocal. The case manager serves as the operational expression of the collaborative's mission to improve coordination around at-risk youth issues. The case manager's experience with that task (particularly the obstacles he or she confronts with real children) should serve, in turn, to keep unresolved policy-coordination issues in front of the collaborative.

This conception of case management is a complex one. Its complexity is evident in the variety of case-management models proposed by the New Futures cities in their initial plans. Pittsburgh's model, for example, stresses the roles of mentor, liaison, and personal advocate. Dayton, Lawrence, and Savannah point more toward the traditional social-agency role of needs assessor and service planner. Little Rock's concept touches both roles and adds an emphasis on case manager as an on-going systems-change advocate.

It is still too early to judge how these broadly defined and varying visions of case management will eventually crystallize into actual jobs and real functions. The most that can be said now is that they represent several communities' acknowledgment that effective and integrated responses to the needs of multiproblem at-risk youth requires completely new institutional mechanisms.

The difficulty that New Futures cities are experiencing with defining this new case-management role indicates what is significant about the whole Casey Foundation initiative. There are, of course, many important things involved in what these cities are trying to do. Reform of schools and curricula are crucial. Models of improved access and quality of adolescent health services are badly needed.

So, too, are exemplary youth training and employment programs. If the New Futures cities advance on any of these fronts, they will have made substantial contributions.

That notwithstanding, more than just program, policy, or even single-institution reform is the goal in this experiment. The ultimate ambition behind the concepts of collaboration and case management is to trigger and sustain a political process that is powerful enough not only to modify established institutions but actually to redefine their objectives, their accountability, and their interrelationships.

Schools alone — even the best ones imaginable — cannot single handedly provide all young people with a real opportunity for a successful adulthood. Nor will the best conceivable job compact, nor the best-funded family or youth service agency achieve this goal. Whole communities just might, however, if a process can be found that allows communities to put the money, the commitment, the people, the expertise, and the imagination that currently resides in organizationally and politically insulated youth-related systems to practical purpose of improving the real life prospects of real live children. Finding the words that capture this hoped-for process is not easy. The concepts of service integration, cooperation, institutional linkage, and system coordination have all been cheapened by years of casual bureaucratic imprecision and by a rich history of failed efforts in their name. Moreover, those terms may not signify the process that is sought.

The development of New Futures collaboratives, combined with the creation of a case-management function under their control is not immediately intended to "link systems." Instead, it is aimed at linking the people who control those systems with the needs and problems of children. It is hoped that collaboratives' connection with those day-to-day problems, and their realization that no one system can solve them, will at some point engender a genuine sense of collective responsibility and collective institutional accountability for what happens to at-risk youth. That collective accountability would in turn provide the political context for building a youth service system that is more than the sum of its parts. If any of the New Futures cities move any distance down this path of change, they will provide a profound insight for public-policy development for youth, as well as for all human services.

The Process and Preconditions for Institutional Change

The Casey Foundation's New Futures initiative rests not only on a particular analysis of at-risk youth problems and the kind of institutional changes that must be undertaken to address them but also on a number of assumptions about where and under what conditions such an ambitious change can be judged even worth trying. These "strategic" assumptions were reflected in the foundation's process for selecting New Futures sites, in its structuring of the required planning process for applicant cities, and in its design of the initiative's evaluation.

Perhaps the most obvious of these assumptions is the idea that difficult changes around youth issues are most likely to be taken on and sustained in communities that perceive a widely held and vital stake in improved youth outcomes. Simply put, the foundation looked for cities where political leaders, school officials, employers, and citizens were able to recognize that high dropout rates, teenage pregnancy, and youth idleness were not only threats to individual futures but also to the long-term productivity, stability, and development potential of the entire community. It was believed that only where these connections were understood and acknowledged would community power structures find the political will and the future resources to undertake meaningful and durable change. In Savannah, for example, the widely publicized concern of city officials about the direct impact of widespread youth idleness and juvenile crime on the future of tourism promotion and business relocations suggested to the foundation that Savannah's potential for real change was good. Similarly, in Little Rock, a widely shared local belief in the importance of taking progressive action in behalf of disadvantaged youth in order to modify the city's racial-discrimination image was seen as a probable motivator of sustained community commitment. In contrast to these examples, places where little connection had been drawn between youth interests and those of other community sectors were judged to be much less likely to take up the difficult parts of the New Futures challenge.

A second, but related, strategic concept was that hard data on outcomes for youth would tend to deepen and broaden community commitments to reform. This assumption was reflected in New Futures planning requirements — particularly in the suggestion that communities begin their proposal making with a concrete assessment, description, and measurement of the extent of local youth problems. It was thought that public confrontations with reliable numbers and trends concerning academic achievement, dropout rate, the incidence of teenage pregnancy and parenting, and the extent of youth idleness would further manifest the broader economic and social arguments for basic change.

It appears that to some degree the strategy has been successful. In most cities, a large part of the planning period was, in fact, devoted to problem analysis and measurement, and respondents in several of the successful cities have reported that their exercise did indeed heighten the engagement of certain community sectors that had felt a fairly remote connection to the youth crisis.

The foundation's strategic emphasis on data, however, has not been limited to the initial planning phase. With technical assistance and supplementation from outside evaluators, New Futures cities are being asked to institutionalize new data-gathering and information-management capabilities within their communities throughout the course of the grant. These efforts are intended to provide the cities with a reliable and on-going picture of what is happening to local youth against a dozen key outcome measures (from course-failure rates to dropout statistics to youth-employment benchmarks). It is assumed that this knowledge, amplified by regular evaluation findings, will inform policy and program management, increase the public accountability of key youth-serving institutions, serve as a stimulus for reexamination when progress is not evidenced, and reinforce political momentum when improvements are achieved.

Conclusion

Neither the Casey Foundation in its conceptualization, nor the five New Futures cities in their response, purport to have all the answers — or, for that matter, any of them. They are embarking, however, on a difficult and complex endeavor. The real work lies ahead, in concretizing reforms and making new interventions operational. To achieve fundamental changes in the way that schools educate and service systems provide help will require hundreds of thoughtful decisions. New staff positions have to be created, staff need to be retrained, eligibility policies need to be revised, services need to be reshaped to reinforce one another, and financing streams need to be modified — in short, the inner workings of a range of public and private organizations need to be restructured singly and in combination if communities are to increase the chances of better futures for all children.

Whether the programs succeed or fail, an enormous opportunity to learn will have been provided. More than that, New Futures may foreshadow a far larger social-policy principle. This initiative is premised on the conviction that all children are entitled to succeed — that they are entitled to the opportunities, supports, and experiences needed to equip them to become contributing adults. It further argues that every sector of the community has both a contribution to make and an interest to protect in seeing that this universal entitlement is realized.

Taken together, these assumptions may point to a social contract as a useful paradigm for describing society's responsibilities toward children. Just as Social Security embodies the principle of a socially insured social covenant among generations to guarantee the aged a secure and dignified retirement, the five New Futures cities may be moving toward an example of a social covenant that ensures that the young have access to a useful and dignified adulthood.

Index